MONUMENTAL CONTROVER

MONUMENTAL CONTROVERSIES

MOUNT RUSHMORE, FOUR PRESIDENTS, AND THE QUEST FOR NATIONAL UNITY

HARRIET F. SENIE

Potomac Books · AN IMPRINT OF THE UNIVERSITY OF NEBRASKA PRESS

∞

Library of Congress Cataloging-in-Publication Data
Names: Senie, Harriet, author.
Title: Monumental controversies : Mount Rushmore, four
presidents, and the quest for national unity / Harriet F. Senie.
Other titles: Mount Rushmore, four presidents,
and the quest for national unity
Description: [Lincoln, Nebraska] : Potomac Books, an imprint
of the University of Nebraska Press, [2023] |
Includes bibliographical references and index.
Identifiers: LCCN 2022045683
ISBN 9781640124998 (cloth)
ISBN 9781640125858 (epub)
ISBN 9781640125865 (pdf)
Subjects: LCSH: Monuments—United States—Public opinion. |
Memorials—United States—Public opinion. | Mount
Rushmore National Memorial (S.D.)—History. | Washington,
George, 1732–1799—Monuments. | Lincoln, Abraham,
1809–1865—Monuments. | Jefferson, Thomas, 1743–1826—
Monuments. | Roosevelt, Theodore, 1858–1919—Monuments. |
Presidents—Monuments—United States. | United States—Race
relations—History. | BISAC: HISTORY / Social History |
ARCHITECTURE / Buildings / Landmarks & Monuments
Classification: LCC E159 .S52 2023 |
DDC 973—dc23/eng/20221007
LC record available at https://lccn.loc.gov/2022045683

Set in Garamond Premier by Mikala R. Kolander.
Designed by N. Putens.

In memory of my parents, Gerda and Ernest Freitag
For my daughter, Laura Kim Senie—like always
And for Bruce Glaser

CONTENTS

ILLUSTRATIONS

PREFACE

The idea for this book was prompted by my experience serving on the New York City Mayoral Advisory Commission on City Art, Monuments, and Markers in the fall of 2017. Formed in the wake of the protests over the Unite the Right white supremacist rally in Charlottesville, Virginia, that led to the removal of Confederate memorials in a number of states across the nation, the nineteen-member commission was charged with recommending best practices for addressing controversial monuments in New York City and applying them specifically to four local works: the plaque to Philippe Pétain in the Canyon of Heroes in lower Manhattan, a statue to Dr. J. Marion Sims on Fifth Avenue at 103rd Street, an equestrian monument to Theodore Roosevelt in front of the American Museum of Natural History (AMNH), and the statue of Christopher Columbus in Columbus Circle. During our three in-person meetings, it became clear that many commission members were locked into a kind of "either/or" thinking—as in either Teddy Roosevelt was a "good guy" or a "bad guy." When the subject of his equestrian monument came up, I recognized it as a fine work of art. So, as the only art historian on the commission, I decided to do some initial research to share with the group in order to better understand its historical context. Subsequently the AMNH hired me to expand that study for use in an exhibition about the controversy. This work enabled me to become more familiar with Theodore Roosevelt's policies as well as the memorials dedicated to him.

Roosevelt is one of the four presidents represented on Mount Rushmore. I had taught several graduate seminars on memorials that included discussions of memorials pertaining to the other three: George Washington, Thomas

Jefferson, and Abraham Lincoln. That experience merged with my participation on the mayoral commission and led me to focus on Mount Rushmore as a way of exploring the divisive, dead-end kind of "either/or" thinking that has become so prevalent and toxic in our culture. In the course of my research, it became clear to me that the controversies focused on Mount Rushmore and other the memorials dedicated to the four presidents were really about definitions of national identity and unity.

I explored these ideas and benefited from feedback in response to several public presentations, in particular a talk I gave at Fairfield University in 2020 on the subject of this book. I also had productive discussions as a panelist on "Contested Legacies: Public Monuments in Global Perspective" (Columbia University, 2020); "Best Practices in Setting Up Commissions" (Organization for Security and Cooperation in Europe [OSCE], The Hague, 2019); "Memorials Reconsidered: Controversies, Resolutions, and Strategies Moving Forward" (The European Fine Art Foundation [TEFAF], New York, 2018); and "Monuments, Memory and the Evolution of Meaning" (City University of New York [CUNY] Graduate Center, 2019).

Publications resulted from two related panels that I co-chaired for annual meetings of the College Art Association. "Teachable Monuments: Using Public Art to Spark Dialogue and Address Controversies" in Los Angeles (2018) resulted in the eponymous anthology co-edited by Sierra Rooney, Jennifer Wingate, and me. "The Challenges of Commissioning Memorials: Symbolic Actions, Political Pressures and Visual Literacy" in Chicago (2020) laid the groundwork for a future work that Cher Krause Knight and I are planning based on our experiences on public commissions in Boston and New York.

I have been fortunate to be able to explore the ideas expressed here with graduate students at City College and the Graduate Center, CUNY. I have also discussed them with an informal group of scholars (many of my former PhD students) who focus on public art: Jennifer Favorite, Sheila Gerami, Marisa Lerer, Sierra Rooney, Sara Weintraub, and Jennifer Wingate. I have benefited from their insights as well as their work. I owe a special thanks to Cher Krause Knight and Sally Webster, close friends and co-editors on several anthologies devoted to public art. Our conversations have always been helpful. Hadley Newton, who worked with me on this book from its inception, is the best research/editorial assistant anyone could hope for. I am also particularly grateful to the people who read my work: first and foremost, my daughter, Laura Kim Senie, who has been editing my writing ever since I realized she had this skill, and whose contributions to this book are immeasurable. Elke Solomon's encouragement and comments have improved this as well as other books I have written. Bruce Glaser has been with me throughout this project in many ways and provided essential valuable insights, most notably suggesting Mount Rushmore as the focus of this book.

Introduction

Mount Rushmore features gigantic heads of four of the nation's most revered presidents: George Washington, Thomas Jefferson, Abraham Lincoln, and Theodore Roosevelt. Located in South Dakota, it attracts millions of visitors annually. Standing for national identity, its image is even on U.S. passports. It has been featured in a range of advertisements from automobiles and beer to toothpaste. Its ubiquitous appearance is internationally recognizable. In today's climate, however, in which national values and their memorials are being questioned, the meaning of Mount Rushmore has been challenged. There have been many projected or substituted images, including those of women or World Wrestling Entertainment's best wrestlers.

What you see when you look at Mount Rushmore, or any memorial, depends on what you know and how you feel about it. For example, because it is on land taken illegally from the Lakota Sioux, Mount Rushmore can be seen as the desecration of a sacred site. Understanding various perspectives is essential to developing a more inclusive and accurate narrative explaining both the country's origins and the divisive and often toxic controversies so prevalent today.

The history of Mount Rushmore begins long before the heads of four presidents were carved into four peaks in the Black Hills, previously inhabited by the Lakota Sioux, whose way of life was alien to the Rushmore presidents. This book begins with a consideration of Native American customs and concepts, followed by a discussion of the origin of the monument and the sculptor who realized it, Gutzon Borglum. Each president is discussed first in terms of other key monuments that honor their contributions in different ways, followed by a reflection on their policies connected to the genocide of Native populations, the continuation of slavery, and expansionism or imperialism.

The Lakota Sioux had a well-organized functioning society with a belief system radically distinct from that of the United States, which was based on the British legal system. The Indigenous way of life remained beyond Euro-American understanding, especially the concept that land was communal rather than private property. This and other essential differences prompted the Rushmore presidents and many others to think of the Natives as savages, providing justification for seizing their land.

The concept for Mount Rushmore originated in the early 1920s with South Dakota state historian Doane Robinson's idea to increase tourism in the area. While Robinson envisioned celebrating heroes of the West, including Native American chiefs, the sculptor of the monument, Gutzon Borglum, wanted to celebrate American expansion. Borglum was also a believer in the Lost Cause mythology and affiliated with the Ku Klux Klan. His previous large-scale project at Stone Mountain in Atlanta celebrated Confederate heroes.

In thinking about how best to portray the Rushmore presidents, Borglum considered how they were depicted in other works of art. Beginning with Washington, the question was what a president, who was neither a king nor exactly a commoner, should look like. Should he be clothed in contemporary or classical apparel? The first sculpted portrait of Washington was created for the capitol of Richmond, Virginia, by the French sculptor Jean-Antoine Houdon. His preference for both the neoclassical style and dress was well known, but Washington preferred a more contemporary depiction. At the time Houdon was commissioned to create a statue of Washington, the commander in chief of the Continental Army had just stepped down from this role and was returning to life as a plantation owner. Creating a visual representation of the man who was the nation's first president and came to symbolize national identity was not easy. The protracted saga surrounding the creation of the later Washington Monument on the National Mall offers ample evidence of this.

All the Rushmore presidents were forward-thinking men; however, they were also products of their time. As politicians they were limited by what was possible while they were in power. Both their contributions to the United States, as well as some of their beliefs and policies that no longer coincide with twenty-first-century values, are still fundamental to national identity. Like all traditional monuments, Mount Rushmore conveys a single message: these men were great, heroes—see how they tower above us. Removing or destroying memorials, a trend that has gathered momentum in the third decade of the twenty-first century, substitutes a different narrative: these men are no longer worthy of our esteem and are considered contemptible. It is time to move beyond a monocular either/or construction to a more inclusive and accurate narrative. We need an account of Mount Rushmore and other memorials that acknowledges that their subjects did many great things but were far from perfect.

Washington's professional life began with a career focused on land. Like his father, he worked as a land surveyor, intent on acquiring property for himself whenever possible and later for the country—even when it involved dire treatment of Native Americans. Although he struggled privately with the issue of slavery throughout his life, in reality he was a harsh taskmaster. Still, while he never took a public stance against the practice, he eventually freed his slaves in his will. He was the only one of the signers of the Declaration of Independence to do so.

Thomas Jefferson, best known as the author of the Declaration of Independence, also defined national values in the Virginia Statute for Religious Freedom, an important document that advocated for freedom of religion and separation of church and state. Among other things, Jefferson was also a talented architect: fittingly, the most famous memorials to the third president are architectural structures. Monticello, the home he designed for himself, presents an image of how he wished to be perceived by the public. It included areas dedicated to the pursuits that were most important to him; meanwhile, slave quarters were largely hidden from view. The Jefferson Memorial on the

National Mall features a larger-than-life-size statue of the third president housed in a circular neoclassical temple containing edited quotes that omit any reference to slavery. Gateway Arch in St. Louis, a striking modern form, bears no obvious relationship to Jefferson, even though it is dedicated to him.

One of Jefferson's goals was to create what he called an "empire of liberty," a concept whose fundamental contradiction did not seem to bother him. Under his presidency, the Louisiana Purchase (which doubled the size of the country) led to the extreme suffering of Native Americans, many of whom were forcibly evacuated from their land in what has become known as the Trail of Tears. Jefferson was also a slave owner who fathered four children with one of his enslaved women—Sally Hemings. She was the daughter of another enslaved woman and Jefferson's father-in-law, making her his wife's half-sister. Initially a strong supporter of emancipation, he came to believe this could only be accomplished by following generations.

Abraham Lincoln's policies followed a different trajectory. He arrived gradually at the Emancipation Proclamation. Although his early statements on slavery were constrained by its legality at the time, his election prompted the secession of a number of states. This led to the Civil War and ultimately the passing of the Thirteenth Amendment abolishing slavery in the United States. Much lauded for his role in freeing enslaved people, he was also responsible for approving the mass hanging of the largest number of Native Americans in the country's history. Although he greatly reduced the number of those originally sentenced, he did next to nothing to improve conditions for Indigenous people. Furthermore, Lincoln adhered to a system of patronage that fostered political appointments of unethical officials who took advantage of the system for personal profits at the expense of Native inhabitants.

The Lincoln Memorial on the National Mall celebrates the sixteenth president as the savior of the Union but makes no reference to his role in emancipation. The earlier Emancipation Memorial, financed by formerly enslaved people but commissioned by whites, is located at a distance from the National Mall in Lincoln Park, a residential area. It depicts a standing Lincoln apparently blessing a kneeling, partially nude Black man with his chains broken. In 2020 it became the object of such intense controversy that it was fenced in for protection; in the same year a copy in Boston was removed from its site. Without a doubt the strangest memorial to a Rushmore president and perhaps any president is the Lincoln Memorial in Hodgenville, Kentucky. The neoclassical temple structure encloses a reconstituted log cabin symbolizing Lincoln as a self-made man who rose to the presidency from humble beginnings. However, it contains no logs from the actual house in which he was born. Although the National Park Service has acknowledged the monument's inauthenticity, apparently this does not matter to its over two hundred thousand annual visitors.

One of the two most important memorials to Theodore Roosevelt proved to be so controversial that it was removed, while the other remains virtually unknown due to its location. The equestrian statue outside the American Museum of Natural History in New York City, based on a Renaissance precedent, was part of the overall design of the building's façade. It became the focus of intense controversy prompted by the perceived inequality between the president on horseback and the standing figures of the Native American and African that flank him. By contrast, the president's national memorial features a standing Roosevelt in contemporary dress delivering a speech. Sited in a discrete location in a large, wooded park closer to Virginia than the National Mall, it is easily missed and remains unknown to many.

Theodore Roosevelt has been widely discredited for his imperialistic policies, particularly in the Philippines, but he did in fact make many positive contributions to the United States. An author of numerous publications on many subjects, he advocated for conservation and implemented positive labor reforms in the various political offices he held over the years. Importantly, in light of today's proliferation of monopolies, he also curtailed damaging practices of large national trusts. On the international front his diplomacy in the Russo-Japanese War earned him the Nobel Peace Prize in 1906.

One thing the Rushmore presidents agreed on was national unity; it was a priority for all of them. It was paramount for George Washington throughout his tenure and featured prominently in his Farewell Address of 1796, in which he warned the nation about the dangers of political parties and regional divides. He implored his listeners and readers, "Properly estimate the immense value of your national union to your collective and individual happiness . . . discountenancing whatever may suggest even a suspicion that it can in any event be abandoned; and indignantly frowning upon the first dawning of every attempt to alienate any portion of our country from the rest, or to enfeeble the sacred ties which now link together the various parts."[1] In 1862, during one of the bleakest moments of the Civil War, citizens from Philadelphia petitioned Congress to read Washington's entire Farewell Address around the time of his birthday. This became a permanent event in the Senate in 1888, the centennial of the ratification of the Constitution; it continues to date.[2]

Thomas Jefferson made national unity a priority in his inaugural address as third president of the United Sates in 1801. He had survived a bitter campaign with former president John Adams but tied with Aaron Burr.[3] The election was ultimately decided by the House of Representatives only after thirty-six runoffs. Acknowledging the animosity expressed during the election, Jefferson stated, "This now being decided by the voice of the nation, announced according to the rules of the Constitution, all will of course arrange themselves under the will of law, and unite in common efforts for the common good." With a view toward unity, he also noted the importance of tolerating opposing views: "If there be any, among us who wish to dissolve this Union, or to change its republican form, let them stand undisturbed as monuments of the safety with which error of opinion may be tolerated, where reason is left free to combat it."[4]

Abraham Lincoln's presidency is defined today by the Civil War and with it the preservation of the Union and the emancipation of enslaved people. In what has come to be known as his House Divided Speech delivered in 1858 he stated, "I do not expect the Union to be dissolved—I do not expect the house to fall—but I do expect it will cease to be divided." In his inaugural address in 1861 he noted that "the Union is much older than the Constitution. It was formed in fact, by the Articles of Association in 1774. It was matured and continued by the Declaration of Independence in 1776." Perhaps most famously, he hoped, "The mystic chords of memory, stretching from every battle-field, and patriot grave, to every living heart and hearth-stone, all over this broad land, will yet swell the chorus of the Union, when again touched, as surely they will be, by the better angels of our nature."[5]

Theodore Roosevelt became president in 1901 after the assassination of William McKinley. Although as president he faced fewer threats to national unity than Lincoln, he nevertheless was conscious of the need to preserve it. In his second annual message to Congress in 1902, he emphasized that "we need to remember that any kind of class animosity in the political world is, if possible, even more wicked, even more destructive to national welfare, than sectional, race or religious animosity." He urged that "no true patriot will fail to do everything in his power to prevent substitution of class hatred for loyalty to the whole American people."[6] In a speech delivered at Everett, Washington, in 1903, he spoke of the dangers of divisions along lines of "caste, creed, or locality."[7] His 1904 campaign button for the presidency featured the phrase "National Unity" directly above his image. In his inaugural address in 1905 he acknowledged that "though the problems are new, though the tasks set before us differ from the tasks set before our fathers who founded and preserved this Republic, the spirit in which these tasks must be undertaken and these problems faced, if our duty is to be well done, remains essentially unchanged."[8]

The Rushmore presidents faced some of the most contentious times in our history but while they acknowledged the prevalent dissention they championed the Union, held together by accepting opposing opinions. This was for them one of the basic premises of democracy; they thought in terms of "and" rather than "or."

1

The Land of the Lakota Sioux

Great civilizations existed in North America prior to European arrival . . .
villages existed all over the Northeast and a network of them stretched into
the Plains. Commerce bound villages together from the Rocky Mountains
to the Atlantic Coast and from Canada to New Mexico. The villages and the
artistry of the people required an advanced ability at organization.

—ALVIN M. JOSEPHY JR.

As a consequence of our preoccupation with development and progress
we have not understood American Indian views on conservation and
protection of the environment.

—PHILLIP DEERE

Native Americans occupied this land long before Christopher Columbus and
the European settlers who followed. Their various self-governing tribes were
independent nations with economically self-sustaining practices and strong
belief systems that were radically different from and often in direct opposition
to most Anglo-American values, centering as they did on a closely knit communal society that shared the land and the animals and plants that sustained

it. The Mount Rushmore presidents made no attempt to acknowledge or understand the mores of this culture. Motivated by an expansionist land grab, based on the concept of private property rather than communally owned land, they tried systematically to convert Indigenous people to American ways. Failing assimilation, they tried to eliminate Native Americans through battle, starvation, and substandard living conditions. The focus here is on the Lakota Sioux who legitimately own the Black Hills—the land on which Mount Rushmore is built and which they consider sacred.

Native American Belief Systems

Native American belief systems infuse all aspects of daily life and are incorporated into each person and celebrated in communal ceremonies.[1] Cardinal virtues are gender specific. For men, they are bravery, honesty, generosity and fortitude; for women, chastity, hospitality, industriousness, and generosity.[2] Any violation of these principles brings shame to one's extended family and kinship. Additionally, history is conveyed through the oral tradition, which fosters skills of narration as well as remembering and listening. It is a sacred responsibility to share this history, which is first learned in a family setting.[3] Native American governmental and educational systems, too, are also based on oral history.[4] However, Western written records are largely narratives of those in power—colonial missionaries, agents, or settlers. These are framed by European perspectives that include the incentive to own property.[5] Many scholars posit that Native languages are more precise and accurate than English; this is especially relevant when considering interpretations of treaties between the United States and the Sioux nation.[6]

The stark distinctions between Western and Native American values are perhaps most evident in their respective views of the land. The Lakota consider the Earth as their mother, a source of nurture and sustenance, and therefore revered.[7] Since they see themselves as stewards rather than owners of the land, selling it is both inconceivable and anathema. In contrast, the capitalist system considers land to be private property, valued according to its potential monetary profits. Land in the United States has become synonymous with the country itself; the national anthem refers to the country as the "land of the free," while Woody Guthrie sings, "This Land is your Land."[8] Thus, in a symbolic but radically different way, land represents national identity for both the Sioux and the United States.

Mount Rushmore is located in the Black Hills (Paha Sapa), which are located at the center of the Lakota nation and considered their most sacred land.[9] The Lakota depend on its rich food resources as well as a variety of plants grown in the area that are used for medicinal purposes. This was especially important at a time when U.S. government representatives were systematically killing off buffalo in order to make Native Americans dependent on farming and federal food rations.[10] Colonial settlers were primarily attracted by flakes of gold floating in the streams and visible on the land. The Lakota did not prize gold practically or spiritually.[11] The goal of accumulating personal riches was virtually unknown to them; instead, group welfare was paramount and individuals behaved accordingly. Leisure time was used for tribal practices,[12] especially the Ghost Dance and Sun Dance ceremonies. Practiced by at least one quarter of the Lakota,[13] the Ghost Dance was essentially a ritual rejection of the non-Native values increasingly being imposed on them. It was also a symbolic return to Native life as it had been lived.[14] The Sun Dance, based on personal sacrifice, was practiced in secret by approximately one-third of the men and took place in a sweat lodge. According to what was told to Dennis Banks, chief executive officer of the American Indian Movement (AIM), men would fast for four days, dance around a cottonwood tree that was sacred to them, and rend their flesh.[15] This ceremony, based on a deeply held belief in a better future, enabled the Lakota to persevere through decades of punishing treatment.

Before the United States profoundly disrupted their way of life, the Lakota had a well-developed system of government headed by council chiefs who functioned as peacekeepers and had final authority in all matters. They made tribal decisions by consensus, not majority rule; dissenting members were asked to relocate.[16] Esteemed for their wisdom, compassion, and generosity, council chiefs represented the best of what it meant to be Lakota. They were supported by warrior societies (Akicita) that acted both as guardians and protectors, a kind of benevolent police force. Among other things, they made sure all families obtained sufficient buffalo meat to feed their members.[17] With their communal focus, the Lakota were committed to care for older and disabled members of the tribe.[18] Concepts of punishment and war also differed widely from Western practices. Criminals, even murderers, were not imprisoned; instead, they were required to pay compensation to the victim's family. In extreme cases, a murderer might be exiled from the tribe. Given the importance of family relationships, this was an extreme form of punishment.[19]

Significant Treaties

Historically, treaties are made only between independent nations, not between a nation and its colonies.[20] The United States made many treaties with Native American nations. The Fort Laramie Treaty of 1868 clearly established Lakota sovereignty and ownership of the Black Hills. It was not, however, the first treaty between the two nations. In nearly all instances there were serious gaps between what the Native Americans were told and what was actually written (in a language they could not read). In his detailed study of treaties and other relevant documents, Vine Deloria Jr. has concluded that the United States consistently misled Native Americans and in so doing behaved illegally.[21]

The gradual erosion of Lakota ownership of and even rights to the lands on which they had lived for centuries began with the 1785 Land Ordinance that permitted the purchase of Native American property. Two years later the Northwest Ordinance of 1787 allowed for the annexation of Native American land once they were outnumbered by U.S. settlers. Subsequent treaties (made in 1805, 1815, 1816, 1825, 1851, 1858, and 1868) were intended to cement the friendship and cooperation between the United States and Native American nations.[22] The 1830 Indian Removal Act, however, was something different. Signed into law by Andrew Jackson, it gave the U.S. president the right to give Native Americans unsettled lands west of the Mississippi in exchange for their lands within existing state borders. Despite widespread tribal resistance to this displacement, the U.S. government persisted.[23] In 1838 the government displaced the Cherokees in a forced march, known as the Trail of Tears, resulting in the death of some four thousand Native Americans.

The Fort Laramie Treaty of 1868 between the Sioux nation and the United States, like most others before it, was intended as a peace treaty. Based on their consistent military victories, the Sioux were negotiating from a position of strength. The treaty clearly established their sovereignty and ownership of the land that included the Black Hills.[24] Article 2 established the Great Sioux Reservation covering an area of some thirty-six million acres west of the Missouri, including the Black Hills, and hunting rights to another thirty million acres. Furthermore, it stipulated that colonial settlers and prospectors were prohibited from passing through it, and the forts built along the Bozeman Trail had to be abandoned. Lakota Sioux chief Red Cloud refused to sign the treaty until the forts were burned down. The U.S. government was willing to give them up because they had become costly to defend. Additionally, the Union Pacific and Northern Pacific Railroads had found alternative routes to Montana and thus did not require the Sioux land. The 1868 Treaty was both an acknowledgment of Native American power and an assurance that there would be no loss of land.[25]

There were, however, some problems with the treaty. Article 11 did not include the forts along the Missouri or potential future routes that might be needed by railroads or wagons heading west, suggesting that the U.S. government anticipated further expansion. While article 12 specified that more land could be ceded only if three quarters of adult Sioux males agreed, subsequently the U.S. either found ways around that provision or simply ignored it. Several other articles were intended to convert the Lakota to an agrarian economy based on individually owned plots (i.e., private property). Instead of depending on the buffalo for survival, they now depended on the U.S. government for rations.[26] The United States, however, regularly reneged on their commitments, creating an ongoing risk of starvation and indebtedness to pay for food, eventually forcing the Native Americans to sell their land.

The 1868 Treaty was abrogated almost immediately by trespassers looking for gold, most famously by Lieutenant Colonel George Armstrong Custer who in 1874 was surveying land for the United States located on Sioux property. His announcement of finding gold in the Black Hills predictably prompted a gold rush and subsequent retaliatory Sioux attacks. These culminated in 1876 with the Battle of Little Bighorn, which resulted in the death of Custer and his entire troop, later celebrated as heroes. John Taliaferro called it "the worst drubbing the Army would ever suffer at the hands of Indians."[27] Led by Sitting Bull and Crazy Horse, the most famous Lakota Sioux warrior, it was their last major victory.[28] Although "Custer's Last Stand" was framed in heroic terms and described as a massacre it was really the U.S. retaliation that should be described as such. The 1877 Treaty (referred to as the Paha Sapa Treaty) ended all appropriations and annuities to the Sioux until they gave up the Black Hills, in effect imposing certain starvation. Even under these dire circumstances the officially designated chiefs refused to sign; instead, the U.S. government obtained unofficial signatures, although far fewer than the three quarters of the male population stipulated by the Treaty of 1868.[29]

After the fraudulently signed 1877 treaty, Crazy Horse surrendered and Sitting Bull went to Canada. This was the last time the Lakota would fight to defend their lands; however, this did not mean that they were resigned to their losses even though they had to live in substandard conditions in often devastating circumstances.[30] Their children were taken from their homes and sent to mission-run schools that forced them to speak English and adopt American ways.[31] They were required to wear uniforms and cut their hair, which was considered a Lakota sign of mourning.[32] Ted Means, from the Pine Ridge Reservation in the Black Hills recalled, "In the mission school I was taught about living a good Christian life. I was told we must become assimilated, become white. While they talked of being Christian, Indian children were being punished for speaking their own language. They were beaten because they could not relate to that educational process. They told us we were dirty. They did not live as Christians in their relations with us."[33]

The Dawes Act of 1887 (sometimes referred to as the General Allotment Act) divided reservation land into individually owned plots. Sponsored by Senator Dawes, who believed that without private property the Native Americans would "not make much progress," the legislation was in direct opposition to Sioux philosophy and practice.[34] After the land had been apportioned to Native families, there was usually a surplus, which could then be sold to colonial settlers or speculators. This policy of assimilation was felt by some to be even worse than previous wars and treaty abrogation.[35]

Acculturation extended to the suppression of key Native ceremonies, among them the Ghost Dance. The War Department, fearing violence that was neither preached nor encouraged by the Lakota Sioux, began an investigation of the Ghost Dance. In response, President William Henry Harrison ordered thousands of troops to surround Lakota reservations.[36] The Seventh Cavalry, the battalion that the Sioux had defeated at Little Bighorn, now attempted to arrest the Lakota chiefs and killed Sitting Bull. The news of his death prompted several hundred Lakota to seek safety on the Pine Ridge Reservation. The U.S. Army, however, proceeded to kill starving, unarmed refugees, including women and children, in what came to be known as the Battle of Wounded Knee. Actually a massacre, it is now seen as marking the end of many things—among them, the Great Sioux Wars and Native American military resistance and, to a large extent, their way of life.

David Treuer in *The Heartbeat of Wounded Knee* described the Native American situation in 1890: "In four hundred years, Indians had lost control of 100 percent of the United States and remained in small clusters scattered like freckles over the face of the country. . . . Tribal government had been replaced by the dismal and crushing paternalism of the Office of Indian Affairs. . . . The entire United States had been 'settled,' and Indians had been broken, removed, and safely 'settled,' too, on reservations where they were expected to either die or become Americans."[37] According to the U.S. Census Bureau, there were fewer than two hundred thousand Native Americans left alive; when the colonists first arrived, Native American populations numbered over twenty million. For many decades the Massacre of Wounded Knee was seen as the end of Native Americans, a view that was widely publicized by Dee Brown's influential book, *Bury My Heart at Wounded Knee* (1970), as well as James Fenimore Cooper's *Last of the Mohicans* (1826). James Earle Fraser concretized this image in his sculpture *The End of the Trail*, first modeled in 1894, just four years after Wounded Knee.

Wounded Knee eventually came to serve as a rallying point for Indigenous activism and self-determination. A hundred years later a demonstration at the site in 1973 was followed in 1977 by the publication *The Great Sioux Nation: Sitting in Judgment on America*, edited by Roxanne Dunbar-Ortiz, which provided important source material for subsequent histories. More recently, Treuer noted the strides Native Americans have made, their accomplishments, and a kind of assimilation that both maintains Indigenous ways and makes accommodations to the modern world.[38] When construction on Mount Rushmore began in 1927, Native American conditions were beginning to change. Seven years after the Indian Reorganization Act ended the policy of allotment and supported tribal economic development. It allowed tribes to adopt their own constitutions and governments, but these had to be approved by the U.S. government.[39] That year, Native Americans were granted citizenship (something they hadn't requested) but were not given the same civil and political rights as other citizens.[40] The 1934 Indian Reorganization Act did not improve matters, creating a system that, although run by Native Americans, essentially ratified government policies that did not reflect local needs.[41] Continuing its policy of seizing lands as needed, in 1942 (the year after Borglum died and construction of Mount Rushmore ended), the government appropriated Sheep Mountain on the Pine Ridge Reservation for use as a gunnery range during World War II. After the war, the government proposed turning it into Badlands National Park.

Native Americans at Mount Rushmore and Beyond

Mount Rushmore, located in close proximity to Wounded Knee, eventually became a site of Native American protest. Three years before the 1973 Wounded Knee demonstration, on 24 August 1970, about twenty Lakota arrived at the monument's parking lot and asked to conduct a vigil in the amphitheater that included praying, drumming, and singing. While there, they informed tourists that the land upon which they stood had been taken from them illegally. Native American speakers referred to the many broken treaties and challenged the monument's association with democracy.[42]

The activity at Mount Rushmore attracted several recently formed Native American organizations, among them the United Native Americans led by Lehman Brightman; members of All Tribes founded the previous year during the 1969 occupation of Alcatraz led by John Trudell; and nearby state chapters of AIM led by Russell Means and Dennis Banks. Brightman's statement was the first public demand for the return of the Black Hills to the Lakota Sioux.[43] Several members of the activist group AIM climbed onto the mountain, camped behind the head of Theodore Roosevelt, and remained there for several days. Park superintendent Wallace McCaw countered Brightman's speech by asserting instead that the Mount Rushmore presidents believed their policies would lead to the assimilation of Native Americans into contemporary society, thereby solving their problems. Since there was no violence or destruction of property, the National Park Service did not interfere. Colder weather eventually prompted the demonstrators to disband.[44] The protest the following year was different. A group of AIM members came prepared for an occupation, bringing camping equipment, provisions, red paint, and a press release. This time the National Park Service forcibly removed them from the mountain and issued a fine.

These protests were evidence of a shift in Native American identity politics as well as national attitudes. By the 1980s there was evidence of a Native middle class. Many had learned some marketable skills in boarding schools, and the allotment that made some of them property owners had led to other financial gains.[45] In 1980 the Supreme Court ruled that the seizure of the Black Hills had been illegal, a violation of the prohibition of taking property without just compensation as stated in the Fifth Amendment. The court awarded the Sioux some $17.5 million in reparations; by 2007 they were owed $750 million dollars. The Sioux, however, continue to refuse to take the money because for them the Black Hills were never for sale.[46]

As Told at Mount Rushmore

For years the official story presented at Mount Rushmore included few details of the history recounted above. In 2004 this changed, with the appointment of the first Native American superintendent of the site, Gerard Baker, a Mandan Hidatsa tribe member. Previously the official introduction offered by park rangers emphasized the praiseworthy deeds of the four presidents and the technical achievements of the sculptor, Gutzon Borglum, and his crew.[47] By the twenty-first century this monolithic narrative had been challenged.[48] A shift in emphasis was evident in the orientation films shown in the auditorium.[49] The 1965 film, titled simply *Mount Rushmore*, focused on Borglum and included details of his other works. However, it omitted Borglum's focus on territorial expansion as the reason for choosing the four presidents as well as his association with the Ku Klux Klan. The 1973 film, *Four Faces on a Mountain*, focused on the problems each of the four presidents faced and overcame. Produced at a time of social unrest and environmental concerns, this film had a decidedly somber and pensive tone. By contrast, the 1986 film *The Shrine* was more celebratory, but instead of Borglum it valorized the workmen who actually built the monument. It also touted the best-known accomplishments of each represented president. These films presented Mount Rushmore in a way that Americans understood it, but none introduced a nuanced or complicated narrative.

Gerald Baker tried to expand the experience of the monument by introducing a Native American perspective. First, he put up a tipi—a visible emblem of Indigenous life that had flourished on the site for centuries. His attempt to include a more broadly based interpretive program prompted a lot of controversy, but he succeeded in creating Heritage Village located along the first section of the Presidential Trail. Here Native American National Park Service rangers convey a sense of the civilizations that once inhabited the land. During the summer season there are performances by Native dancers and musicians, demonstrating that their culture is ongoing. Baker's vision was inclusive. As he said in Ken Burns's documentary on the national parks, "This is Mount Rushmore! It's America! Everybody's something different here; we're all different. And just maybe that gets us talking again as human beings, as Americans."[50] Since Baker's retirement in 2010, his position was held by three interim appointments—all white women. In March 2021 Michelle Wheatley was selected as superintendent of the memorial. She promised to engage "with community members to protect the incredible resources and tell the many stories Mount Rushmore has to offer."[51] Arguably it may prove difficult for ancillary programs to cut into the uninflected heroic message of the monument itself. Nevertheless, introducing a Native American perspective would introduce an alternative view of national identity.

2

Gutzon Borglum's Mount Rushmore

The initial impetus to build Mount Rushmore was typically American, or in any event, entrepreneurial. In 1923 Doane Robinson, secretary and superintendent of the South Dakota State Historical Society, was thinking about how to increase tourism to the Black Hills.[1] Locally well-known for his work on Native Americans, especially the Sioux, he had established the monthly magazine *South Dakota*, which in 1901 was the springboard for the society he still ran.[2] Robinson imagined something radically different than the final result, and Gutzon Borglum was not his first choice as sculptor. Based on the success of Chicago-based sculptor Lorado Taft's gigantic *Big Injun*, he inquired if he might be interested in carving figures into one of the pinnacles of the Black Hills. Robinson had in mind "some notable Sioux such as Red Cloud, who lived and died in the shadow of these peaks."[3]

Taft did not initially refuse and Robinson expanded his vision: "In my imagination I can see all the heroes of the old west peering out from them [the pinnacles]; Lewis and Clark, Fremont, Jed Smith, Bridger, Sa-kaka-wea, Red Cloud, and an equestrian statue [Buffalo Bill] Cody and the overland mail." Subsequently he added, "Custer and his gold-discovering cavalcade winding its way through the Needles, with Red Cloud and a band of Sioux scouts, resentful and suspicious, spying on it through rifts in the pinnacles of the opposite wall, while above, a great mountain buck, wary but unafraid, inspects the pageant with curiosity."[4] Taft, however, was in poor health and declined the commission. Some historians have noted that Robinson next considered Daniel Chester French, well-known for his sculpture of Abraham Lincoln in the Lincoln Memorial, but there is no documentary evidence.[5]

In the summer of 1924, he wrote to Gutzon Borglum who was then working on the head of Robert E. Lee for Stone Mountain near Atlanta: "In the vicinity of Harney Peak, in the Black Hills of South Dakota are opportunities for heroic sculpture of unusual character. Would it be possible for you to design and supervise a massive sculpture there? The proposal has not passed beyond the mere suggestion, but if it would be possible for you to undertake the matter I feel quite sure we could arrange to finance such an enterprise."[6] Since Borglum was engaged in a losing struggle with his Atlanta patrons, this commission provided a perfect escape hatch.

Borglum had a complicated family history. His Danish-born Mormon father, Jens (called James in the United States) had two wives, the second of whom, Christina, was mother to both Gutzon and his younger brother Solon.[7] When Borglum was a young child, James gave up Mormonism, moved the family to Nebraska, and went to medical school there. In 1871, when Borglum was four, Christina was sent away, since it was illegal to have two wives. This called into question Borglum's legitimacy. The children were told never to speak of her and Borglum never mentioned his Mormon past; usually he just said his mother died, sometimes embellishing this narrative with a last bedside moment.

His artistic training began in the late 1880s when he took painting lessons from Elizabeth "Liza" Jaynes Putnam. He married her in 1889 when he was twenty-two and she was forty; they subsequently divorced. Shortly after their marriage, at her suggestion, they moved to Paris in 1891, where he studied at the Académie Julian and the École des Beaux Arts and exhibited at the Salon. While there, he befriended the French sculptor Auguste Rodin, who became a decisive and formative influence. On their return voyage to the United States, Borglum met Mary Williams Montgomery, whom he married in 1909, after he divorced his first wife. Montgomery took charge of his business affairs,[8] and the following year they moved to a four-hundred-acre estate known as Borgland near Stamford, Connecticut. In 1912 their son Lincoln was born; he would eventually work on Mount Rushmore and take over the project after his father died.

Although Borglum was widely known to be very difficult, he could also be as charismatic as he was cantankerous, and he came to know many influential people. Among the most important for his career was Jessie Benton Fremont, daughter of Missouri senator Thomas Hart Benton (great-grandfather of the artist) and wife of California senator John C. Fremont. They met when she commissioned a portrait of her husband, and she became his life-long patron and friend. Borglum knew how to network; he was an active member of the Masons and the Players, as well as the Century Club in New York and the Metropolitan Club in Washington.[9] He was also on good terms with Presidents Theodore Roosevelt and Franklin Delano Roosevelt, as well as the Wright brothers and Frank Lloyd Wright, among others. His assistants over the years included Marian Bell (daughter of Alexander Graham Bell), Malvina Hoffman, and Isamu Noguchi.

Borglum before Mount Rushmore

Although Borglum today is primarily known for Mount Rushmore, he had a successful art career well before then.[10] In 1908 he completed on his own initiative a forty-inch-high head of Abraham Lincoln carved directly into a block of marble. Lincoln was one of his great heroes. He may also have been influenced by recent biographies that mentioned that Lincoln's mother may have been illegitimate, which was something he could relate to.[11] Borglum initially hoped to display his sculpture in the Theodore Roosevelt White House in time for the anniversary of Lincoln's birthday. Instead it was purchased by Eugene Meyer Jr., the future owner of the *Washington Post*, and exhibited in the Capitol Rotunda. It remained there until 1979 when it was moved and installed in the crypt below.[12]

On Memorial Day 1911, Borglum's *Seated Lincoln* was installed in front of the Essex County Court House in Newark. President Theodore Roosevelt gave the dedication speech to some twenty-five thousand spectators, following a parade of six thousand soldiers, including Civil War veterans.[13] The commission for the statue was funded by the estate of Amos H. Van Horn, a Civil War veteran who made his fortune in the furniture business.[14] His executor, Ralph Lum, had been impressed with Borglum's *Lincoln* in the Capitol Rotunda and used his influence to hire the sculptor. Rather than the typical formal portrait, Borglum depicted a tired humble president seated on a bench with room for visitors to join him. Roosevelt supposedly remarked, "Why this doesn't look like a monument at all."[15] Borglum explained that he wanted to portray Lincoln as worried and grieving about Civil War casualties and initially titled the sculpture *Lincoln in Gethsemane*. However, it has always been referred to as the *Seated Lincoln*. Immediately accessible, the work attracted widespread press and was immensely popular.

Wars of America (1920–24) was an early indicator of Borglum's propensity for large-scale works. Also funded by the Horn estate, the sculpture was dedicated on Memorial Day 1926, in Newark's Military Park. This large complex sculpture features two horses and forty-two large figures depicting fighters in the Revolutionary, Civil, and Spanish-American Wars, as well as World War I. It also includes a Red Cross nurse, scenes of civilian life such as leave-taking, and portraits of the donor, the artist, and his son. The mass of figures surges forward up a hill overlooking a reflecting pool in the shape of a sword, visible only from the air.[16] Later the pool was filled with flowers.

Wars of America rests on a base made of granite taken from Stone Mountain where Borglum had been working on a monument to the Confederate heroes of the Civil War.[17] The Atlanta monument was initially suggested by local newsman Jack T. Graves. His idea appealed to Mrs. C. Helen Plane, leader of the United Daughters of the Confederacy who commissioned the *Stone Mountain* sculpture in 1915. The property was leased from Samuel Venable, the owner of the granite company and a Ku Klux Klan member.[18] The original plan called for a bust of Robert E. Lee; Borglum, however, had a larger vision. He wanted to include figures of Jefferson Davis and Stonewall Jackson on horseback, followed by a vast relief of cavalry, artillery, and foot soldiers. At the base of the mountain he envisioned a hall of records containing Confederate documents, as well as a large open amphitheater.[19]

The project presented many technical challenges, but there were other obstacles as well. When the United States entered World War I in 1917, the commission had to be put on hold. Then, too, Borglum's cavalier spending led to ongoing financial problems that, in turn, led to issues of control with the Board of the Confederate Memorial Association. In 1925 they fired him; in turn, he destroyed his models, leaving the project unfinished and prompting the board to put out a warrant for his arrest. Leaving this aborted commission, Borglum headed straight for Mount Rushmore, writing to Doane Robinson, "I want the vindication it would give me."[20] According to his granddaughter Robin Borglum Carter, "The Stone Mountain defeat remained Gutzon's biggest disappointment in life," and he always hoped someday to finish it.[21]

Ideologically, *Stone Mountain* aligned with Borglum's political beliefs. He told a reporter, "I am celebrating an idea, the idea of strength, courage, self-sacrifice and love. These men who fought for a lost cause went forth fearlessly to do their best as they saw it."[22] An ardent white supremacist, Borglum was closely associated with the Ku Klux Klan.[23] There is no documentary proof that he actually joined it, but his various prejudices became more pronounced after 1923 when he became directly involved with the group.[24] Today *Stone Mountain* is situated in a three-thousand-acre state park with multiple tourist attractions. Visited by some four million visitors annually, it too has become a site of controversy.[25] In this and in many other ways, it was a preview of Mount Rushmore. Both monuments presented daunting technical challenges, and Borglum enlarged the original scheme of both to include additional figures and elements. Both projects were plagued throughout by financial problems and struggles over control created by Borglum; at Rushmore these were consistently resolved by others. In addition to Doane Robinson, U.S. senator Peter Norbeck, U.S. congressman William Williamson, and business-man John Boland all lobbied to make Mount Rushmore possible.[26] Without their support, Borglum's vision, his art, and the technical knowhow of his assistants, the monument would never have been built.

The Realization of Mount Rushmore

When Borglum arrived in South Dakota, the location for Mount Rushmore had not yet been determined and there were no easy roads leading to the Black Hills. Within three days he selected the peak that had been named in 1885 for a young New York lawyer, Charles Rushmore, sent by the Harney Peak

Consolidated Tin Mining Company to handle mining claims. As the story goes, when he asked his guide and the miners and prospectors accompanying him about the name of the mountain, they told him that it didn't have one so they joked that they would name it after him.[27]

Once the location was set, the subjects had to be determined. Borglum argued that Robinson's original focus was too local. He envisioned a grand national monument and began sketching a standing figure of George Washington. Soon after, he added Lincoln and then Jefferson, and by 1925 he had included Theodore Roosevelt. Borglum intended the monument to commemorate "the foundation, preservation, and continental expansion of the United States."[28] Although Roosevelt was a controversial choice since he had only been dead for sixteen years, he and Borglum were friends with similar personalities, and the sculptor admired his role in building the Panama Canal.[29] Both Borglum and Norbeck had campaigned for Roosevelt's reelection in 1912.

Each head on Mount Rushmore is 60 feet tall and all four together measure 180 feet across. In photographs taken from a parallel height they appear gigantic. Seen from the ground they seem much smaller. At the site, it is possible to climb a stairway that provides various closer views. The carving of Mount Rushmore was both a huge sculptural and engineering challenge, not the least of which was getting men and materials up the mountain.[30] They had to deal with punishing South Dakota winters and ongoing funding crises, including the Great Depression, all of which stopped work for a time. That Borglum managed to get it built at all is a tribute to his skill and determination. Setting up a studio at the site, he entertained visitors throughout the process. Fortunately, he was able to hire many workers, some through the New Deal. He carved one head at a time based on models built on a scale of one to twelve feet. Washington was dedicated in 1934, Jefferson in 1936, Lincoln in 1937, and Roosevelt in 1939.

Dedication ceremonies were important and Borglum was very good at staging them. They attracted national press and engaged public opinion— much of it translating into public support and funding opportunities. In *The Carving of Mount Rushmore*, Alan Smith described the initial dedication on 1 October 1925: "A typical Borglum production, it contained drama and inspiration in flowing abundance. The band played; a group of Sioux Indians did a war dance, and, later, a grass dance; and interspersed among these activities were speeches and more speeches . . . upon the top of the cliff [there was] the distance-dwarfed figure of a Sioux Indian chief, Black Horse, in full tribal regalia. Representing the land's original owners, he remained there, regal and unmoving, throughout the rest of the ceremony."[31] It ended with the singing of "The Star-Spangled Banner" and Borglum planting the American flag on the mountain. The greatest public relations impact, however, was the appearance of the president of the United States.

Borglum enlisted supporters to make every effort to persuade President Calvin Coolidge to vacation in the Black Hills, ensuring that he had a good time and would attend the dedication of the cornerstone in 1927.[32] The South Dakota legislature issued a formal invitation, delivered to the president by Senator Norbeck. Since Coolidge suffered from chronic bronchitis, the invitation emphasized the benefits of the South Dakota climate. He liked to fish so a local creek was reserved for him and stocked with old trout that were easy to catch. The state changed the name of Mount Lookout to Mount Coolidge and that of Squaw Creek to Grace Coolidge Creek. A delegation of Sioux made the president an honorary member of the tribe (although this may not have been legitimate), gave him a Sioux name, and presented him with a headdress. It worked.

Coolidge gave a ringing endorsement of the project, totally ignoring the Native American history of the site: "Its location will be significant. Here in the heart of the continent, on the side of a mountain which probably no white man had ever beheld in the days of Washington, in territory acquired by the action of Jefferson, which remained an unbroken wilderness beyond the days of Lincoln, which was especially loved by Roosevelt."[33] Coolidge's interpretation of what the presidents symbolized aligned with Borglum's: "The union of these four presidents carved on the face of the everlasting hills of South Dakota will constitute a distinctly national monument. It will be decidedly American in its conception, in its magnitude, in its meaning and altogether worthy of our country."[34] Coolidge went on to promise federal support and urged private contributions as well.[35] As part of the day's pageantry, Borglum asked the president to hand him the first drill bits that would be used on the project. After drilling symbolic holes, he gave one bit each to Coolidge,

Norbeck, and Robinson. Prompted by the president's unexpected but exceedingly welcome financial endorsement, Borglum invited him to write the text for the entablature: "As the first president who has taken part in the great undertaking, please write the inscription to be carved on that mountain!"[36] Although that sounded promising, it did not end well.

The subsequent unveiling of Washington's head on 4 July 1930 coincided with the beginning of the Great Depression, so the overall tone was subdued and there were no celebratory speakers.[37] Nevertheless, the event was widely filmed and featured in the press, including the front page of the *New York Times*. Improved roads now made it possible to reach Mount Rushmore by car, and Borglum's studio had become an added tourist attraction. Around this time, the chairman of the recently formed Mount Rushmore Memorial Commission, Joseph Cullinan, a Texas oil man and personal friend of the sculptor, suggested adding the words "America's Shrine for Political Democracy" to the organization's letterhead. This was subsequently shortened to "The Shrine of Democracy," which caught on immediately.

Six years later, in 1936, Franklin Delano Roosevelt attended the dedication of the as yet unfinished head of Thomas Jefferson. Even though he hadn't intended to speak, the president was so impressed with the monument that he changed his mind: "I had seen the photographs, I had seen the drawings, and I had talked with those who are responsible for this great work, and yet I had no conception, until about ten minutes ago, not only of its magnitude but of its permanent beauty importance."[38] Since the project now depended on federal funding, FDR's presence and endorsement was a critically important vote of confidence.

The dedication of Lincoln's head took place on 17 September 1937, the 150th anniversary of the ratification of the Constitution, but with no president there.[39] Nevertheless, attendance was about double from the previous year and Borglum, as always, was able to supply some drama. He began with a recollection of some of the most important supporters of the monument who had since died, including Calvin Coolidge, Andrew Mellon, Coleman Dupont, Edward Rushmore, and Peter Norbeck. Following the playing of "Taps," he stated, "This monument has but a single purpose, to borrow a line from Lincoln's Gettysburg speech: 'That these men shall not have lived in vain; that under God the nation they built shall have a new birth of freedom, and that a government of the people, by the people, and for the people shall not perish from the earth.'"[40] Borglum spoke of his own grandiose ambition to carve a work that would stand with the colossal statues of Egypt and the classical world.[41] He concluded the day's proceedings with a blast of dynamite as Lincoln's face was revealed from behind the American flag.

The same year Congress cut funding for the planned inscription and the Hall of Records and recommended that Borglum's studio be repurposed as a museum. Two years later, on 2 July 1939, South Dakota's fiftieth anniversary of statehood, Borglum dedicated the head of Theodore Roosevelt.[42] William S. Hart, a famous actor who had appeared as a cowboy in many westerns, and whom Borglum inexplicably referred to as the heir to Crazy Horse, appealed for justice for Native Americans in both English and Lakota. A number of Lakota Sioux were present and participated in the pageant. Again, the ceremony ended with a display of fireworks, these outlining images of, among other things, a Native American and a white man, a map of the state, and the American flag. Finally, the four presidents were revealed together for the first time, illuminated in the night sky by twelve enormous spotlights that gradually gained in brightness. The audience was the largest yet. But within two years Gutzon Borglum would be dead and his son Lincoln would take over work on the monument.

Unfinished and Unbuilt Elements

Mount Rushmore remains unfinished. Even the heads are not quite complete although that is not apparent. Borglum at first considered head-to-waist figures that would have been some four hundred feet high. He envisioned an entablature on the same side of the mountain and a hall of records behind it as essential parts of his conception. Inspired by inscriptions on ancient monuments such as the Arch of Constantine, Borglum said, "You might as well drop a letter into the World's Postal Service without an address or signature as to send that carved Mountain into history without identification."[43] The entablature was publicized in 1927 when Borglum on the spur of the moment invited President Coolidge to write it.[44] It was intended to cover an area of some 120 by 80 feet with an outline shaped like the Louisiana Purchase, which in 1803 doubled the size of the country. Three-foot-high letters would list key events in American history in the area where Lincoln's head was eventually carved. Although Coolidge complied, Borglum took it upon himself to edit his text and submit it to the press in his revised form. The president found out about it the next day only when he read the words attributed to him in the paper, and promptly withdrew from the project.[45]

After Coolidge's death in 1933, Borglum arranged to have the Hearst newspaper chain, with a circulation of some five million, run a contest to sum up the history of the country in six hundred words or less for the inscription on the entablature. The sizable Hearst fortune had come in part from goldmining in the Black Hills. Borglum provided a list of events to be included: "the Declaration of Independence, the Constitution, the Louisiana Purchase, the cession of Florida to the United States, the rise of the Republic of Texas and its entry into the United States; the Mexican War and the acquisition of a huge swath of land that included California, Nevada, Utah, most of New Mexico, Arizona and Colorado, and parts of Texas, Oklahoma, Kansas, and Wyoming; the settlement of the Oregon boundary dispute; the Alaska Purchase; and the Panama Canal."[46] Like his choice of the Rushmore presidents, these subjects were based on the territorial expansion of the country.[47] Prizes were to include medals and cash, a college scholarship, and the honor of having your words inscribed on the monument. Thousands entered, although sources disagree about who won and how the prize money was used.[48] In any event, the contest generated a great deal of publicity for Mount Rushmore.

Borglum's plan for the Hall of Records was even more ambitious. His inspiration came from *She*, a 1935 Hollywood film directed by Henry Rider Haggard based on his eponymous novel; the film starred Randolph Scot as the hero and Helen Gahagan as an African queen who remained forever young and lived in an underground temple.[49] Located behind the presidents, Borglum's museum was to be reached by a grand stairway at Lincoln's left, leading to a sixty-foot-high entrance similar to the one leading to Queen Ayesha's Temple of Kor in the film; Borglum envisioned it as comparable only to the steps leading to the Parthenon from the Acropolis. Cast glass doors were to be topped by a giant eagle with a wingspan of thirty-eight feet, while the inner entrance wall would be made of a blue-and-gold lapis mosaic. Interior walls would feature a frieze with historic events, while a series of carved recesses with bronze and glass cabinets would contain archival records that included inventions (such as electricity, radio, motion pictures, and aviation) and a sealed time capsule.

Borglum was adamant about the exclusion of Native American history: "Neither will the records contain more than a brief resume of the Indian occupancy here but will be specifically devoted to the progress that has changed the country since the first white man sighted America."[50] He planned a series of busts of famous men: Benjamin Franklin, Alexander Hamilton, John Hancock, Patrick Henry, Andrew Johnson, John Marshall, Thomas Paine, Daniel Webster, among others, as well as the men who had made Mount Rushmore possible: Robinson, Norbeck, Williamson, John Boland, Kent Keller, and Key Pitman. There was a brief campaign to have Susan B. Anthony included on the front of the mountain along with the four presidents and a bill to that effect was introduced in Congress. Although Borglum never intended to comply, he did at one point tell FDR that he planned to include a bust of Anthony with those of the men named above.[51]

In proposing the Hall of Records, essentially a museum, the sculptor was somewhat prescient. Plans for both the Oklahoma City National Memorial (2000–2001) and the National September 11 Memorial (2014) included a museum from the start, and a proposed addition of an education center to the Vietnam Veterans Memorial remains unrealized due to insufficient funds. That, too, was the fate of Borglum's Hall of Records. By 1938–39, the entire cavern had been blasted and hollowed out but nothing was done until the 1980s, when the sculptor's daughter, Mary Ellis Borglum, presented a much-reduced plan to the National Park Service. In 1998 a few porcelain panels inscribed with the Declaration of Independence and the Constitution, a biography of Borglum, some historical information about the four presidents, and a brief history of the United States, together with a few other things, were placed in a box and sealed in a titanium vault. The granite chamber was covered with a granite stone inscribed with an explanation of how the Hall of Records relates to the project.

Although only a fraction of Borglum's vision was realized, over time the Mount Rushmore complex was enlarged to include a Memorial View

Building with a restaurant and gift shop as well as an amphitheater with a two-thousand-person capacity. There are also administrative buildings and a large parking lot, as well as an Avenue of Flags. A Lincoln Borglum Museum was added below the Grand View Terrace, including two theaters that feature a thirteen-minute film. These additions are indicative of the gigantic tourist attraction that the monument has become, well beyond the scale of anything Doane Robinson could have imagined. Approaching Mount Rushmore from Highway 16 today, one experiences what has been described as "one of the most orgiastic tourist corridors in the world. The buffer of roadside attractions include but is by no means limited to Reptile Gardens, Black Hills Maze, 1880 Train, Sitting Bull Crystal Caverns, Fort Hays Dances with Wolves Film Set, Cosmos Mystery Area, Old MacDonald's Farm, and Bear Country USA. . . . For sheer density and intensity, Highway 16 rivals not so much the Strip in Las Vegas as the Via Dolorosa in Jerusalem, where the Stations of the Cross today are scrunched between shops offering everything from sheep heads to knock-off crowns of thorns."[52]

Almost everyone today recognizes Mount Rushmore, whether or not they've actually seen it in person; if they visit the site it has been preframed for them, perhaps most famously by *North by Northwest*, Alfred Hitchcock's 1959 thriller starring Cary Grant and Eva Marie Saint. Three years later, in 1962, the first American Telstar satellite contained images of "a baseball game (Cubs versus Phillies), a presidential press conference, and Mount Rushmore, including a lingering pan of the actual face of Ben Black Elk, a Lakota Sioux. Thus, a Native American was one of the very first people in the world to have his image broadcast by satellite across the Atlantic. . . . As the camera panned over the faces on the mountain, an announcer solemnly spoke of the presidents and their contributions to our nation's history."[53] Today Mount Rushmore has been enculturated through various media including television, films, and all manner of advertisements.[54] There are also countless satirical suggestions for a fifth head or four different heads.

Mount Rushmore has remained a site for political rallies and statements. On 11 June 1953, President Dwight D. Eisenhower addressed the Young Republicans League convention there using the monument primarily as a backdrop. Fifty years after Borglum's death, on 3 July 1991, President George

H. W. Bush dedicated the completion of the monument, marking the sixth time that Mount Rushmore had been dedicated. Produced by Radio City Music Hall, it was quite an extravaganza. Introduced by actor Jimmy Stewart, Bush quoted a visitor who likened their experience to "a communion with the very soul of America."[55] He praised the four presidents for their best-known accomplishments, and called the Louisiana Purchase an opportunity for all Americans. He cited Theodore Roosevelt's Nobel Prize for Peace and his love for the wilderness, which Bush considered the property of all future Americans. In sum he deemed Mount Rushmore a "symbol of the American character soaring and unafraid." Lakota Chief White Eagle, a token Native American presence, stated: "I can feel the dignity and the pain of my fathers as we stand together on this land we call *Paha Sapa*." There was, however, no mention of broken treaties or stolen property. White Eagle sang "So Many Voices Sing American Songs," but the dominant note was sounded by Rose-mary Clooney's performance of "America the Beautiful," followed by Woody Guthrie's "This Land Is Your Land."

President Clinton's visit on 6 July 1996 was radically different. He gave no speech, mingled with visitors on the observation terrace, and stayed only about an hour, but spent nearly twice as long at the memorial to Crazy Horse some seventeen miles southwest of Mount Rushmore. Most of the next day he visited the Pine Ridge Reservation, located in what was then the poorest county in the United States, and concluded: "We have to find a way to fix this. We cannot rest until we do better, and trying is not enough."[56] When President George W. Bush visited Mount Rushmore on 15 August 2002, he spoke mainly about contemporary political issues. In 2014, two years after the United Nations recommended returning the Black Hills to the Sioux, President Barack Obama visited the Standing Rock Reservation and reviewed his administration's various efforts on behalf of Native Americans, acknowl-edging both their status as nations as well as the many problems they faced.[57]

President Donald Trump visited Mount Rushmore on 3 July 2020. The media featured articles on environmental concerns about the fireworks, his racist speech (remarkably similar in tone and substance to Borglum's views), and the revival of Native American claims.[58] The monument was temporarily closed except for this event due to the coronavirus pandemic. Trump mentioned neither the pandemic rapidly spiraling out of control in many states nor the significance of the growing Black Lives Matter movement. Instead he focused on preserving monuments to an uninflected national history.[59]

Given the myriad references and reproductions, it is sometimes difficult to remember that Mount Rushmore is also a work of art. When we compare Borglum's sculpture to the nearby memorial to Crazy Horse (also unfinished), it is clearly of a higher aesthetic quality. The easily recognizable portraits project from the mountain so that they are widely visible and are carved to take advantage of natural light. Korczak Ziolkowski, the self-taught sculptor of Crazy Horse, spent some time as an assistant at Mount Rushmore but apparently was fired after he got into a disagreement with Lincoln Borglum.[60] The finished Crazy Horse monument is intended to depict him sitting on a horse, pointing ahead with his left arm at a scale that will dwarf Mount Rushmore. Brooke Jarvis in a 2019 *New Yorker* article noted that at "an over-all height nearly four times that of the Statue of Liberty; the arm long enough to accommodate a line of semi-trucks; the horse's ears the size of school buses, its nostrils carved twenty-five feet around and nine feet deep, it will be the largest sculpture in the history of the world."[61] Although begun in 1948, so far all that has emerged from the mountain is his face—not even his entire head—and it is very crudely carved.

Like Mount Rushmore, the history of the Crazy Horse memorial is riddled with disturbing ironies. Although commissioned in 1939 by a Lakota elder, Henry Standing Bear, who considered a memorial to Crazy Horse a response to Rushmore, a statement "that the red man had great heroes, too," it is seen by many Native Americans as an insult to the warrior who would have been appalled by its grandiosity. Crazy Horse was known for his humility; he never allowed himself to be photographed and asked to be buried in an unmarked grave. He fought his entire life to keep the Black Hills sacred, yet this monument was created by blowing up another mountain. The AIM leader Russell Means likened it to "carving up the mountain of Zion," and Charmaine White Face, spokesperson for the Sioux Nation Treaty Council, called it "a sacrilege." Some say the face on the mountain resembles Ziolkowski. When the project was announced in 1948, plans included the Indian University of North America and Medical Training Center, the Indian Museum of North

America, the Native American Educational Cultural Center, and recreational facilities.[62] A scaled down version of the university exists today in the form of a summer program offered by the University of Iowa in conjunction with the Memorial Foundation.[63] There is also an Indian Museum but the authenticity of some of its objects has been challenged.[64] While there is something called the Native Educational Cultural Center at the memorial, there is also one located at Purdue University.[65]

The film shown in the theater includes laudatory testimonials from Native Americans, and there are all kinds of efforts to link the subject with the sculptor. More than anything the memorial functions as a Ziolkowski family business. Even though it exists in a barely realized form, it has become a tourist attraction and a money maker. The family has refused funding from the federal government to complete the monument since they are doing very well on their own. In 2018 the Crazy Horse Memorial Foundation had $77 million in assets and reported $12.5 million from annual admissions (it costs $125 to visit the top) and donations from over a million visitors. There is a general perception that fees and contributions go to local reservations. However, that is not the case and Native Americans resent this. Jim Bradford, who worked at the site after serving in the South Dakota state senate, observed that it seemed to start as "a dedication to the Native American people." He continued, "But I think now it's a business first . . . one non-Indian family has become millionaires off our people." Meanwhile Native Americans at the nearby Pine Ridge Reservation continue to live in deplorable conditions and their visitors' center has few tourists.

The Mount Rushmore story is nothing if not complex and contradictory, a history of willful greed and cruelty. Until recently it has been obscured by an unquestioned tribute to American greatness. Borglum's intention of celebrating territorial expansion has been largely masked by the patriotic rhetoric surrounding the four presidents. The treatment of Native Americans by the U.S. government is characterized by one betrayal after another, although a kind of reckoning has slowly begun. Signs appeared at the site with the burgeoning of Red Power and the acknowledgment by the Supreme Court that the Lakota Sioux still own the land that was ceded to them by the 1868 Fort Laramie Treaty and upon which Mount Rushmore stands. Finally, ongoing

Native American issues are featured in the press, even if only to highlight continuing problems. The protest and lawsuit by the Standing Rock Sioux Tribe against the Dakota Access Pipeline garnered broad attention and support ending in a victory for the Standing Rock Sioux Tribe.[66] In the spring of 2020, the *Washington Post* noted that the coronavirus pandemic was taking an extraordinarily high toll on Native Americans, largely due to inadequate health care.

Mount Rushmore today is so closely linked to national identity that removing it, as some have suggested, is neither viable or even desirable.[67] We can acknowledge that while for many it remains "a shrine to democracy," it was intended to celebrate American expansion. We can make the national narrative pertaining to Mount Rushmore more inclusive by consulting with Native Americans, hiring them in positions of authority, and electing them to local, state, and federal office. We can update programs at the site and in American history textbooks and always continue to ask what and whom we have left out.

3

George Washington Imagined

Before there was a nation—before there was any symbol of that nation (a
flag, a Constitution, a national seal)—there was Washington.

—GARRY WILLS

George Washington's face is immediately recognizable from its appearance
on dollar bills, quarters, and postage stamps.[1] However, the works of art on
which they, as well as his image on Mount Rushmore, are based are not nearly
as familiar. George Washington stood for national identity and portraying
him in a neoclassical style (the preferred style in Europe from roughly the mid-
eighteenth to the mid-nineteenth century and which was based on Greek and
Roman art and architecture) indicated an adherence to traditional visual and
cultural values. By contrast, a distinctly American style based on naturalism
(a style concerned with depicting actual appearances) rather than idealism
was intended to convey that the former colonies were an entirely new entity.
Borglum was committed to an independent American style.[2]

 Borglum's first idea for Mount Rushmore appeared in a 1924 sketch of
standing figures of Washington and Lincoln seen in profile.[3] He had looked
closely at the portrait by the American Rembrandt Peale (son of Charles

Willson Peale), painted after Washington's death, and the terra cotta bust by the French sculptor Jean-Antoine Houdon.[4] Borglum's Washington also resembles some of Gilbert Stuart's better known paintings, in particular the *Landsdowne Portrait* (1796) and the much reproduced but unfinished *Athenaeum Portrait* (1796). At the unveiling of Washington's head, Borglum remarked, "On Mount Rushmore, there has been produced a forehead of Washington twenty feet from wig to nose, as animate and carefully constructed as the Houdon mask which I have followed, together with the portraits of Peale and Stewart [*sic*]. The brow has emerged, amazing in mass, vigor and beauty of form; the nose seems better than the Stewart nose."[5] Borglum acknowledged that Houdon's life mask was "the most valuable document extant . . . and I have followed it more than any or all others."[6]

Houdon was commissioned by the Virginia state legislature to create a statue to celebrate Washington's leadership as commander in chief during the Revolutionary War.[7] In 1784 there were no American sculptors thought capable of executing such a work, so Governor Benjamin Harrison sought advice from Thomas Jefferson, who was then in France. Jefferson, in consultation with Benjamin Franklin, recommended Houdon. Governor Harrison offered to send a full-length image of Washington by Charles Willson Peale to Paris to serve as a model but Houdon preferred to work directly from the subject. Washington, then fifty-three, had just resigned his military commission and was returning to life as a gentleman farmer after eight and a half years of war. Houdon spent several days with him at Mount Vernon, took careful measurements, and created a life-size terra cotta bust that he gave to Washington, who kept it in his study for the rest of his life. His family and many others considered it the best existing likeness.[8] Houdon submitted copies of the bust and the life mask to the Continental Congress in New York as his bid for a pending commission for a bronze equestrian statue of Washington "represented in a Roman dress, holding a truncheon in his right hand and his head encircled with a laurel wreath."[9] This unrealized commission rather than the Virginia statue was likely what prompted Houdon's trip to the United States.[10]

The issue of how the Richmond statue should be clothed was emblematic of the importance of style in conveying content. Houdon made two scale models, one dressed in the traditional neoclassical style and the other in contemporary dress. The American painter Benjamin West, then living in London, had been lauded for his use of modern uniforms in *The Death of General Wolfe* (1770) commemorating the 1759 Battle of Quebec, in which James Wolfe died at the moment of victory. Washington, hearing of West's success, replied to Jefferson's query about dress: "A servile adherence to the garb of antiquity might not be altogether so expedient as some little deviation in favor of the modern costume. This taste which has been introduced in the painting by Mr. West I understand is received with applause and prevails extensively."[11] Surprisingly, Jefferson concurred: "I think a modern in antique dress as just an object of ridicule as a Hercules or Marius with a periwig and chapeau-bras."[12] Washington and Jefferson were advocating for an independent American style (as Borglum was to do later) even though both Jefferson's and Houdon's abiding preference for the neoclassical was evident elsewhere.[13]

In Houdon's standing sculpture Washington is depicted putting his military cloak aside, surrounded by symbols that convey his transition from one life to another.[14] The plow behind Washington indicates his return to agriculture, as does the walking stick he carries in his right hand, typical of gentlemen farmers. There are also some classical references. He leans on the fasces, a bundle of rods with an extended axe blade that symbolized power and legal authority in the Roman republic. Because Washington relinquished his powerful military commission for a civilian life, he was compared to Cincinnatus, the Roman statesman and military leader famous for resigning from power after a crisis had passed.[15] Houdon's six-foot-two marble statue, completed in 1788, was installed some eight years later in the Virginia State House, where it still stands today. In 1814 James Madison added an inscription on the pedestal, typical of the veneration of Washington: "The General Assembly of the Commonwealth of Virginia have caused this Statue to be erected as a monument of affection and gratitude to George Washington, who, uniting to the endowments of the Hero, the virtues of the Patriot, and exerting both in establishing the Liberties of his Country, has rendered his name dear to his Fellow-Citizens, and given the world an immortal example of true Glory." The images Houdon created of Washington during the latter's lifetime—the statue, the bust, and the life mask—became the primary models for sculptors going forward.[16]

Unlike George Washington, Thomas Jefferson preferred the classical style. This was evident in the 1818 commission of a monument to Washington for the state house in Raleigh, North Carolina. In a letter to North Carolina senator Nathaniel Macon, he wrote, "As to the style or costume, I am sure the artist, and every person of taste in Europe would be for the Roman, the effect of which is undoubtedly of a different order. Our boots and regimentals have a very puny effect."[17] Jefferson recommended Antonio Canova, who created a greater-than-life-size statue of a seated Washington writing his Farewell Address, dressed as a Roman general wearing a knee-length toga and sandals. Following Jefferson's suggestion, Canova used the classicizing marble bust created from life by Giuseppe Ceracchi for the face.[18] The reliefs around the base of the statue depict scenes from Washington's life. These were taken from engravings by John Trumbull: Lord Cornwallis surrendering his sword to Washington; Washington resigning his military commission after the war; Washington receiving a unanimous vote to head the new government; and Washington in front of a cottage holding a plough drawn by two oxen with figures of Ceres (the god of agriculture) and Mercury (the god of war).

Although Canova's statue eventually became the most famous and admired work in the country, initial response to the work was mixed. Some local residents and visitors were shocked by the appearance of a partially nude Washington, while more esthetically sophisticated viewers were appreciative; after a time, popular opinion evolved.[19] State architect William Nichols rebuilt the North Carolina capitol rotunda, which was to house the statue, in a neoclassical style that by the early nineteenth century was considered conservative, in alignment with the status quo. In this way it was related to the political ideology of the ruling planter class.[20] Slavery had become a contentious issue and Washington's association with the Roman Cincinnatus, also a slave owner, was interpreted as a validation of the first president's participation in the practice. The statue was destroyed in a fire in 1831; plans to restore it never materialized. However, a plaster cast can be seen in the North Carolina Museum of History and a marble replacement of the statue was installed in the rotunda in 1970.[21]

Objections to the neoclassical style of Canova's statue were minor compared to responses to Horatio Greenough's *George Washington* (1832–41), commissioned for the Capitol Rotunda in DC to mark the centennial of the first president's birth. Greenough, the first American sculptor to receive a federal commission, had trained in Italy. His statue of Washington, inspired by Phidias' fifth-century BCE sculpture of Zeus at Olympia in Greece, depicts a ten-foot-high, seated president, partially clad in classical drapery.[22] This limited nudity as well as the implicit comparison of Washington to a Greek god were shocking to the American public. The negative reaction was so intense that the sculpture was moved to the Capitol grounds; there, it did not fare well exposed to the elements. After extensive conservation it was relocated several times. Today it is in the National Museum of American History in Washington DC.

By midcentury, adherence to neoclassicism had lessened considerably.[23] Equestrian monuments, however, which had a long tradition in classical and Renaissance art, were still in vogue. Henry Kirke Brown and Clark Mills, creators of the first equestrian monuments of George Washington, would have been familiar with well-known surviving examples: *Marcus Aurelius* (ca. 173–76 CE) now in the Capitoline Museum, Rome; Donatello's *Erasmo da Narni*, better known as *Gattamelata* (1445–53), in Padua; and Andrea del Verrocchio's *Colleoni* (1481–95) in Venice. Brown and Mills were part of a new generation of artists who, although well-versed in European traditions, were more interested in developing a naturalistic American style.[24]

Despite objections to Greenough's neoclassical Washington for the Capitol, in 1851 the sculptor was commissioned to create an equestrian monument for Union Square in New York. Sometime later, Henry Kirke Brown was apparently asked to work as his assistant. Greenough, however, quarreled with the committee that had requested the statue, and the commission went to Brown when Greenough died in 1852.[25] John Q. Quincy Adams Ward was then hired to assist Brown. In this monument, Washington is portrayed reclaiming the city from the British on Evacuation Day, 25 November 1783. The sculpture uses both naturalistic and historical references. The general's head is based on a copy of Houdon's bust, while the horse and overall composition evoke the calm dignity of both the *Marcus Aurelius* and Donatello's *Gattamelata*. Washington's right arm is stretched forward in command and one of the horse's front legs is raised, suggesting movement. Unveiled on the eightieth anniversary of the signing of the Declaration of Independence in 1856, the statue was originally sited on a traffic island on the southeast corner of Union Square.[26] In 1930 it was relocated to its present location at the center of the south side, where it has served as a focal point for various demonstrations. On and after 9/11 it became a locus of mourning for those lost in the attack and an expression of patriotism, symbolized by the numerous American flags on and surrounding the statue.

Brown's equestrian monument was the second to be cast in the United States. The first was Clark Mills's *Andrew Jackson* (1848–53) in Lafayette Square, Washington DC.[27] Within weeks of its installation, Mills was commissioned to create an equestrian statue of Washington for Washington Circle in the nation's capital, which was dedicated by President James Buchanan on Washington's birthday in 1860. On the eve of the Civil War sectional conflict and partisan animosity ran high,[28] but Washington was valorized by both the North and South, and his image was used to reinforce a sense of national unity even in the face of impending civil war.

The very first monument dedicated to the first president was a column and the most famous an obelisk; both were by the architect Robert Mills, one of the first professional architects born in the United States. The cornerstone of the Washington Monument in Baltimore was dedicated on 4 July 1815. A little over a decade later, a statue of Washington resigning his commission as commander in chief of the Continental Army by the Italian sculptor Enrico Causici was installed on top of the 178-foot, 8-inch column. In many ways problems with this commission prefigured Mills's later problems realizing the Washington Monument in the nation's capital. Both were delayed by external circumstances and an inability to decide on an appropriate form. Both used ancient architectural precedents (a classical column and an Egyptian obelisk) modified for a contemporary audience and budget. Significant stylistic changes were made to the winning design—in Baltimore by Mills himself, and in DC after the architect's death by Lt. Col. Thomas Casey of the Army Corps of Engineers. Modifications and embellishments continued even after the monuments were dedicated.

The Baltimore monument was commissioned by a group of the city's most prominent residents led by its foremost patron of the arts, Robert Gilmor Jr., in an effort to prevent the demolition of a cluster of townhouses then located around a courthouse.[29] Robert Mills was not their first choice.[30] The twenty-three-member Board of Managers initially invited Maximilian Godefroy, a French architect then living and teaching in the city, to submit a proposal. Although they did not accept any of the five ideas he presented, Godefroy's Doric rotunda with a statue of Washington on top appeared in one version of Mills's winning design for the Washington Monument in DC.[31] After delays caused by financial difficulties and the War of 1812, the design committee for the Baltimore statue considered commissioning Canova or holding a limited competition; they chose the latter. Mills was the only American among the five entrants, a factor that he emphasized in his presentation.[32] He thought his Doric column appropriate for Washington's "solidity and simplicity of character."[33] The column, however, was far from what would be characterized as simple today. A circular stairway was divided into galleries and walkways that featured inscriptions and reliefs. The even more elaborate base consisted of a grand arch with thirteen segments, each to be inscribed with the emblem of a state. For the top, Mills planned an equestrian statue of Washington led by a figure of Victory placed so high it is hard to see. Installation was completed in 1829, while decorative iron railings and gates were finished later, as were the promenades. Four large trophies planned for the corners of the pedestal were never realized. Without them Mills and the Board of Managers considered the monument unfinished. Kirk Savage concluded that "Baltimore elevated Washington's achievement in order to elevate its own column, to be the 'largest and finest' monument ever erected in the country."[34]

In 1845, after many years and many design submissions by many architects and sculptors, Robert Mills won the competition to design the Washington Monument in DC. This protracted process revealed widely differing views of what Washington stood for and how he should be commemorated.[35] Mills proposed a five-hundred-foot-tall obelisk with a nearly flat top, covered with inscriptions and ornamentation. The base consisted of a rotunda (one hundred feet high, two hundred feet in diameter), punctuated by thirty twelve-foot-wide Doric columns, representing the existing states. This "National Pantheon" was intended to include statues of the signers of the Declaration of Independence on the outside behind a colonnade and statues of heroes of the Revolution inside the rotunda gallery. It would also have been decorated with a series of paintings depicting major events of the war. A monumental statue of Washington was planned for the center while one of him driving a chariot drawn by four horses (a quadriga) was planned for the entryway with four columns (tetrastyle portico). This complex, highly embellished design is in stark contrast to the minimal form the monument eventually took. The 555-foot-tall obelisk on the National Mall today bears only scant resemblance to the design accepted by the Washington National Monument Society.[36]

The cornerstone of the Washington Monument, laid on July 4, 1848, contained copies of the Declaration of Independence, the Constitution, coins, and newspapers. It was located in the center of the city at the site originally chosen for a monument dedicated to the first president by Pierre Charles L'Enfant, designer of the capital. Congress had asked Mills to modify his original design but the Monument Society ran out of funds in 1854, and Mills died a year later. In 1876, Congress took ownership of the project and finally replaced the unfinished work that had been at the site for years.[37] Once funding was in place, Lt. Col. Thomas Casey, working behind the scenes with next to no interference, radically simplified Mills's design into an obelisk.[38] The interior elevator, powered by steam and lit by electric lights, a technological marvel at the time, provided an exciting ride to the top. Dedicated on Washington's birthday in 1885, the Washington Monument's only relationship to the nation's first president is its name. It includes no image of him, nor any texts pertaining to his life or accomplishments. He is not buried there, nor did any significant event in his life take place there. As such, it is a blank slate suitable for any interpretation.[39]

By contrast, John Quincy Adams Ward's over-life-size bronze statue of Washington, which stands in front of Federal Hall in downtown Manhattan, commemorates a specific event—the inauguration of the first president in 1789. The commission specified, "Said statue shall be in all respects a complete embodiment of the exalted character of Washington, together with the great event the statue commemorates, and that no expense be spared to make it in all respects worthy of the cause."[40] Washington is depicted lifting his hand from the Bible as he completes the swearing-in ceremony. At his inauguration he expressed anxiety about accepting the presidency and concern about his limitations, a Cincinnatus-like attitude toward power he did not seek but accepted as his duty. He declined payment for his services except for expenses, as he had previously as commander in chief of the Army. Dedicated just two years before the Washington Monument, this statue, like so many others, was largely dependent on Houdon's marble work in Richmond (especially in the stance of the figure and inclusion of the fasces), and Stuart's *Athenaeum Portrait* for the face.[41]

One hundred and fifty years after Washington's inauguration a colossal statue of the first president was placed at the crossroads of the 1939 New York World's Fair in Flushing Meadows–Corona Park.[42] The sixty-one-foot-tall statue was by James Earle Fraser, who around this time was working on the statue of Theodore Roosevelt for the front of the American Museum of Natural History. His statue of Washington was sited at the center of Constitution Mall surrounded by the Court of States, with buildings including Federal Hall recreated in the architectural style popular during Washington's time. The fair featured an official ceremony overseen by Albert Einstein with a light show entitled "The Spirit of George Washington."

Today Washington is increasingly viewed critically because of his treatment of Native Americans and enslaved people. These issues came to the fore in a 2019 controversy over a series of thirteen murals created by Victor Mikhail Arnautoff for George Washington High School in San Francisco. A Russian émigré, Arnautoff had worked with the Mexican muralist Diego Rivera who believed in the social mission of art.[43] Covering sixteen hundred feet, the murals were completed in 1936, one of six Works Progress Administration (WPA) commissions for the high school. They included images of Washington as a slave holder and participant in a westward expansion that trampled on Native American rights and lives.[44] Located in the lobby entrance and main stairway, these images prompted objections based on a complete misreading of the visual evidence. Many students understood them to be a celebration of the first president rather than an implicit critique of these injustices. Interpreting the murals as condoning the depicted crimes, they complained of feeling distressed, and even traumatized and unsafe. Responding to #paintitdown advocates, the school board in 2019 voted to cover the murals with white paint. Subsequently the school administration backtracked and chose to hide them behind removable panels. Unfortunately, there were no explanatory labels, no school-wide introduction to the content of the murals, and no strategies for incorporating them into class curricula.[45] This was truly a lost teaching opportunity to address Washington's legacy.[46]

The controversy raised issues of censorship and the valorization of emotional reactions over factual evidence.[47] Amos C. Brown, president of the San Francisco branch of the NAACP, lamented, "We haven't been taught to be critical thinkers. It's cotton candy politics—a 'feel good' for progressive liberals that has no substance to it."[48] The dispute also demonstrated the importance of visual literacy—the ability to interpret images correctly in a historical context and not exclusively through a presentist lens.

Indeed, it turns out that the 2019 controversy was not the first time that the interpretation of the Arnautoff murals proved problematic. In response to earlier student protests of the late 1960s against the mural, Dewey Crumpler, an African American painter who had been involved with civil rights, was commissioned to create a new mural cycle.[49] After an in-depth study of Arnautoff's murals and a trip to Mexico to view Rivera's work, he created *Multi-Ethnic Heritage: Black, Asian, Native/Latin American* (1974). This triptych on removable panels was intended as an affirmation of the contributions of so-called others to the history of the nation. It was meant to supplement, not replace, Arnautoff's work. As Crumpler saw it, "My mural is part of the Arnautoff mural, part of its meaning, and its meaning is part of mine. If you destroy his work of art, you are destroying mine as well."[50]

The history portrayed in Arnautoff's murals—Washington's policies toward Native Americans, Black people, and American expansion—have thus far been largely omitted not only from visual depictions but also from textbooks and school curricula in the United States. Yet these, too, are part of U.S. history. While the first president's contributions to the nation have been widely celebrated, his policies were not without problems. He struggled with his position on slavery and made decisions that prioritized national unity above all.

4

George Washington's Mixed Messages

George Washington has been honored, if not revered, for leading the Continental Army in the Revolution, his role in framing the Constitution, and most importantly his service as the nation's first president. The policies he established were followed for decades if not centuries. Unfortunately, this is also true of his treatment of Native Americans and Black people.

Although the Constitution gave the president authority over Native American affairs, it provided no specifics. Washington developed his policy toward the Indigenous nations together with Secretary of War Henry Knox, suggesting an implicitly adversarial stance. The lands occupied by Native Americans were a direct obstacle to his vision of territorial expansion under federal control.[1] Prior to the Revolution, the British government had imposed a limit on westward expansion in response to Native American resistance and rebellion during the French and Indian War. This prompted the allegiance of many tribes to the British and further unified Washington and the colonists against them.[2]

On a personal level, Washington was interested in owning land from the start of his working life. His first job was as a surveyor when he was still a teenager, measuring and mapping the land so that it could be bought and sold to speculators or settlers.[3] He learned about the profession from his father, who had also been a surveyor. It was a fairly common way for young men to earn good money, both generating sizable fees from large landowners or companies and occasionally providing the opportunity to purchase property. At the age of eighteen, Washington bought 1,459 acres in Frederick County, Virginia, and within three years used his surveying fees to purchase 2,315 acres in the state's Shenandoah Valley. At the time of his death, he had acquired title to some 52,000 acres.[4] With his marriage to the widow Martha Dandridge Custis, he gained an additional 17,500 acres as well as a sizable fortune, making him a landowner of considerable substance, an important factor at a time when owning land was a prerequisite for participation in government.

Washington viewed Native American lands as an obstacle that stood in the way of expanding the country with private property that could be sold to pay off national debts incurred during the Revolution.[5] The individual right to private property was established by the Constitution in 1791 with the Fifth Amendment.[6] Washington considered owning property a hallmark of American freedom, a marker of the best possible way of life. He believed that Native Americans were savages (as they were described in the Declaration of Independence), who had not attained this enviable level of civilization. As a result, he developed what he called "conversion policies" intended to force them to convert their communally administered land to privately owned plots devoted to farming. These policies involved treaties that promised animals and plows that would support this basic change to the Indigenous communal way of life and established Native American trading posts that were not structured to their advantage.[7]

These transformations affected Indigenous domestic life and radically revised gender roles. Although Native women had typically farmed the land and enjoyed considerable equality and influence within their culture, the first president envisioned a patriarchal family with women confined to the home in a subservient role, as part of a total assimilation of Natives into an American way of life. As he prepared for retirement, he compared his situation inappropriately to theirs: "What I have recommended to you, I am myself going to do. After a few moons are passed I shall leave the great town and retire to my farm."[8]

Washington never wavered in his determination to obtain Native American land. He would have preferred to acquire it in a peaceable manner, but he was prepared to take extreme measures, inflicting what by today's standards would be called war crimes. The Six Nations of the Iroquois Confederacy were of particular concern to Washington: at stake was whether they would support the British or side with the French and Americans in the Revolution. He initially tried to negotiate with Native American leaders, but after their attack on Mohawk Valley settlements in upstate New York he retaliated in devastating fashion.[9] At that time the Iroquois referred to him as Town Destroyer (*Conotocarious*, or "devourer of villages").

Still, Washington held various attitudes and deployed different policies toward the Native Americans, as evidenced by the names the Iroquois had for him: Brother, Destroyer, Father.[10] At first, following precedents established by the British, Washington approached Native Americans as a Brother, as equals. He negotiated with them according to their customs, establishing treaties and giving gifts. During the Revolutionary War, as Destroyer, he ordered a scorched earth policy, destroying crops and trees, as well as homes, often killing inhabitants and in some instances setting the houses on fire with people inside. Washington instructed his forces to "chastise and intimidate" and "cut off their settlements, destroy their next year's crops, and do every other mischief of which time and circumstances will permit."[11] This included taking women and children as hostages to use as bargaining chips. He believed that Native Americans gave up any claim to their lands when they supported the British in the Revolution, and therefore it was generous to let them keep any property at all.[12]

After the Revolution, as Father, Washington again followed British and French practice, at least nominally, aimed at protecting the Iroquois from continued encroachment by settlers and speculators. This, however, was consistently subordinated to the priorities of white settlement.[13] In the end, it is this aspect of the first president's legacy that is most difficult to reconcile with the way most Americans view him. Washington gave Native Americans a choice between acculturation and excessive hardship.[14] His policies evidence a monocular cultural arrogance that justified hypocrisy, outright deceit, and excessive cruelty.

Washington's policies toward slavery were even more complex, influenced by his primary concern to save the Union as well as his personal ownership of enslaved people. Africans were imported to Jamestown in 1619; by the 1630s it had become customary to enslave them. Earlier, England, wanting to limit their poor, unemployed, and criminal population, sent these individuals to the colonies where Washington's grandfather, among others, hired them.[15] When England's need for cheap labor increased, the country stopped exporting this population, and consequently plantation owners in Virginia made up the labor shortage with slaves. When Washington was born in 1732, slavery had existed in the colonies for about thirty years. By the time he was a young man, it had become almost impossible to employ white laborers. Since Virginia planters exclusively used slaves for labor, the enslaved population increased from 13,000 in 1700 to 105,000 in 1750. By then, almost 80 percent were born in the United States.[16]

In colonial Virginia, slavery was supported by the powerful Anglican Church, which functioned as the moral and political center for much of contemporary life. Washington was a member of a class that was taught that a person's station in life was defined by God.[17] While slavery originated as a system of free labor, it increasingly became intertwined with other public and private networks.[18] Enslaved people were considered property that could be sold, auctioned and raffled; separating families was common. Hard field labor and long hours were the norm, and perceived slacking was routinely punished by beating. Slaves who worked in the house received better shelter, food, and clothing; the further they worked from the main house, the shabbier these basic elements became.

When Washington was eleven years old his father died and left him ten slaves.[19] Over the next few decades, he purchased more slaves whenever he could afford them, just as he purchased more land. He also married well.[20] When Martha Dandridge Custis's first husband, Daniel Parke Custis, died unexpectedly in 1757 at the age of forty-six, the twenty-six-year-old widow was left with two young children as well as 17,500 or, according to some estimates, 18,000 acres and nearly three hundred slaves.[21] This dower property was neither at her disposal nor Washington's; rather, it remained in the estate of her first husband and his heirs. When Washington married Martha, he assumed temporary ownership and the responsibility of managing the estate and became legal guardian of her children. Even though he formally adopted them, they kept the Custis name as family connections were a critical factor in business as well as politics.[22] By 1770 Washington owned eighty-seven enslaved people. Although he stopped buying slaves, their number grew to 135 through births, some as a result of marriages to Martha's slaves. This created complicated bookkeeping and legacy challenges.[23]

Washington's taste for an elegant lifestyle (made possible by slavery), together with his plantation expenses, resulted in a state of almost perpetual debt, a fate of many plantation owners. The Custis fortune initially solved Washington's accumulated debt problems. Additionally, Washington proved to be exceptionally adept at farming and managing a complex plantation. Starting as a tobacco farmer, he switched to grains when tobacco ceased to be profitable. He experimented with different types of manure and cultivation techniques, always looking to become more productive and financially solvent.[24]

Washington's attachment to Mount Vernon and his lifestyle there was profound. He returned there whenever he could and throughout his two terms as president dreamed of resuming his civilian life; his will contained a provision that he be buried on the estate.[25] Washington wanted Mount Vernon to be as grand and impressive as possible, a reflection of his own ambitions, and perhaps an attempt to match the style to which his wife and her children were accustomed. At the time of his death, Mount Vernon encompassed around eight thousand acres and housed more than three hundred people.[26] It included "a storehouse, smokehouse, washhouse, stable, coach house, overseer's quarters, ice house, greenhouse, and farther off from the house, a gristmill and even a distillery."[27]

By all accounts, Washington was a harsh taskmaster, expecting his slaves to have the same work ethic he did. Apparently not understanding why they might not, he never instituted any kind of reward system. Enslaved people were required to work six days a week from 5 a.m. to sundown and expected to be productive even if they were physically impaired. Washington was raised to be indifferent to the feelings of those he considered inferior.[28] Despite making many remarks about not selling slaves in a way that would break up families, he repeatedly did just that.[29] He also resorted to whipping, occasionally meting out punishment personally. Sometimes he threatened slaves with being sent to the West Indies, where they would be worked to death, and actually dispatched a few.[30] Washington's records document that his slaves were shabbily dressed and lived in dismal conditions, forced to use the blankets they slept on to carry leaves that served to line the beds of livestock.[31] Mary V. Thompson, research historian at Mount Vernon, has acknowledged that "some of the worst things one thinks about in terms of slavery-whipping, keeping someone in shackles, tracking a person down with dogs, or selling people away from their family—all of those things happened either at Mount Vernon or on other plantations under Washington's management."[32] He even had slaves raffled off in a sporting atmosphere with drinking and bawdy songs. This practice, which resulted in more profitable sales, has largely gone unmentioned in nearly all accounts of the first president.[33]

When the nation's capital moved from New York to Pennsylvania in 1790, Washington faced a legal problem related to keeping slaves. Pennsylvania's 1780 Gradual Abolition Act stipulated that nonresidents could continue to own slaves only for a six-month period, after which time they would have to be freed. To circumvent this law, Washington arranged to have his slaves sent back to Mount Vernon periodically and then returned to Philadelphia so the clock would start again. In order to preserve their freedom, Ona Judge, Martha's personal maid, and Hercules, the family cook, escaped before Washington retired to Mount Vernon permanently where they would be enslaved. Ona was a dower slave, so Washington would have to reimburse the Custis family for her loss. He unsuccessfully used every means possible to reclaim her—legal or not—including the power of the federal government.[34] Washington complained at the inconvenience of losing his cook because he "had resolved never to become the master of another slave by purchase."[35]

Washington's position on slavery was challenged during the American Revolution as debates over the subject raged around him. Initially, he did not consider including Black soldiers in the army, apparently because he shared a common belief among the upper classes that their presence would bring dishonor.[36] Free Black people, however, had enlisted from the start, and de facto, the army had become integrated. In 1775 Washington issued an order excluding all Black people, whether they were free or enslaved. Around the same time John Murray Dunmore, British governor of Virginia, promised slaves their freedom after the war if they joined the British. In order to keep them from signing up with Dunmore, Washington allowed free Black people to reenlist. However, he still refrained from recruiting slaves, largely due to their status as property.[37] However, during the Valley Forge winter of 1777–78, at a low point for the revolutionary army, Brigadier General James Mitchell Varnum of Rhode Island asked for permission to enlist Black troops from his state. Washington not only approved but suggested that the two Rhode Island regiments be reorganized to equalize the number of white and Black soldiers in each. This would avoid the appearance of a distinct Black corps and coincidentally integrate the troops.[38] As it turned out, George Washington's winning army was more integrated than any American military force until the Vietnam War. In fact, Black soldiers were so common that their presence was not considered newsworthy.[39] Although Washington's actions seem to have been prompted by pragmatic concerns of military strategy, his experience of the courage and contribution of Black troops may have had some influence on his future policies.

The integration of the army prompted talks of freeing the slaves after the war. This initiative was spearheaded by Colonel John Laurens, who believed that it was the right thing to do, even though most of his vast family fortune came from slave trading.[40] Washington initially approved the plan although he expressed empathy for the slave owners' loss of property. Initially, Col. Laurens's father, Henry Laurens, president of the Continental Congress from 1777–78, did not agree with the initiative and the colonel temporarily shelved the plan. Henry Laurens's position changed when South Carolina was at risk of falling to the British. In 1779, when Laurens's plan was sent to John Jay, the new president of the Continental Congress, Washington rejected it based largely on financial considerations and the fear that it might prompt rebellion among existing slaves, including his own. After the war, Washington was unwilling to free the slaves who had fought for the British although they had been promised their liberation. Again, this was essentially a property issue; slaves were valuable not just for their labor but also their fertility. The British were baffled at Washington's position and feared that some of the slaves might become suicidal; as it was, many chose to go to Africa rather than return to the system of slavery they had previously endured.[41]

Washington's stance on slavery evolved during his lifetime. Although he expressed his conflicts in private, he never spoke of them in public, even in a period when antislavery views were being widely expressed and the heritage of the American Revolution was passionately debated. Even before the war, Abigail Adams, who had grown up in a slaveholding family, wrote to her husband, "I wish most sincerely there was not a single slave in the province; it always appeared a most iniquitous scheme to me [to] fight ourselves for what we are daily robbing and plundering from those who have as good a right to freedom as we have."[42] After the conclusion of the Revolutionary War, two states abolished slavery completely: Vermont in 1777, and Massachusetts in 1783. Two years earlier Pennsylvania had instituted laws enabling a gradual emancipation. In 1782–83 some southern states, including Virginia, passed legislation allowing owners to free their slaves under certain conditions.[43]

In the time between the end of the Revolutionary War and the start of his presidency, abolitionists tried to enlist Washington's support for their cause. While he consistently replied that he shared their beliefs and expressed these sentiments verbally to local politicians, he refused to sign their petitions.[44] After the war Washington's protégé the Marquis de Lafayette approached him with a proposal that they buy a small property and try an experiment for freeing slaves by treating them as tenants. Washington admired the proposal, indicating that he would consider it, but never agreed to the plan. Lafayette eventually tried the experiment on his own in Cayenne on the coast of French Guiana.[45]

During the Constitutional Convention of 1787, slavery became an officially sanctioned national practice.[46] Although Washington was elected only to preside—not participate in—the convention, he could have made his position clear had he chosen to do so. His silence appeared prompted by his concern over maintaining the Union. Representatives from New England and most of the Middle Atlantic states advocated for an immediate end to the slave trade, as well as a plan for gradual emancipation, and against expansion of slavery into western territories. The Deep South, however, petitioned for a continuation of the slave trade and a constitutional prohibition against the federal government interfering with their property rights. South Carolina and Georgia threatened not to sign the Constitution unless slavery was allowed to continue. The compromise solution allowed the slave trade to continue for twenty years until 1808. In return the North got an agreement that federal regulation of commerce would be determined by a majority rather than two-thirds vote; a slave would count as three-fifths of a person in order to limit Southern representation.[47]

Many of those who agreed to the compromise believed that slavery would cease to exist of its own accord. However, the ongoing influx of slaves guaranteed otherwise.[48] Even with Washington's support it is doubtful that emancipation could have been achieved at this time. The antislavery movement appeared to be ebbing and the South reacted forcefully to any legislative progress in the direction of emancipation.[49] The word slavery was never used in the Constitution (enslaved people were referred to as property of man).

Washington's Farewell Address in 1796 presented one more opportunity to make a plea for emancipation, but again he chose to remain silent. The outgoing president's primary concern continued to be maintaining the Union. Washington believed that unity and liberty were inextricably linked; he called them "sacred ties" that guaranteed the freedom that Americans so prized.[50] Nearly a quarter of the address dealt with the threat of foreign powers, specifically the efforts by Spain and Britain to annex areas of the United States. Washington considered these potential foreign infringements as domestic issues because they might threaten the fragile unity of the young republic. In the context of the sanctity of the Union, any kind of partisanship was defined as disloyal.[51] Again, slavery was never mentioned. In fact, Washington signed the Fugitive Slave Act in 1783, enabling the South to maintain and enforce the institution while compelling those states that outlawed slavery to become complicit by allowing masters to cross state lines to recapture their runaway slaves.[52]

Still, in 1794, two years before his Farewell Address, Washington was secretly making plans to free his own slaves. In a letter that year he instructed his private secretary, Tobias Lear, to look for a buyer for a large portion of his land, describing his intention "to liberate a certain species of property which I possess, very repugnantly to my own feelings."[53] He intended to sell four of the five farms at Mount Vernon to English farmers, with the hope that new owners would free some 170–80 slaves and rehire them as employees. It's possible that Washington had become exhausted managing this large property and his ongoing debt.[54] If he wished to free the dower slaves in addition to his own, he would have had to compensate the Custis heirs, who might not have agreed to sell them.[55] Since Washington could find no buyers for his lands, it is impossible to know if such a plan would have worked.

Washington's will finally made public his intention to free his slaves—but only after Martha's death. When he died in 1799, he owned 124 slaves and rented 40 from a neighbor; the remaining 153 were dower slaves.[56] He wrote his twenty-nine-page will himself, detailing the critical and complicated section pertaining to their distribution.[57] Complications existed because there had been frequent intermarriage among Washington's and Martha's slaves. He may have been hedging about this provision up until shortly before his death. Finally, he asked his wife to burn his previous will, created after accepting the role of commander in chief of the Continental Army in 1775. It is safe to assume that the earlier version contained no provisions for freeing slaves, given that his views then were typical of most Southern plantation owners.[58]

Martha realized that Washington's final stipulation might put her in danger as some of his slaves may have been tempted to harm her to ensure their freedom as soon as possible. Thus, she proceeded to free all of them at once.[59] It seems odd that Washington, the ultimate strategist, did not foresee this potential consequence. Martha, in her will, did not free any of her own slaves; she bequeathed them to her grandson. None of the other Custis heirs freed more than a few slaves. Washington's own nephew, Bushrod Washington, who became a Supreme Court justice, inherited Mount Vernon and four thousand acres of the estate but freed no slaves at all and even sold some in a way that split up families.[60]

In addition to granting their eventual freedom, Washington considered the welfare of freed slaves in ways that were unusual for his time. His will stipulated that the young be educated to read and write and learn some employable skills. This would suggest that he believed that Black Americans were not inherently inferior but rather that slavery was responsible for their current condition. Further evidence of this was apparent in 1775 when he invited former slave Phillis Wheatley, who had sent him one of her poems, to visit him at his headquarters.[61] Washington also provided a fund to care for slaves who were too sick or too old to manage freedom on their own. He made no provisions to send the freed slaves elsewhere as Jefferson did, further indicating that he was perhaps able to envision the development of an integrated society.[62]

Washington's evolving positions on slavery have been variously characterized. Some writers saw them as vacillation, while others attributed them to moral confusion, and still others observed that financial concerns were always primary for the first president.[63] During the formative years of the nation, however, it was Washington's concern over unity that overrode everything else, including his beliefs regarding slavery. Many writers have praised Washington for his final act as an affirmation of his belief in emancipation.[64] A few, however, suggested that Washington might have found the money to free his slaves by setting aside a portion of his estate.[65] After a lifetime of vacillating between his public statements and acts, including some evasions of the law (his Philadelphia ruse not to free his slaves and the measures he took to track down Ona Judge), it is fair to conclude that his commitment to ending slavery was not complete. He struggled with the issue and finally took what he knew would become a public position in his will. This document was so widely circulated that it has been suggested that it should be seen as a national text, comparable to the Declaration of Independence.[66]

Most of the signers of the Declaration of Independence also held slaves, but Washington was the only one of the Founding Fathers to free his, even if he specified that it was only to be after Martha's death. From a contemporary vantage point, it is impossible to know if or how things might have been different if Washington had taken a more public proactive stance on abolition. Would the Union have survived? In any event, the gap between Washington's private and public positions made it possible for both the North and South to claim him as their own during and after the Civil War.[67]

5

Thomas Jefferson's Architectural Monuments

Today it seems surprising that a national memorial to Thomas Jefferson was by no means assured as late as 1920.[1] Like all the Mount Rushmore presidents, at different times Jefferson has meant different things to different people. Although initially a Republican, in the nineteenth century he was revered and claimed by the Democratic Party, based primarily on his authorship of the Declaration of Independence.[2] He was admired variously for his advocacy of religious freedom, national expansion, and the creation of the University of Virginia.

Among Thomas Jefferson's astounding number of talents was architecture, an interest that began while he was still a student at the College of William and Mary in the early 1760s. At that time he purchased his first book for what later became one the largest architecture libraries in America. He designed the Virginia State Capitol in Richmond, the first major building constructed in the United States after the Revolution. It was based on the Maison Carrée in Nîmes, a Roman-era building Jefferson saw while traveling in France when he was ambassador there (1784–89). As secretary of state under Washington (1890–93), he supervised the eventual planning of the nation's capital by Pierre L'Enfant. He was also involved with designing many of the first government buildings in the nation, including the White House by James Hoban and the United States Capitol by William Thornton. He planned the entire University of Virginia campus (1817–26), an undertaking he referred to as "the hobby of my old age." However, the architectural project that consumed nearly all of his adult life was Monticello, his beloved homestead in Albemarle County in Virginia. Jefferson was greatly influential in establishing neoclassicism as a style for official buildings in the United States, thereby concretizing an image of national identity that linked the country to European precedents.[3]

It is fitting that the three most important memorials to Jefferson are architectural in nature: Monticello; the Thomas Jefferson Memorial in Washington DC; and the Jefferson Memorial Arch in Saint Louis. Monticello reflects Jefferson's ideas about architecture and the diversity of his many interests. It also reflects the image he wished to convey to the many people who visited its public rooms.[4] Monticello existed for Jefferson as an idea and an ever-evolving reality.[5]

Monticello

While in Paris serving as ambassador to France, Jefferson longed for the domestic reprieve provided by his home and family. He assumed this post after the death of his beloved wife, Martha Wayles Skelton Jefferson, in 1782 at the age of thirty-four. Initial work on Monticello (referred to as Monticello 1) began in 1769, on a hill overlooking Shadwell in Piedmont, Virginia, where he had grown up. The elevation of the site and its view of the surrounding countryside (including the village of Charlottesville) reflected his appreciation of the beauty of the landscape in which he was raised and then chose to live. At this time Jefferson's architectural influences came from books, primarily those of Andrea Palladio, the sixteenth-century Italian architect whose work referred to the classical tradition. Jefferson's attraction to all things classical reflected the ideas of the Enlightenment, which were basic to his outlook and writings, most specifically the Declaration of Independence.[6]

In the five years Jefferson spent in France, he had ample time to experience contemporary French neoclassical architecture directly and this in turn had an impact on the further design of Monticello, called Monticello 2.[7] While in Paris he purchased furniture, mirrors, kitchen supplies, and art, much of which he brought back with him. Arguably the most important room at Monticello 2 was the two-story entrance hall.[8] All visitors were ushered into this room, which Jefferson intended as a museum but which might more accurately be called a cabinet of curiosities—a variety of notable objects, rather than a logically curated collection.[9] It contained paintings, sculptures, and Native American artifacts (gathered by Meriwether Lewis and William Clark at Jefferson's request during their exploration of the vast territory he purchased from France in 1803). These included animal and mineral specimens, as well as maps and clocks. Jefferson believed profoundly that the education of general citizens was an essential element of democracy. He wanted to inform his visitors about the history of the United States and, through maps, its place in the wider world.

The parlor at Monticello was less public than the entrance hall. It was the site of family gatherings where visitors might be invited to have tea, make music, or play games. It, too, contained works of art: portraits of the Enlightenment thinkers Jefferson most admired (John Locke, Sir Isaac Newton, and Francis Bacon); explorers (Christopher Columbus, Ferdinand Magellan, Hernán Cortés, and Sir Walter Raleigh); and heroes of the Revolution (George Washington, John Adams, James Madison, Benjamin Franklin, and the Marquis de Lafayette). Select guests were also entertained in the adjacent dining room and tea room. Jefferson's interest in innovations was evident in the dumbwaiters he installed that brought bottles of wine directly to diners without requiring slaves.[10] His taste, cultivated during his stay in Paris, was expressed in the French cuisine prepared by James Hemings, his slave who had accompanied Jefferson to France and was trained there. The tea room featured more portraits and a special chair and lap desk where Jefferson wrote the Declaration of Independence.

Monticello's private rooms (his library, study, and bedroom) were reserved for Jefferson, his daughter, Martha Jefferson Randolph, and presumably Sally Hemings, his slave and the mother of four of his children. These were attached to a greenhouse that contained Jefferson's prized flowers, plants, and seed collection that included many non-native specimens. Jefferson's extensive book collection eventually formed the core of the collection of the Library of Congress.[11] His bed was in an open alcove that contained storage space for clothing and a handsome clock that he designed. There were separate guest rooms for frequent visitors, such as James Madison.

Jefferson also designed a separate residence that functioned as his private retreat at Poplar Forest in Bedford County. There he experimented with an octagonal shape, allowing for more windows, increased lighting, and views in eight directions. Located at the center of the house, the dining room was a perfect square with a sixteen-foot-high skylight. Jefferson was so obsessed with the perfect geometric realization of this house that he forgot to include a stairway from the lower level to the main floor, so one had to be built outside. Jefferson included fifteen fireplaces, which fed into only four chimneys and in 1845 the roof burned, leaving the house in ruin. Poplar Forest is emblematic of Jefferson's striving to express ideal values in architecture, at times to the point of ignoring practical realities.

In a different way, Monticello represents Jefferson's ideal concept of national identity: the United States was to be an informed, sophisticated nation based on Enlightenment principles, a worthy part of the larger international world. It was an astronomically expensive enterprise and by the end of his life Jefferson was overwhelmed with debt. His possessions, including his slaves, were sold off after his death, as was the house itself. The restoration of Monticello began in 1923 with the founding of the Thomas Jefferson Memorial Foundation (TJMF). It featured an educational program that expressed Jefferson's key ideas.[12] The restoration was completed on the hundredth anniversary of Jefferson's death, on 4 July 1926.

The Thomas Jefferson Memorial in Washington DC

First proposed in 1903, the Thomas Jefferson Memorial in Washington DC was not dedicated for another four decades, after overcoming many obstacles, including protests over the destruction of some cherry trees that required the intervention of President Franklin Delano Roosevelt. Although considered by many to be the most beautiful memorial in the nation's capital, today there are calls for its removal based on a reevaluation of Jefferson's legacy, including one by Lucian K. Truscott IV, a descendant of Jefferson and Sally Hemings.[13]

The initial proposal for a memorial came from the Thomas Jefferson Memorial Association (distinct from the later foundation).[14] The U.S. Commission of Fine Arts had been considering a memorial since 1914 although at a different site, either Union Station or close to the State Department.[15] The Tidal Basin site, originally a beach, was first mentioned in 1925 for a memorial to Theodore Roosevelt, to be designed by John Russell Pope. Objections arose over building a memorial to Theodore Roosevelt in Washington before there was one honoring Jefferson, and also to building a tribute to Jefferson in St. Louis (then being proposed) before there was one in the nation's capital. The Thomas Jefferson Memorial Commission (TJMC) was created in 1934 and charged with selecting the site and design as well as overseeing the construction. The twelve-member commission consisted of senators, representatives, the undersecretary of the Treasury Department, and Fiske Kimball, known for his expertise on Jefferson's architecture and at the time director of the Philadelphia Museum of Art. The commission finally approved the Tidal Basin site, thereby linking the Jefferson Memorial visually to the Lincoln Memorial, the Washington Monument and the Capitol.

The selection of John Russell Pope, who was then working on the Washington National Gallery, guaranteed a neoclassical memorial. This prompted a slew of objections from the Fine Arts Commission as well as architects and others in the field who favored a more modern style.[16] Suggestions for a living memorial, including a national auditorium, were rejected by FDR, who approved both Pope's plan and the site in 1937. Although Congress once again blocked funds to construct a Jefferson memorial, the cornerstone was laid by FDR in 1939, using the same silver trowel that Washington had used to lay the cornerstone of the Capitol and tamping it down with a wooden gavel made from an elm tree that Jefferson had planted at Monticello.[17] FDR praised Jefferson as the founder of the Democratic Party and a firm believer that the "average opinion of mankind is in the long run superior to the dictates of the self-chosen," segueing into praise for a republican form of government.[18] Inside the cornerstone was a copy of the Declaration of Independence; the Constitution; Jefferson's *Life and Morals of Jesus of Nazareth*; a copy of the ten volumes of *The Writings of Thomas Jefferson* by Paul Leicester Ford; the 1939 annual report of the Memorial Commission; and the day's editions of the four Washington newspapers.

FDR's support for the Jefferson Memorial was critical at several points, perhaps none more so than the so-called Cherry Tree Rebellion. Using the

Tidal Basin site required removing some of the three thousand cherry trees that had been gifted to the city by the mayor of Tokyo in 1912. As soon as construction started in 1938, a group of approximately fifty women marched on the White House protesting the removal of the cherry trees, a few even chaining themselves to trees. As the momentum of the protest and the publicity it prompted increased, FDR intervened, announcing that only eighty-eight trees would be removed and hundreds more would be planted to take their place.[19]

The final design of the Jefferson Memorial was modified after Pope's death in 1937 by Otto Reinhold Eggers and Daniel Paul Higgins, resulting in a reduced version, but still essentially based on the Pantheon.[20] As it now stands, the Jefferson Memorial consists of a domed open structure supported by a circular colonnade of twenty-six Ionic columns and four wide openings, each with four columns. The entrance from the Tidal Basin is reached by a flight of stairs leading to a portico topped by a triangular pediment with a relief sculpture by Adolph A. Weinman depicting the five men submitting their draft of the Declaration of Independence to Congress (Jefferson, John Adams, Benjamin Franklin, Robert R. Livingston, and Roger Sherman). The nineteen-foot bronze statue by Rudulph Evans of Jefferson holding a copy of the Declaration faces away from the Potomac, apparently looking past the Washington Monument toward the White House.[21]

Each of the four interior walls features a quote from Jefferson's writings; there is also a fifth quote encircling the frieze. All were chosen by a committee headed by Senator Elbert Thomas of Utah.[22] Located on the southeast wall, the most important quote from the Declaration of Independence is an edited version, partially explained by the imposed 325 letter limit per panel.[23] After much discussion, including input from FDR, the final quote omitted any mention of the people's right to abolish a government that no longer protected their rights, even though this was the very purpose of the document. In its truncated version it reads, "We hold these truths to be self-evident: that all men are created equal, that they are endowed by their creator with certain inalienable rights, among these are life, liberty and the pursuit of happiness, that to secure these rights governments are instituted among men." FDR wanted words from the final paragraph of the Declaration of Independence included with the edits imposed by Congress rather than Jefferson's original submission. The final version reads, "We . . . solemnly publish and declare, that these colonies are and of right ought to be free and independent states . . . and for the support of this declaration, with a firm reliance on the protection of divine providence, we mutually pledge our lives, our fortunes and our sacred honour [*sic*]."[24]

There were arguably more problematic edits to the six quotes on the northeast wall, mainly from Jefferson's 1786 *Notes on the State of Virginia* and *Summary Views*, which expressed his opinions on slavery and the need to educate the general public. The quotes on the northeast wall begin, "Nothing is more certainly written in the book of fate, than these people are to be free," but critically omits what follows in the original text—the insistence that the two races could not live together under the same government and that Black people should be deported to a place where they might establish a separate system granting them the right to self-rule.[25] Jefferson's complex and evolving views on slavery are not conveyed by these misleading edits.

The northeast wall contains a quote from the Statute of Religious Freedom adopted by Virginia in 1779, including Jefferson's opinions on the separation of church and state. The quotation from the southeast wall is taken from a letter that Jefferson wrote in 1816 to Samuel Kercheval, a Virginia lawyer and author of *A History of the Valley of Virginia*, which included information about the interactions between early white settlements in the Shenandoah Valley with local Native Americans. The quote conveys Jefferson's belief that institutions, and even the Constitution, should be adapted periodically to reflect changes in society.

The quote encircling the interior came from a letter written in 1800 to Benjamin Rush, a signer of the Declaration of Independence who attended the Continental Congress and was also a civic leader in Philadelphia, a physician, politician, social reformer, and founder of Dickinson College in Carlisle, Pennsylvania. This quote reads, "I have sworn upon the altar of god eternal hostility against every form of tyranny over the mind of man." Visitors to the Memorial will understandably consider the quotes as entirely representative of Jefferson's writings. There is no information at the site noting or explaining the edits.

In one essential way, however, the Jefferson Memorial is an appropriate tribute. Since the third president was one of the first to introduce neoclassical architecture to the United States, John Russell Pope, arguably the last great practitioner of the style, was certainly a fitting architect to build his monument. As the sculptor James Earle Fraser stated: "I believe Pope's Jefferson Memorial . . . is eminently fitting, because it suggests Jefferson's Monticello home with its dome, columns and pediment. In fact, the design is an heroic and symbolic Monticello."[26]

The Jefferson Memorial Arch

At first glance it is hard to determine what the 630-foot-high gleaming arch on the west bank of the Mississippi River in St. Louis is commemorating. Attracting some three million visitors annually, the National Historic Landmark is nevertheless one of the most recognized structures in the world. Variously referred to as Gateway Arch or the Gateway to the West, its official name until recently was the Jefferson National Expansion Memorial. This was a reference to his Louisiana Purchase, which doubled the size of the United States. In essence then, the tallest monument in the country was intended to celebrate precisely those values that determined Gutzon Borglum's choice of presidents for Mount Rushmore—expansion. Its name was changed in 2018 to the more neutral Gateway Arch National Park, omitting the reference to Jefferson at a time when many tributes to slave owners were being questioned. As with most memorials, there is a backstory—here one that has nothing to do with Jefferson and is not a part of the standard information presented to the public. It involves the redevelopment of the St. Louis riverfront, driven by a profit motive based on ownership of land.

The St. Louis riverfront was once a thriving area home to banks and businesses, as well as the center of western fur trading.[27] By 1900 it was the second largest railroad hub in the United States, the site of a group of architecturally important cast-iron buildings, and one of the nation's first skyscrapers (Louis Sullivan's Wainwright Building). The downtown riverfront was also the site of the courthouse where the infamous Dred Scott slavery case was heard.[28] The Civil War and a significant fire prompted an economic downturn. To counteract this there were attempts throughout the 1870s to have the nation's capital moved to St. Louis. The 1904 World's Fair commemorating the Louisiana Purchase opened by then-president Theodore Roosevelt attracted over twenty million visitors during its first few months. Subsequently, however, the riverfront was vulnerable to the effects of the Great Depression of 1929, which resulted in disproportionately high rates of unemployment among Black people, who moved to East St. Louis in increasing numbers.

The idea for a memorial was suggested by Luther Ely Smith, a local lawyer active in civic affairs, as a way to counteract the decline. He considered a range of possible subjects: Daniel Boone, Jefferson, Lewis and Clark, Robert E. Lee, Ulysses S. Grant, and John C. Fremont (presumably for his role as an explorer and mapmaker of the West).[29] Smith was joined in his efforts by Mayor Bernard Dickmann (elected in 1933), who was also president of the St. Louis Real Estate Exchange. The following year the Jefferson National Expansion Memorial Association was formed, and the year after that then-president Franklin Delano Roosevelt signed a resolution establishing the United States Territorial Expansion Memorial Commission. FDR liked "the principle underlying the thought of a memorial to the vision of Thomas Jefferson and the pioneers in the opening of the west."[30] The focus on Jefferson appeared to have been prompted by the president's comments and its presumed value in obtaining federal funds.

In early conversations about what might be an appropriate memorial, former secretary of war Newton Baker urged the commissioners to "proceed as if they were building a cathedral," a remark repeated often through the protracted process.[31] The charge for the first major national architectural competition after World War II was "memorializing Thomas Jefferson, his Louisiana Purchase, and the expansion of the American nation by creating a national park and monument on the west bank of the Mississippi River at St. Louis."[32] The commission was headed by George Howe, whose preference for a modern style was well known.[33] At this point modern meant abstract and not naturalistic. The extensive design requirements included a place for sculpture depicting historical scenes, landscaping, a living memorial to Jefferson's vision, and a number of parking spaces.[34] In 1947 architect Eero Saarinen's submission was selected by unanimous vote from among the five finalists. It was not, however, the first arch envisioned for the site.

A parabolic arch had been suggested as early as 1933 by Geneva Abbott, a student at Central High School, in response to an assignment to imagine the future of the St. Louis riverfront. In 1945 National Park Service engineer Julian Spotts observed that the area needed a symbol, something like the Washington Monument. His plan suggested a hollow arch that would frame the Old Courthouse and include a structure containing a museum as well as visitor observation opportunities. He saw the arch as "representative of the Gateway to the West, that is a symbol of strength, progress, and expansion."[35] Arches have a long history and Saarinen knew of and had seen various examples in Europe. Visiting the St. Lquis riverfront convinced him that an arch was indeed the appropriate form both from a design perspective and also for Jefferson: "A monument to him should not be something solid and static but something open—a gateway for wider vistas—because one of his many great qualities was the ability to look towards the future."[36] The jury had decided that the memorial should be striking, something visible from a distance but also "a notable structure to be remembered and commented on as one of the conspicuous monuments in the country. Its purpose should be to attract in the interest of the multitude as well as that of the connoisseur of art."[37] Indeed, Saarinen's arch proved to do just that. Although it made the architect famous, it took another couple of decades to be built and he died in 1961, before it was finished. The project was completed by his associates, Kevin Roche and John Dinkeloo.

The project was delayed by unanticipated engineering and funding problems, as well as the Korean War. The groundbreaking finally took place in 1959, with President Truman speaking briefly at the dedication. In 1961 the United States Territorial Expansion Commission referred to the work as the Gateway Arch for the first time and spoke of the intention to encompass "migration and travel as well as [the] frontier" and symbolize the conquering of "Indians, vast distances, and arid lands as well as the greater obstacles that lay ahead: alien ideologies, popular pressures, and the challenges of outer space."[38] Construction began in 1962; the keystone was put in place in 1965. Three years later the arch was finally dedicated—some thirty-five years after Smith first publicized his idea for a memorial.

The building of the St. Louis arch is more than the story of the evolution of a memorial; it is also a reflection of ill-fated urban renewal policies, de facto segregation, and the time during which it was built. From the start the real estate board chair was clear about the purpose of the project, including the memorial: "It has always been my idea that if we could make 4th Street valuable, it is absolutely a certainty that Sixth and Seventh Streets would continue to get the rent they contracted to get for the next 35 years."[39] Indeed, real estate companies and bankers did well, but small businesses suffered or disappeared, and architecturally significant cast-iron buildings were destroyed. In all thirty-seven blocks were demolished and eighty-two acres cleared, which had been largely inhabited by Black people. At the time this kind of urban renewal was a popular practice; only later was it seen as destructive to the urban core.

There was another problematic element of the design. Immediately after it was published, Gilmore D. Clarke, then chair of the Fine Arts Commission, noted its similarity to an arch planned for E 42, a 1942 exposition in Europe intended to celebrate the twentieth anniversary of Mussolini's March on Rome that marked the start of the fascist era in Italy.[40] Designed by Pier Luigi Nervi, Adalberto Libera, Gino Covre, Vincenzo di Berardino, and others, it was often remarked that had it been built it would have become the symbol of modern Rome.[41] Libera, the primary designer of the parabolic arch, envisioned it as an icon for the European fair, comparable to what the Eiffel Tower had been for the 1889 Universal Exhibition in Paris. Intended to be installed five miles south of the center of the city, the 420-acre site was to feature a new city that was the most ambitious of Mussolini's building projects. Plans for E 42 were delayed during World War II and canceled after the fall of Mussolini's regime in 1943. The potential lawsuit against Saarinen for using this design was dropped on the basis that the parabolic arch was a standard architectural form. Nevertheless, there are disturbing similarities about its use in St. Louis. As William Graebner concluded, "What Saarinen could not effectively address . . . was the larger issue: that his design for an American arch had appropriated a form—the great arch—that in the late 1930s and early 1940s had been held out to the world as a symbol of Italian fascism. . . . Saarinen was tapping into a constellation of meanings and messages, heightened in intensity by the planning for E 42, that by the mid-1940s were part and parcel of the very idea of the arch: spectacle, urban planning, a coupling of nationalism with universality and, most importantly, empire."[42]

Memorials always reflect the time in which they were built. By the middle of the twentieth century, the United States was a rich nation. It had won World War II and there were plans for a trip to the moon. Tracy Campbell concluded that the St. Louis arch can be seen as "a symbol of affluence and influence, a bold statement of national strength."[43] But it can also be understood as an emblem of the failure of a policy of urban renewal that favored automobile over foot traffic rather than the urban core represented by the riverfront. And, as with so many things motivating American society early on as well as now, the acquisition of land, valued in terms of its ability to generate personal wealth, was a powerful factor. That was the basic contention between Native American communal views of the land and those of the new colonists, who saw it only in terms of private ownership, evident and indeed writ large in the building of Mount Rushmore.

6

Thomas Jefferson's Complicated Legacy

When we think of Thomas Jefferson today what likely springs to mind are the Declaration of Independence and the Sally Hemings story. The declaration continues to be a foundational element of U.S. national identity, but few people know that it is a version based on congressional edits of Jefferson's original submission. Although Jefferson's relationship with Hemings was denied for many years, DNA evidence leaves no doubt that he fathered at least four children with Hemings, who was his slave as well as his wife's half-sister. Both stories are even more complicated than these factual statements suggest. They highlight a legacy filled with conflict and contradiction.

Jefferson died on the fiftieth anniversary of 4 July 1776, the date now celebrated as the signing of the Declaration of Independence. He left instructions that his tombstone acknowledge just three things: his authorship both of that document and the Virginia Statute for Religious Freedom, and the founding of the University of Virginia. He made no mention of his impressive record of public offices: ambassador to France (1784–89); secretary of state (1789–93); vice president (1797–1801); and two terms as president (1801–9). He also did not list the 1803 Louisiana Purchase, which doubled the size of the country. In addition to the above, Jefferson was an accomplished architect, city planner, agriculturist, inventor, and much more.

Jefferson and the Declaration of Independence

Jefferson, like many colonists, resisted making a final break with England for many years. The Second Continental Congress was convened in May 1775 because the king failed to address repeated petitions objecting to unfair taxes.[1] The break, however, did not come easily. Jefferson wrote that he "would rather be in dependence on Great Britain, properly limited, than on any nation upon earth, or than on no nation."[2] Pauline Maier noted that even after the outbreak of the war, for Jefferson and many others, "reconciliation was still the American Dream."[3] The reluctance of the thirteen colonies to give up British rule was partially explained by their admiration for Britain's unwritten constitution that distributed power among the king, lords, and commons, rather than concentrating it in a single individual or entity.[4] There was also a sense that the colonists had more in common with Britain than with each other. In the end, there were two tipping points that led to war. One was that the king hired German soldiers to fight the colonists. The other was the royal governor of Virginia Lord Dunmore's 1775 offer to grant freedom to any slave who fought for Britain. The colonies needed funds to finance a war against Britain, and such funds could only be solicited from another country (in this case France) by an independent nation.

Jefferson joined the Second Continental Congress late, taking the place of his mentor, Peyton Randolph, who had been called back to Virginia to preside over its legislative body, the House of Burgesses.[5] The congress charged a committee of five, consisting of Jefferson, John Adams, Benjamin Franklin, Robert R. Livingston, and Roger Sherman, with preparing a Declaration of Independence, and a scant seventeen days later they presented a draft based on several sources, including Jefferson's own writings. The preamble that contained many of the most quoted phrases was taken from his Virginia Declaration of Independence (June 1776).[6] Jefferson also used George Mason's Virginia's Declaration of Rights (adopted in June 1776),[7] as well as the British Declaration of Rights (1689) that marked the end of the reign of James II.

The most frequently cited source, however, is John Locke's *Second Treatise of Government* (1689), which noted man's right to life, liberty, and property; the separation of legislative and executive powers; and the right to rebel against a government that did not serve the needs of the people.[8]

Jefferson readily acknowledged that the ideas he articulated were not new; rather, he was combining them in a way that he hoped would persuade a general public that the Revolution was necessary at a time when the war was not going well.[9] The Declaration of Independence has remained what has been called "America's mission statement."[10] The document that we read and quote today, however, is not the one that Jefferson wrote; it is the version that Congress edited.[11] Most of their changes were to the list of grievances.[12] Of these, by far the most significant was the deletion of the last one (number twenty), which implicated King George III in the international slave trade.[13] In response to Lord Dunmore's 1775 offer of freedom to those Black people who fought on the side of Britain in the Revolution, it included a reference to inciting enslaved people to rise up against the colonists. Jefferson did not accuse the king of introducing slavery to America (this was done by the Dutch in 1619) but instead challenged his claim to be a Christian king. Since at least one-third of the signers of the declaration owned slaves, the Continental Congress did not want to include any references to the practice of slavery in the United States.[14] Here, as in the Constitution, all references to slavery were omitted. This failure in our founding documents only postponed the reckoning that eventually erupted in the Civil War.

The language used in the Declaration of Independence was that of the Enlightenment and often meant something quite different from contemporary interpretations.[15] Most misunderstandings pertain to the much-quoted statement: "All men are created equal." What Jefferson meant is that all men are equal in terms of "benevolence, gratitude, and unshaken fidelity, the cardinal virtues of moral-sense-theory."[16] For Jefferson their emotional capacity was the only way that all men could be considered equal. That significant limitation, however, has been ignored over time. Instead, it has been understood in a much wider context, as it was reinterpreted by Lincoln in the context of the Civil War.

Similarly, the declaration's guaranteed right of the pursuit of happiness is now typically misunderstood as the right to live a good life in terms of material wealth and well-being. Jefferson, however, saw happiness in a civic context, something that government should make possible, at least for white men.[17] He considered property (as cited by Locke) a means of achieving happiness.[18] Therefore, Jefferson substituted the word "happiness" for Locke's "property."[19]

Jefferson and Freedom of Religion

Although Jefferson listed the Virginia Statute for Establishing Religious Freedom as the second of three things he wished to be listed on his tombstone, it has been discussed much less often than his other contributions.[20] Drafted in 1777, it became law in 1786, after what Jefferson characterized as politically "one of the severest conflicts in which I have been engaged."[21] The statute stated that "no man shall be compelled to frequent or support any religious worship, place, or ministry whatsoever, nor shall be enforced restrained, molested, or burthened in his body or goods, nor shall otherwise suffer on account of his religious opinions or belief; but that all men shall be free to profess, and by argument to maintain, their opinions in matters of religion, and that the same shall in no wise diminish, enlarge, or affect their civil capacities."[22] Jefferson considered these among the natural rights of mankind, essential to the functioning of a democratic society.[23] He championed individual freedoms, including "the right to the unbounded exercise of reason and freedom of opinion," and worried that early religious indoctrination of children would limit their freedom of thought.[24] He insisted that they should not even be given access to a Bible until they were able to freely form their own opinions.

Jefferson's firm belief in the separation of church and state was influenced at least in part by his experience of the Anglican Church in Virginia prior to the Revolution. The church imposed taxes for its own support, as well as penalties for dissenters and for anyone failing to attend services. Jefferson's commitment to freedom of religion as broadly defined in the Virginia statute has remained a constitutive element of our definition of democracy.[25]

Jefferson and the University of Virginia

Jefferson's association with the University of Virginia (UVA) is well-known, but his commitment to public education is less so. Since the Revolution and long before he retired to Monticello, he envisioned a statewide public education system for all ages that, unlike the European model that educated only the elite, would include lower-class white males.[26] In the end Virginia agreed to fund only a state university to be sited just outside of Charlottesville in Albemarle County near Jefferson's home. UVA was chartered in 1819, some forty years after Jefferson first proposed a bill for a widespread system of public education funded by the state. In keeping with his advocacy of the pastoral life of the yeoman, or private farmer, Jefferson believed that education in a rural setting was best for learning. He considered this project "the last act of usefulness" he could contribute to his country.[27]

Designed by Jefferson, UVA opened in 1825, although construction on the rotunda and other elements continued after his death. Jefferson focused on a number of small buildings that would create an academic village rather than one large extensive structure that was then the norm. Each faculty member would have their own residence with one or two lecture rooms while students would have distinct dormitories. Housing for laundry workers, gardeners, and cooks, along with other enslaved workers who kept the university running, was located below the academic village in basement-level quarters and screened off behind eight-foot-high brick walls.

The library, a central feature of Jefferson's design, was housed in the university's rotunda and was to contain some seven thousand books concentrating on what was considered scientific knowledge at the time; this separated UVA from religious institutions found at other universities of the period. Jefferson was also directly involved in developing the curriculum. There would be no required courses: "This institution of my native state, the hobby of my old age, will be based on the illimitable freedom of the human mind to explore and to expose every subject susceptible of its contemplation."[28] The subjects that Jefferson envisioned included ancient and modern languages, mathematics, astronomy, geography, physics, chemistry, botany, zoology, anatomy, medicine, history, government, law, general grammar, ethics, and the fine arts. He also had plans for a botanical garden as well as an experimental farm and agriculture school, but these were not built until later.

Jefferson failed to consider that the initial group of students who enrolled at UVA had been brought up under a system of slavery that instilled in them a sense of entitlement, evidenced in all kinds of raucous and abusive behavior in general, but especially toward enslaved people.[29] Their comportment, modeled on that of their parents, was not punished. Jefferson, who had experienced precisely this type of conduct as a student at the College of William and Mary, hoped to create a different type of institution. Many years would pass before UVA became the type of university Jefferson envisioned, on a par with esteemed New England schools. Jefferson's ideas were often more admirable than he was able to realize. This was certainly true with regard to slavery.

Jefferson and Slavery

According to Annette Gordon-Reed and Peter Onuf, "Property in land and property in slaves were the engines that drove Virginia society from its earliest days, giving Jefferson and those in his class wealth, independence, and liberty—their sense of identity. It was the dividing line between those who could participate in republican society by voting and those who could not, between those who were respectable and those who were not."[30]

Emancipation and how to achieve it were never far from Jefferson's mind, yet there is no issue about which he, as well as historians who wrote about him, were in more conflict. In 1757, at the age of fourteen, Jefferson inherited fifty-two slaves from his father; he acquired 135 more in 1773 when his father-in-law, John Wayles, died. When he wrote the Declaration of Independence he owned over 175 enslaved people, at a time when some of his contemporaries were freeing theirs.[31] After the age of thirty-one he owned approximately two hundred; over his lifetime he owned some six hundred. Although there is some disagreement as to how harsh a plantation manager Jefferson was,[32] there is no question that, like Washington, he was concerned with maximizing productivity and expanding profits. Toward that end, he built a nailery as well as a textile factory and trained his slaves in a variety of skills. Unlike Washington, Jefferson also provided some profit incentives for his enslaved laborers.

No aspect of slavery related to Jefferson has received more attention than his relationship with Sally Hemings, daughter of John Wayles and his slave Betty Hemings, and therefore the three-quarter white half-sister of his wife Martha Wayles. For many years scholars and others argued about the very existence of this relationship and questioned whether Jefferson had fathered her four children. This was not surprising given prevailing prejudices and Jefferson's often expressed views on the abomination of intermarriage between Black and white people.[33] In 1998, however, DNA evidence provided proof positive. Their relationship began when Hemings accompanied Jefferson's daughter to Paris in 1787 where he was serving as ambassador to France, an appointment he accepted two years after his wife died. When Jefferson's appointment ended, Hemings was only sixteen and pregnant. She could have remained in Paris as a free woman but agreed to return to Monticello as a slave after she was promised certain personal benefits and guaranteed freedom for her unborn child and any future children with Jefferson.[34] At Monticello her life and the chores assigned to her siblings were distinct from those of the rest of his slaves.[35] The only slaves Jefferson freed either in his will or during his lifetime were members of the Hemings family.[36]

During the time he lived in Paris, Jefferson's attitude toward emancipation evolved from unequivocal advocacy into something approaching acceptance of a practice by trying to reform it. Somehow he was able to convince himself that treating enslaved people better, more humanely, according to what he perceived to be in their best interests would result in their acceptance of their situation with equanimity.[37] Eventually, he came to consider slavery a pernicious practice that could be left to the future generations to eradicate.

It is difficult to reconcile Jefferson's early writings championing emancipation with his life at Monticello. While he was writing the Declaration of Independence he was also working on a model constitution for Virginia prohibiting slavery.[38] At the same time, he expressed overtly racist views in *Notes on the State of Virginia* (1781): "I advance it therefore as a suspicion only that the blacks . . . are inferior to the Whites in the endowments both of body and mind."[39] He also claimed that Black people lacked intelligence, beauty, most skills except music, and were weak in aesthetic appreciation. Furthermore, he believed that Black men preferred white women, much as orangutans desired Black women more than their own species.[40] The *Notes* appeared in some nineteen editions during his lifetime but the publication did not appear in the United States until 1788.[41] Although Jefferson was opposed to slavery, he felt strongly that Black and white people could not live together given the insurmountable hostility fostered by the system that had prevailed for so long.[42] Therefore, he supported freeing slaves only if they were sent elsewhere—initially to Africa, then possibly to the West Indies, or west of the Mississippi after the Louisiana Purchase in 1803.[43] According to Jefferson's plan, all slaves born after a designated date would be taken from their parents and educated at public expense and eventually freed. To ensure that they would be ready to live as freedmen, they would be trained in a variety of fields according to their aptitude and inclination. When men reached the age of twenty-one and women eighteen, they would be sent elsewhere and given what they needed for sustenance. The colony of emancipated slaves would thus be independent.[44]

Jefferson was convinced that a homogenous society was necessary for democracy, which precluded both integration and intermarriage. In the late 1770s while working on a revision of the *Notes*, he suggested a law that would exile a white woman who had a Black man's child; failing expulsion, she would be vulnerable to beating or worse.[45] Even so, as late as 1821 he wrote in his autobiography, "Nothing is more certainly written in the book of fate than that these people are to be free." Like many others, he was convinced that slavery would die off on its own accord.[46]

Whatever his commitment to emancipation, it was trumped by his unwavering belief in the sanctity of states' rights and the separation of powers between the federal and local governments. In response to the Missouri Compromise of 1820 when Congress admitted Maine as a free state and Missouri as a slave state, Jefferson remarked, "But as it is, we have the wolf by the ear, and we can neither hold him, nor safely let him go. Justice is in one scale, and self-preservation in the other."[47] This neatly summarized Jefferson's quandary—the disjuncture between his deeply held beliefs and actual practice.[48]

Jefferson and Native Americans

In the Declaration of Independence, Jefferson charged that King George III had incited "domestic insurrections amongst us, and has endeavored to bring on the inhabitants of our frontiers, the merciless Indian Savages whose known rule of warfare is an undistinguished destruction of all ages, sexes, and conditions of existence." This was a reference to the Native American attacks along the northern border of the United States that occurred during the French and Indian War. It did not reflect his opinion of Native Americans in general.

Although Jefferson saw integration between Black and white people as both impossible and undesirable, he firmly believed in the assimilation of Native Americans into Western ways and approved their intermarriage with whites. Assimilation depended on the adoption of a system based on private property and individual farming. In his first inaugural address in 1805, he insisted, "Humanity enjoins us to teach them agriculture and the domestic arts; to encourage them to that industry which alone can enable them to maintain their place in existence, and to prepare them in time for that state of society, which to bodily comforts adds the improvement of the mind and morals."[49] He frequently told Native American tribes, "A little land well stocked and improved, will yield more than a great deal without stock or improvement," or "A little land, and a little labor, will procure more provisions than the most successful hunt."[50]

The central component of Jefferson's pastoral vision for an ideal democratic state was the yeoman farmer. He advocated allocating fifty acres to all free men, including Native Americans, thereby ensuring their financial independence and leaving them with sufficient leisure time to pursue their private and public interests. Jefferson planned to provide them with the necessary farming tools and equipment as well as an education that included some rudimentary English to facilitate communication. He believed such a life would elevate Native Americans to a higher state of civilization. Secretary of War Henry Knox first proposed such a plan to Washington, and Jefferson continued it when he became president.[51] This meant a total dismantling of the Native American way of life that was structured around communal ownership of land, not private property. Since Native American women were traditionally responsible for farming, it also meant a radical change of gender roles. Jefferson's ethnocentrism led him to assume that Native Americans would happily abandon their well-established cultural ways.[52] When this did not happen he did not respond kindly.

Jefferson instructed local officials to encourage Native Americans to incur debt at local company stores, thereby forcing them to sell some of their land to pay off creditors and obliging them to take up farming.[53] While he encouraged his agents to do everything possible to get them to cede their lands, including threats, bribery, and intensive negotiation, he continued to believe that this was in their best interests.[54] Some of the land thus acquired was offered to white settlers or sold to land companies, some of which included Jefferson's investments, to pay off national debt.[55] Jefferson was active in developing a national policy for the handling of public land that became codified in land ordinances of 1784, 1785, and most famously in the Northwest Ordinance of 1787.[56] These laws ruled that lands west of the Appalachian Mountains were to be purchased by peaceful means by the U.S. government or its agents. After he became president, Jefferson's priorities changed and the acquisition of Native American lands took priority over his desire for peace and his civilization program. This resulted in the movement of Indigenous people to smaller and smaller areas of land, either through assimilation or eradication.[57]

The Louisiana Purchase from France in 1803 was one of the most consequential land purchases ever made and has been counted among Jefferson's greatest accomplishments. However, it was primarily enabled by Napoleon's need for funds rather than any action on the president's part. Consisting of over eight hundred thousand square miles in the heartland of the continent, it nearly doubled the territory of the United States. Eventually it encompassed all or parts of fifteen new states spanning the width of the continent from Louisiana to Montana. It meant that the country no longer had to guard against foreign powers in its midst. As a result of this acquisition, Jefferson began to consider a more comprehensive policy for removing Native Americans from the area.[58] He wrote to President William Henry Harrison, "As to their fear, we presume that our strength and their weakness is now so visible that they must see we have only to shut our hand to crush them, and that all our liberalities to them proceed from motives of pure humanity only. Should any tribe be foolhardy enough to take up the hatchet at any time, seizing the whole country to that tribe, and driving them across the Mississippi, as the only condition of peace, would be an example to others, and a final furtherance of our final consolidation."[59]

At the time of the Louisiana Purchase Jefferson was concerned that Napoleon might close the Mississippi River to American use; this would have a dire impact on the economy.[60] He instructed his minister in Paris, Robert R. Livingston, to reach out to his Napoleonic counterpart, Charles Maurice de Talleyrand, on the subject of purchasing the territory and sent James

Monroe (a former governor of Virginia and congressman) to assist Livingston, empowering him to spend as much as $9,375,000. By the time Monroe arrived, Napoleon had decided to sell much more land than Jefferson envisioned in order to help finance his future campaign against the British. What remained was to agree upon a price, which was settled at $15 million. All Jefferson had to do was agree. This amount was more than what was then in the United States treasury, but the government was able to negotiate a loan with Britain's Baring and Company Bank. They bought the territory and turned it over in return for bonds that were paid off over a fifteen-year period. This brought the cost up to $27 million—still a bargain, but not typically recorded as the purchase price.

Jefferson has been called "the most expansion-minded president in American history," as well as "our first truly imperial president."[61] His ambitions extended even beyond this continent to include the possible annexation of Cuba. In 1809 he told President James Madison that if this were accomplished, "we should then have such an empire of liberty as she has never surveyed since the creation and I am persuaded no constitution was ever so well calculated as ours for extensive empire and self-government."[62] Jefferson envisioned this extensive "empire of liberty" as inhabited by yeomen farmers of similar ethnicity, creating small communities of like individuals who would need very little governance due to their shared values and satisfying lives. Such farmers would include assimilated Native Americans.

Jefferson, the most erudite of the Rushmore presidents (and possibly all presidents), had scant personal experience of Native Americans. He considered them from an intellectual remove, approaching them anthropologically by collecting as many of their artifacts as possible. He displayed these in an Indian Hall at Monticello.[63] Jefferson's concept of the American Indian was close to Jean-Jacques Rousseau's noble savage, or natural man.[64] He considered them at the level of whites in an uncultivated state. Native Americans provided a model for his idea of small ward-republics, largely homogenous self-governing groups held together by shared values.[65]

Within this paradigm, Jefferson considered Native Americans ungrateful when they showed any resistance to his efforts to govern them. In a way this echoed Washington's inability to understand why his slaves didn't share his work ethic. Both presidents evidenced a distinctly ethnocentric perspective.

Jefferson's Concept of National Identity

Jefferson believed that a strong central government would not be necessary because the like-minded communities he envisioned would largely be able to regulate themselves.[66] Native Americans would have either been assimilated, exterminated, or relegated to reservations, while slavery would be ended by a subsequent generation educated according to republican principles in a system of widespread public education. Freed Black people would be relocated to a different continent, since Jefferson could not imagine an integrated society and continued to oppose racial intermarriage.

Jefferson's most radical concept was that the country should redefine and renew itself by reconsidering all laws including the Constitution every nineteen years to evaluate their ongoing validity. The impracticality of such an idea is immediately apparent. Jefferson's true legacy is as a visionary thinker, someone who was able to imagine a more ideal society even if he wasn't able to realize it. His conceptual blueprint contained goals that are central to national identity: all men are created equal; freedom of religion; separation of church and state; public education at all levels. Although the three things he wanted to be remembered for have become bedrocks of our democracy,[67] today Jefferson's reputation is decidedly tarnished. In a very real sense, as Scot A. French and Edward L. Ayers observed, "Jefferson's life has come to symbolize America's struggle with racial inequality, his successes and failures mirroring those of his nation."[68]

7

Abraham Lincoln Commemorated

The key issue in deciding how to commemorate Abraham Lincoln was to determine which aspect of the president to celebrate. The Emancipation Memorial of 1876, sited in Lincoln Park in Washington DC, was commissioned and paid for by newly freed slaves; it was designed by a white sculptor who was selected by an all-white committee. The image of a standing Lincoln and a kneeling former slave eventually proved to be controversial. The Lincoln Memorial Building in Hodgenville, Kentucky, completed in 1911, celebrates Lincoln's humble beginnings with a replica of a log cabin similar to the one in which he grew up, enclosed in a neoclassical temple. The Lincoln Memorial on the National Mall, dedicated in 1922, the most famous memorial dedicated to the sixteenth president, celebrates him as the savior of the Union. Over time, however, its meaning has evolved to emphasize his role in freeing enslaved people and civil rights in general.

Emancipation Memorial, Lincoln Park, Washington DC

Thomas Ball's 1876 Emancipation Memorial (also called Emancipation Group or Freedmen's Memorial) was intended to express the gratitude of formerly enslaved people. It depicts a standing Lincoln apparently blessing a kneeling half-naked Black man, in a gesture evocative of Christ. The inscription on the front of the statue reads:

FREEDOM'S MEMORIAL

In Grateful Memory of

ABRAHAM LINCOLN

This monument was erected by the western sanitary commission of Saint Louis MO: With funds contributed solely by emancipated citizens of the United States declared free by his proclamation January 1st A.D. 1863. The first contribution of five dollars was made by Charlotte Scott a freed woman of Virginia being her first earnings in freedom and consecrated by her suggestion and request on the day she heard of President Lincoln's death to build a monument to his memory.

While the memorial was intended to commemorate the Emancipation Proclamation that ended slavery in the Confederacy, the unequal relationship of the depicted figures is problematic. The barely clothed Black figure is kneeling at the feet of the president towering over him. There is no sense of Black agency nor any indication of possible equality between Black and white people. The kneeling figure was actually a representation of Archer Alexander, a Black man who had escaped slavery, joined and aided the Union Army, but was then enslaved again under the Fugitive Slave Act.[1] He is neither named nor acknowledged.

At the dedication, Frederick Douglass spoke of the status of recently freed Black people: "Harmless, beautiful, proper, and praiseworthy as this demonstration is, I cannot forget that no such demonstration would have been tolerated here twenty years ago. The spirit of slavery and barbarism, which still lingers to blight and destroy in some dark and distant parts of our country, would have made our assembling here the signal and excuse for opening upon us all the flood-gates of wrath and violence."[2] Later Douglass critiqued the statue, noting, "Admirable as is the monument by Mr. Ball in Lincoln Park it does not as it seems to me, tell the whole truth, and perhaps no monument could be made to tell the whole truth of any subject which it might be designed to illustrate." He also expressed a wish: "What I want to see before I die is a monument representing the Negro, not couchant on his knees like a four-footed animal, but erect on his feet like a man."[3]

Although not what Douglass wished, the Mary McLeod Bethune Memorial by Robert Berks was installed in the park in 1974 opposite the monument to Lincoln, which was turned to face it.[4] Bethune, the daughter of former slaves, was a groundbreaking Black educator who founded the school that became Bethune-Cookman College. An important civil and women's rights activist, she also served as an advisor to Franklin Delano Roosevelt. Her statue was the first of a woman and the first African American figure on public park land in Washington DC. At the time it was commissioned, Lincoln Park had fallen into disrepair and become a local eyesore as well as a crime scene, so the municipal authorities decided to renew the space. The seventeen-foot-high tribute to Bethune was installed on a lower level than the Lincoln so that it would not exceed it in height. Funded by the National Council of Negro Women (NCNW) that Bethune founded, the memorial to the civil rights activist, presidential advisor, and educator was the first monument to a Black person or any woman on federal property.[5] A boy directly to her right receives a scroll containing her will, and a girl in the center slightly behind them echoes her gesture of outstretched arms. Both can be interpreted as inheriting her legacy. An inscription taken from her will reads: "I leave you love. I leave you hope. I leave you the challenge of developing confidence in one another. I leave you a thirst for education. I leave you a respect for the use of power. I leave you faith. I leave you racial dignity. I leave you a desire to live harmoniously with your fellow men. I leave you a responsibility to our young people."

An NCNW fundraising booklet issued at the time of the commission explained that the juxtaposition of the two statues was meant "to convey the message that the children of slaves had progressed from servitude."[6] Arguably the space between the two statues is too wide to make comparisons inevitable, but the opportunity is there. Jenny Woodley concluded that "Bethune was remembered as both a black American and an American; she is both the freedman and the Great Emancipator."[7] Yet, when I visited Lincoln Park in June 2021, I saw two young Black women photographing Freedom Monument in apparent admiration but paying no attention to the Bethune Memorial.

In spite of her impressive accomplishments, apparently Bethune is still not a well-known figure.

In June 2020 Ball's statue of Lincoln became the object of such intense controversy that for a time fences were erected around both it and the Bethune monument to protect them from destruction or vandalism; these were removed some three months later.[8] By contrast, a copy of Ball's statue that had been located in Boston's Park Square just off Boston Common since 1879 was eventually removed from its site. On 1 July 2020, amid the nationwide protests over the murder of George Floyd, the Boston Arts Commission voted unanimously to relocate the statue. At the public hearing Boston artist Tory Bullock, the author of an online petition that received more than twelve thousand signatures, observed, "This image is problematic because it feeds into a narrative that Black people need to be led and freed." Hannah Bessette, a Howard University student and Massachusetts resident, felt the statue was demeaning: "Regardless of what the intentions were, it is important to note that the intentions were white based intentions."[9] At the same time, Keith Winstead, a distant relative of Archer Alexander, opposed removal because he found it a powerful depiction of an American hero and a significant moment in Black history.[10] Although the statue has since been removed, the base remains. Neither the eventual location of the memorial nor what will occupy the base was known at the time of this writing.

The difference between the DC and Boston cases may be understood in terms of site—one in a residential section removed from the Capitol, the other in a prominent civic location. The public meeting held by the Boston Art Commission was evenhanded, with opinions on both removing and keeping the statue listened to with respect. Commission members appeared especially moved by testimony that spoke of the pain people of color felt when seeing the statue. Hopefully the monument's new location and the new use of the base will foster an open dialogue addressing the various issues prompted by the sculpture in 2020.

Abraham Lincoln Birthplace Memorial Building, Hodgenville, Kentucky

Built between 1909 and 1911 by the Lincoln Farm Association (LFA), this memorial to Lincoln has a complicated history.[11] By the time fundraising began in 1906 the log cabin where he was born no longer existed. Records indicate that it had disappeared by 1860 when Lincoln was elected president. In 1894 the land where it had been located was purchased by Alfred W. Dennett, a New York entrepreneur, who bought logs of an old cabin nearby and asked his agent in Kentucky, the Reverend James W. Bigham, to build one similar to the Lincoln family's original home; both the photograph and the newly erected cabin were generally accepted as authentic. In 1897 it was displayed at the Tennessee Centennial Exposition in Nashville next to a log cabin that was allegedly the birthplace of Jefferson Davis, the president of the Confederacy. This was also purchased by Dennett; subsequently he leased both to Frederick Thompson and Elmer Dundy, entrepreneurs in the amusement business. They furnished and displayed them at the Pan American Exposition in Buffalo in 1901. At some point during transport back to New York for storage the logs from the two cabins were intermingled.

After Robert Collier, publisher of *Collier's Weekly*, purchased the Lincoln farm in Hodgenville, he created the LFA and appointed a board of directors that among others included author Samuel L. Clemens (Mark Twain), labor leader Samuel Gompers, sculptor Augustus Saint-Gaudens, President William Howard Taft, and writer and muckraker Ida Tarbell. One of the board members, influential writer Norman Hapgood, purchased the 146 logs from David Crear, who had been in charge of them since Dennett had been hospitalized due to mental illness. The logs were transported to Kentucky on a flatcar in celebratory fashion, decorated with red, white, and blue bunting and portraits of Lincoln; by then there was no longer any mention of Jefferson Davis. For a time the cabin was set up in Central Park in Louisville. The men who created and exhibited this ersatz memorial were businessmen looking to make a profit comparable to what their amusement park ventures earned.

When the board hired John Russell Pope to design a building to protect the cabin, they initially envisioned something that would resemble the front of the White House, with an interior court containing a copy of Saint-Gaudens's statue of the president in Lincoln Park, Chicago. Financial constraints prompted a reduced plan. In 1906 President Theodore Roosevelt laid the corner stone on the centennial of Lincoln's birth, and some two years later his successor, William Howard Taft, dedicated the Memorial Building that enclosed the so-called birth cabin. Since the number of logs of both cabins combined exceeded the size of a single cabin, Pope had to alter his building in order to allow for enough space for visitors to move freely; this required trimming three or four feet in width and one or two feet in length. The combination of the "birth cabin" and Pope's surrounding neoclassical temple is jarring. Most visitors will likely miss the symbolism of the fifty-six steps leading up to the building representing the fifty-six years of Lincoln's existence, as well as the sixteen windows and sixteen rose-shaped designs on the ceiling intended to indicate that Lincoln was the sixteenth president.

By 1938 National Park Service Historian Roy Appleman noted many errors in the information provided at the memorial. He concluded, "This is the grossest example of mistreatment of an historic structure that has ever come to my attention. It is apparent that a problem exists relative to the representations made to the public concerning this building."[12] In September 1948 the insurance investigator Roy Hays published an article in the *Abraham Lincoln Quarterly* denouncing the memorial as a hoax, relying on evidence that had already been noted by the president's son Robert Todd Lincoln in 1919. Until Hays's article appeared, the National Park Service (NPS), which had managed the site since 1933, endorsed the local tradition that it was authentic. Benjamin Davis, the park's historian, did his own research confirming the inauthenticity of the cabin, which was supported by three Lincoln scholars. Once the NPS confirmed the evolution of the Hodgenville memorial, they added signage to convey the facts. Nevertheless, some three hundred thousand visitors annually respond to the log cabin as if it were authentic. This rather amazing story suggests that illusion may be as powerful as reality when it comes to memorials.[13]

The Lincoln Memorial, National Mall

Dedicated in 1922, the Lincoln Memorial was the work of architect Henry Bacon and sculptor Daniel Chester French. Its focus is a gigantic figure of Lincoln enthroned in a Greek temple-like structure, whose walls are inscribed with quotes from his Gettysburg and second inaugural addresses. His hands are poised above bundles of thirteen fasces, Roman symbols of power and authority repeated throughout the memorial, alluding to the unification of the original thirteen states and the preservation of the Union accomplished by Lincoln.[14] The dedication directly above him reads, "In This Temple as in the Hearts of the People for Whom He Saved the Union the Memory of Abraham Lincoln Is Enshrined Forever."

As early as 1867, Congress passed a bill to create a private Lincoln Monument Association (LMA) similar to the one that was created for Washington. After some initial funds were raised, Clark Mills was asked to develop a design but nothing came of the elaborate structure he proposed; when the sculptor died in 1883, the LMA seemed unsure how to proceed.[15] In 1904 the McMillan Commission, charged with overseeing the redesign of the Mall, authorized Representative James T. McCleary of Minnesota to consider memorials in Europe for possible inspiration. Four years later he proposed a memorial road from Washington to Gettysburg, with each state along the route creating its own memorial. This idea continued to have sizable support. For those who preferred a built memorial rather than a road, there was controversy over whether it should be sited in Potomac Park or nearer Capitol Hill. During the course of lengthy and heated debates, President Theodore Roosevelt created the Council of Fine Arts and the Senate named the Lincoln Memorial Commission (LMC) in 1911.

The next debate centered on whether an architect should be invited to submit a design or if there should be an open competition. The LMC chose to invite architect Henry Bacon to propose a memorial for Potomac Park and later asked John Russell Pope to create designs for two nearby hilltop locations. After the commission selected the Potomac site, both architects were asked to submit final proposals, prompting more controversy over which was the better design. Bacon's proposal for the structure was selected in 1913, and a year later the LMC announced that Daniel Chester French had been chosen to realize the sculpture of Lincoln. Construction took eight years. The Lincoln Memorial was finally completed in 1922. Bacon's temple-like structure evoking classical Greece features thirty-six columns symbolizing the number of states in the Union at the time of Lincoln's presidency. Lincoln's quotes reference slavery, but the interior mural by Jules Guerin did not include any Black figures. At the time of the dedication there was segregated seating.

The overall decision by Congress to avoid citing Lincoln's role as the Great Emancipator was determined by the need for Southern support, similar to the concern that prompted the omission of the word "slavery" in the Constitution.[16] The meaning of the memorial began to shift in 1939 when Marian Anderson held a concert there.[17] Segregation was rife in the nation's capital and Anderson was prohibited from singing at Constitution Hall, which was owned by the Daughters of the American Revolution (DAR). At the time the concert was scheduled to take place there, the hall was open only to white artists. As a result, Eleanor Roosevelt resigned from the DAR in protest, and the concert venue was moved to the memorial. Since no reputable hotel was open to a Black person, Anderson had to sleep in a private house. The concert program quoted the Gettysburg Address on its cover, and she began by singing "America." The peaceful concert, implicitly also a protest, provided a model for Martin Luther King Jr.'s use of the memorial in 1963 for his March on Washington and his "I Have a Dream" speech. This, too, began with a quote from the Gettysburg Address. The new emphasis on emancipation and Black rights at the Lincoln Memorial signaled that these now were integral to national identity.[18]

Over the years presidents of both parties have visited the Lincoln Memorial to embrace its implicit content and importance in defining national identity as they saw it.[19] Notably, Barack Obama, the country's first Black president, used the same Bible that Lincoln used at his swearing in ceremony. The theme of his inaugural speech given in front of the U.S. Capitol, "A New Birth of Freedom," was inspired by Lincoln's Gettysburg Address. In sharp contrast, when Republican President Donald Trump gave a speech at the Lincoln Memorial on 4 July 2019, it seemed to many as a kind of national sacrilege. Philip Kennicott, writing in the *Washington Post*, stated, "It is difficult to express how deeply repugnant his effort to politicize this space is to commonly held American ideals. . . . The Fourth of July, [in] Washington, is beloved because for a moment, the city feels whole, and one can imagine that perhaps someday the country will feel whole, too. It is a fantasy, but a fantasy we abandon at our peril."[20]

In May 2020 a number of memorials throughout the country were defaced in protest in the aftermath of the police killing of George Floyd. The words "Y'all Not Tired Yet?" were spray-painted on a base leading to the Lincoln Memorial, apparently challenging the appropriateness of honoring the sixteenth president.[21] Today the focus is more on Lincoln's limitations: the fact that the Emancipation Proclamation freed only slaves in the Confederacy, that he came to this action rather late, and that he long supported a policy of the deportation of freed slaves. These problematic issues should be seen in the context of his contributions and insistence on his interpretation of Jefferson's founding principle that all men are created equal, which continues to resonate as a central facet of national identity and the basis of national unity.

8

Abraham Lincoln's Evolution

Traditionally celebrated for emancipating the enslaved and saving the Union (not necessarily in that order), Lincoln is also admired for being a so-called self-made man. After a childhood marked by poverty, truncated schooling, and hard work, he went on to hold the highest office in the land. Lincoln was an autodidact, determined to educate himself on a wide range of subjects, including the law; he eventually worked in a thriving law firm. However, politics was always his primary passion, and he had a number of skills that enabled his success in this arena. A good listener who liked to mingle with people after a day's work, he valued public opinion and always considered it in establishing policy.[1] Lincoln was a gifted orator who punctuated his remarks with anecdotes and jokes. He wrote and delivered some of the nation's most memorable and often repeated speeches, some of which are now considered foundational to national identity. Yet today his status is being challenged, primarily because of his treatment of Native Americans and some of his policies regarding Black people.

Unlike the other presidents carved on Mount Rushmore, Abraham Lincoln's primary occupation and passion was always politics. George Washington had a military career and a plantation. Thomas Jefferson had Monticello and a host of other interests, including architecture and education. Theodore Roosevelt was a proponent of the active life, an avid hunter, and a prolific writer.

Since Lincoln's untimely death he has been variously described by those writing about him, as well as by the general public. Merrill D. Peterson in *Lincoln in American Memory* identifies five main themes: "Lincoln as Savior of the Union, Great Emancipator, Man of the People, the First American, and the Self-made Man."[2] The word "Savior" in particular has a decidedly religious connotation, enhanced by the date of his assassination, which occurred on Good Friday, 15 April 1865. After his assassination, references abounded to Lincoln's apotheosis, thereby deifying the former president.[3]

The salient facts of Lincoln's biography justify his definition as a self-made man. Growing up poor in a log cabin, splitting rails as a young man, and his lifelong pursuit of knowledge as an autodidact—all these resonate in the abiding American dream of upward mobility. Yet, though it has been much romanticized over time, Lincoln never idealized this aspect of his life. At the time of his first presidential campaign in 1860, he described it succinctly as "the short and simple annals of the poor."[4] In addition to hard work, Lincoln's early life was marked by tragic loss; his mother died when he was nine. His future wife, Mary Todd, suffered a similar loss; she was six when her mother died. Mary was born into a wealthy family and by marrying her, Lincoln married well. Nevertheless, Lincoln's belief in the potential for self-improvement remained a significant theme in all his political policies and informed his initial objections to slavery.[5]

Lincoln and Slavery

Lincoln's attitudes toward slavery and concomitant policies evolved over time with his circumstances. Kentucky, where he was born, was a slave state. Indiana, where he moved at the age of seven and stayed until he was twenty-one (1816–30), became a free state in 1816 but previously enslaved people continued to live there. Illinois, where he launched his legal practice and political career, allowed indentured servitude until 1848, when a new constitution made it a free state that outlawed slavery. When Lincoln married Mary Todd in 1842, he became part of a very well-connected political family, many of whom owned slaves. Lexington, Kentucky, where Mary grew up, was a major slave trading center, and one of her uncles actively participated in the slave trade.[6] Lincoln's marriage thus brought him into an environment that not only tolerated but profited from slavery.

On the issue of slavery, Lincoln typically aimed at a middle-ground political position.[7] He never declared himself an abolitionist. Up until the time of the Emancipation Proclamation (1863) and thereafter, he spoke only against the spread of slavery since, according to the Constitution, it was still permitted where it already existed. Lincoln's first public statement on the subject was made in 1854 after the passage of the Kansas-Nebraska Act, giving newly established territories the right to decide whether they wished to adopt slavery.[8] Up to that time he believed (as did many others, including Washington and Jefferson) that slavery would ultimately disappear of its own accord. In his efforts to halt the spread of slavery he invoked the Declaration of Independence. Going forward, however, it would be Lincoln's broad interpretation of the statement that all men were created equal that prevailed, and not Jefferson's limited meaning that they were equal only in their emotional capacity.

Lincoln framed his argument against the extension of slavery in terms that resonated with a broad spectrum of the population. His insistence on the evil of slavery appealed to the abolitionists. His opposition to its further extension, based on the threat that freed Black people might pose to the existing workforce in the North, appealed to those who might not otherwise support limiting the practice.[9] These basic arguments formed the basis of all his speeches on the subject, including those in his 1860 campaign for the presidency. Lincoln, however, did not consider Black people equal to whites. Speaking to a delegation of freed slaves in order to convince them that it was in their best interests to leave the country and move to Africa or the Caribbean, he stated, "The aspiration of men is to enjoy equality with the best when free, but on this broad continent, not a single man of your race is made the equal of a single man of ours."[10] He reasoned they would be better off elsewhere—in African or the Caribbean—living among similar people. This position, held by many others, arose in part from the fear that slaves in the United States might rebel, as they had in Haiti and Santo Domingo in 1791, thereby posing a threat to the practice of slavery that would have wide-reaching repercussions.[11] In 1816 Reverend Robert Finley, along with others including Henry Clay, Daniel Webster, and Francis Scott Key (author to the lyrics of "The Star-Spangled Banner"), formed the American Society for Colonizing the Free People of Color of the United States (the American Colonization Society or ACS) with aid from Protestant and Presbyterian churches as well as federal government officials. Thomas Jefferson was an early and ardent advocate of this solution to the United States' race problem. Unable to imagine a way that freed slaves with no education or professional skills could make a living, its supporters linked colonization with emancipation.[12] Neither Washington, Jefferson, nor Lincoln (initially) could envision an integrated society. After Lincoln met and befriended Frederick Douglass, even inviting him to the White House, his opinion of Black people changed.[13]

While advocating against the expansion of slavery, Lincoln continued to reassure the Southern states that he would not interfere with the practice as it existed. Nevertheless, upon his election to the presidency, seven states seceded: Alabama, Florida, Georgia, Louisiana, Mississippi, South Carolina, and Texas. In Lincoln's first inaugural speech he tried to minimize national differences and affirm the integrity of the Union, concluding, "The mystic chords of memory, stretching from every battle-field, and patriot grave, to every living heart and hearthstone, all over this broad land, will yet swell the chorus of the Union, when again touched, as surely they will be, by the better angels of our nature."[14] In spite of this, after his inauguration four more states seceded: Arkansas, North Carolina, Tennessee and Virginia.

Lincoln insisted that the federal government would not attack the seceding states, and that they would have to be the aggressors to start a war. To that end, he succeeded in provoking an attack on Ford Sumter located in Confederate territory by sending a ship with provisions to the Union soldiers who were stationed there. Once the fort was attacked, war would follow; if it were left in peace, there would be continued Union occupancy. Either would be a political setback and a huge loss of prestige for the South. The Civil War began with the Confederate attack on Fort Sumter on 12 April 1861.[15]

Lincoln continued to support financed colonization for freed Black people who wished to leave the country, publicly until 1863 and privately for a period thereafter. As the impetus for emancipation gathered support, he came to realize its obvious advantages: it would strip the Southern states of a vital source of free manual labor and allow the formerly enslaved to serve in the Union army. Viewed as a military necessity, the Emancipation Proclamation issued in the midst of the Civil War came under the purview of the president.[16] Lincoln's acknowledgment of the pragmatic expediency of allowing Black people to enlist was similar to Washington's evolving policy during the American Revolution. The valiant service of Black soldiers changed both Lincoln's and Washington's opinion of Black people.

The Emancipation Proclamation freed enslaved people in Confederate States that had not rejoined the Union. The specific states to which it applied were later added to the document on 1 January 1863, and included Alabama, Arkansas, Florida, Georgia, Louisiana, Mississippi, North Carolina, South Carolina, Texas, and Virginia.[17] The executive order did not apply to those still enslaved in the border states: Delaware, Kentucky, Maryland, Missouri, and West Virginia. The border states had neither supported Lincoln in the 1860 election nor seceded; thus they became a battleground for both the North and South. To complicate matters further, each state was deeply divided on the slavery issue.[18] Lincoln was convinced that victory depended on the border states and that victory was necessary to enforce the Emancipation Proclamation going forward. A different administration could rescind a proclamation that was not law. Still, the effect of the Emancipation Proclamation was immediate and profound, changing the history of the country and promoting national unity. In its immediate wake, Frederick Douglass proclaimed that "the cause of the slaves and the cause of the country had become one."[19]

Late in 1863 Lincoln delivered the Gettysburg Address at the military cemetery where more than forty thousand Union and Confederate soldiers were buried, framing the war as having both national and spiritual significance, in language that invoked the Bible. Lincoln defined the essential goals of the Civil War as freeing the slaves and saving the Union, reiterating Jefferson's words in the Declaration of Independence that all men were created equal. According to Lincoln, the purpose of the Civil War in which so many had died was making certain "that this nation, under God, shall have a new birth of freedom—and that government of the people, by the people, for the people, shall not perish from the earth."[20] Most significantly, he spoke of slavery as a national problem that must be resolved for the nation to survive.

In his 1864 campaign for the presidency Lincoln went further, emphasizing the need for a constitutional amendment to abolish slavery and demanding the surrender of the Confederacy. His second inaugural address frequently invoked God and stated again that the war was waged over slavery, making the South responsible for the bloodshed.[21] Nevertheless, he ended with a resounding plea for unity: "With malice toward none; with charity for all; with firmness in the right, as God gives us to see the right, let us strive on to finish the work we are in; to bind up the nation's wounds; to care for him who shall have borne the battle, and for his widow, and his orphan—to do all which may achieve and cherish a just, and a lasting peace, among ourselves, and with all nations."[22]

As the war drew to an end, Lincoln used the considerable influence of his office to campaign actively for the passage of the Thirteenth Amendment, which would prohibit slavery permanently: "Neither slavery nor involuntary servitude, except as a punishment for a crime whereof the party shall have been duly convicted, shall exist within the United Sates, or any place subject to their jurisdiction. Congress shall have the power to enforce this article by appropriate legislation."[23] Introduced in January 1865, it was passed by Congress and ratified by twenty-seven of the existing thirty-six states in early December of that year, becoming the law of the land by the end of the month. Lincoln was assassinated on Good Friday, 15 April 1865, and did not live to see its ratification or enactment.

The evolution of Lincoln's policy on slavery was perceived to be too slow by some abolitionists and too extreme by Southern slave holders. It demonstrated Lincoln's ability to reconsider his own deeply held beliefs and change his position in response to events and public opinion. Focused on maintaining the Union, he offered both Southern and border states incentives to rejoin or remain, but these were rejected. Lincoln's tone remained conciliatory, above all to maintain the Union. His vision of national identity was based on his interpretation of the Declaration of Independence and his firmly held conviction, based on his own life experience, that every individual should have the right and opportunity to prosper.

Lincoln's Native American Policies

Lincoln's first encountered Native Americans in the context of his family history. His paternal grandfather, for whom he was named, was killed by a

Native American while he was working on his farm. Lincoln's father, a witness, was left orphaned at the age of six.[24] This traumatic event, which imposed hardships on his family that he still felt growing up, did not appear to make Lincoln an "Indian hater," but he had an uncle who was.[25] In 1832 the twenty-three-year-old Lincoln volunteered to fight against Native Americans in the Black Hawk War waged by the eponymous Native American chief who refused to leave his home; Black Hawk was eventually subdued by U.S. forces after a conflict that resulted in some five hundred deaths. Lincoln dismissed this military experience, making humorous remarks referring to struggles with his weapon and mosquitoes. Still, at the time he ran for president in 1860, his biography focused on his being selected as a captain during that war.[26]

Once Lincoln assumed the office of president in 1861, he participated in a well-established patronage system that awarded positions for political reasons in what was then called Indian country.[27] Congressionally approved treaties were ignored, leading to a land grab by whites of territory officially ceded to Native Americans, who were then moved to reservations. White contractors and traders consistently stole goods and funds allocated to Indigenous people, so that they never reached their intended population. Additionally, whites could make claims to the government for alleged damages to their property by Native Americans. All this was widely known, including by Lincoln's Commissioner of Indian Affairs William P. Dole. The president, nevertheless, followed well-established political precedent and continued to make politically advantageous appointments.[28] As a result of this systemic corruption, Native Americans lived in deplorable conditions. They were deprived of rations as well as arable land to raise their own food and often starved to death.

This situation prompted the Dakota Wars of 1862, in which the Santee Sioux in Minnesota attacked white settlers in order to remove them from land that was legally theirs and gain access to a warehouse where food was stored.[29] Following Lincoln's instructions to "Attend to the Indians" quickly, the Union Army, led by General John Pope, murdered Native American civilians, including women and children, and took several hundred men prisoner, sentencing some three hundred to be hanged.[30] Although there was widespread support for this wholesale execution among Minnesota officials and the general public, Lincoln decided to review the charges.[31] He and his lawyers began by looking for Native men accused of rape, reflecting a widespread fear among whites (similar to their fear of Black people), but found only two. After evaluating the rest of the charges, Lincoln deemed thirty-three valid enough for hanging. Apparently distressed, he spent a considerable amount of time mulling over alternatives, including leaving the decision in the hands of the governor. After he was informed that this was illegal, he issued the order for the largest single hanging of Native Americans in United States history. It is seldom noted that this was also the nation's largest pardon of those spared from execution.

Subsequently, Lincoln signed a bill for removing the Sioux as well as the Winnebago from Minnesota, continuing their harsh treatment by those who benefited from the politics of patronage.[32] He then turned away from what he viewed as a troublesome problem, resulting in the death of many more who remained in Minnesota prison camps, including women and children who died from disease or starvation—in total many more than were actually hanged.[33] Lincoln's overall actions and inaction in the Minnesota case resulted in inestimable suffering.[34] At that time Minnesota was important politically and Native Americans couldn't vote. In 1859, shortly before his election, Minnesota had become a nonslave state, and during the Civil War Lincoln needed it to stay that way. There were also widespread rumors that the South was actively campaigning for Native American support. Although this was not actually the case, the rumors were credible because some Southern tribes had aligned with the Confederacy early on since they, too, owned slaves.[35] As soon as Lincoln was inaugurated, the Confederate government created a Bureau of Indian Affairs charged with negotiating treaties and later that year organized what was known as Indian Territory into a separate military department. While the Union abandoned that land and continued to ignore Native Americans, the South tried to win them over. They gave their Native American troops the right to select their own officers and promised them representation in the Confederate Congress.[36]

The Minnesota Indian War of 1862 was waged against white settlers by the Santee, or Eastern Dakotas, over broken treaties that had resulted in increased white settlement on their land. Many of the Santee were starving, and out of desperation attacked settlements. Hundreds died in a series of battles along the Minnesota River. When the Civil War began Lincoln sent troops then stationed in the west that were charged with protecting Native Americans to the eastern front—in effect abandoning them.[37] At the time the Civil War was going badly for the North. The president instructed Union forces under General John C. Pope to take care of the Native American problem as quickly and completely as possible. The consistent need for manpower, exacerbated by the Minnesota Indian War, may have been a factor in Lincoln's decision to finally enact the Emancipation Proclamation.[38] Even though some linked abolitionism with reforms to benefit Native Americans (most notably William Lloyd Garrison as early as 1829),[39] the central importance of the Civil War to maintaining the Union has overshadowed historical assessments of Lincoln's treatment of Native Americans.

Part of the problem was Lincoln's basic attitude toward Native Americans, one shared by a wide segment of the population. Unlike his connection with Frederick Douglass and other Black people that he came to respect, Lincoln had no personal relationships with Native Americans either before his presidency or after. When he met with a group of fourteen chiefs of western tribes at the White House in 1863, he condescendingly informed them that the world was round, strongly urged them to take up farming, and told them to become less warlike by adopting the peaceful ways of white people—this in the midst of the Civil War.[40] In this way Lincoln invoked a number of stereotypes embraced by many white leaders.[41] Some insisted that the plight and condition of Native Americans was their own fault. No one, it seemed, was able to acknowledge the sophisticated system of Indian governance and agriculture that had contributed to their sustained existence before white interference.

This was true even among reformers who petitioned for better treatment of Native Americans, most notably Bishop Henry Benjamin Whipple, the first Episcopalian bishop of Minnesota. Persistent in trying to get the president's attention, he identified both the problem and the solution: in his view, what was needed was reform of the patronage system. However, any attempts to investigate corrupt practices were squelched by Lincoln's high-ranking appointments, including William P. Dole, who was a beneficiary of the system.[42] Still, Whipple's demands appeared to impress Lincoln when they met in 1862. By the end of the year the president in his annual message to Congress asked members to give special consideration to remodeling the Indian System, although he gave no specifics.[43] In 1863 he spoke of the urgent need for legislative action to address the needs of Native Americans, but this followed praise for actions that led to their removal from lands that then became available for white settlement. By 1864 Lincoln had stopped asking for reform and Whipple had given up on the president. During that year's presidential election he voted for his opponent, James McClellan.[44]

Congress was finally prompted to investigate the widespread problem by the 1864 Sand Creek massacre. Some four hundred or possibly even five hundred men, women, and children in a village of Cheyenne and Arapaho Indians in Colorado were slaughtered even though they had not been charged with any crime. Congress specifically investigated the role of Dole, Lincoln's commissioner of Indian Affairs; he resigned after President Lincoln's assassination in 1865.[45]

Throughout his presidency Lincoln participated in a corrupt patronage system and thought about Native Americans only in the context of the Civil War when he was forced to. Although he considered their needs briefly, he did nothing to address them because he was more committed to national expansion, as were the other Mount Rushmore presidents. Toward that end he championed the Transcontinental Railroad, resulting in the displacement of more Native Americans. He committed his administration to a policy of resettling them on reservations with all their attendant abuses. This has been compared to his support of colonization of Black people. Seen in the most positive light, however, it is possible that Lincoln's public expression of concern for Native Americans planted a seed that made it easier for Congress eventually to consider their plight more seriously.[46]

1. Gutzon Borglum and Lincoln Borglum, Mount Rushmore National Memorial, cornerstone dedicated in 1925, Keystone, South Dakota. Photograph by Zachary Frank. Alamy Stock Photo.

2. *Above:* Gutzon Borglum, *Seated Lincoln*, 1911, Essex County Courthouse, Newark, New Jersey. Photograph by Richard Levine. Alamy Stock Photo.

3. *Opposite:* Jean-Antoine Houdon, *George Washington*, installed 1796, Virginia State Capitol Rotunda, Richmond, Virginia. Courtesy Visions of America, LLC. Alamy Stock Photo.

OLD HOUSE CHAMBER

GEORGE WASHINGTON

4. Antonio Canova, model for *George Washington*, plaster, 1818, collection of Gypsotheca e Museo Antonio Canova. Courtesy Museo Gypsotheca Antonio Canova, Possagno, Italy.

5. Robert Mills (initial architect) and Thomas Casey, Washington Monument, 1884, Washington DC. Photograph by Clarence Holmes Photography. Alamy Stock Photo.

6. *Opposite:* Robert Mills, Washington Monument, masonry completed in 1829, Baltimore, Maryland. Antique halftone photographic print published by the Saalfield Company, 1908. Courtesy Antiqua Print Gallery. Alamy Stock Photo.

7. *Above:* Victor Mikhail Arnautoff, "Westward March" of *Life of Washington*, mural, 1936, George Washington High School, San Francisco. Courtesy Tammy Aramian. Artam Studio.

8. Thomas Jefferson, Monticello, completed circa 1809, Albemarle County, Virginia. Photograph by Edwin Remsberg. Alamy Stock Photo.

9. John Russell Pope, Jefferson Memorial, completed 1943, Washington DC. Photograph by Blakeley. Alamy Stock Photo.

10. Eero Saarinen, Gateway Arch National Park, Jefferson National Expansion Memorial, arch completed 1965, St. Louis, Missouri. Courtesy Library of Congress, Prints & Photographs Division, LC-USZ62-123456. Photograph by Carol M. Highsmith.

11. John Russell Pope, Abraham Lincoln Birthplace Memorial Building, dedicated 1911, Hodgenville, Kentucky. Courtesy Library of Congress, Prints & Photographs Division, LC-USZ62-123456. Photograph by Carol M. Highsmith.

12. Interior of Abraham Lincoln Birthplace Memorial Building with log cabin. Photograph by Daniel Dempster Photography. Alamy Stock Photo.

13. Henry Bacon (architect) and Daniel Chester French (sculptor), Lincoln Memorial, dedicated in 1922, Washington DC. Photograph by Alan Novelli. Alamy Stock Photo.

14. *Opposite:* Thomas Ball, Emancipation Memorial, dedicated 1876, Lincoln Park, Washington DC. Courtesy Renée Ater.

15. *Above:* James Earle Fraser, *Theodore Roosevelt*, 1939, American Museum of Natural History, New York City (removed 2022). Photograph by Robert K. Chin—Storefronts. Alamy Stock Photo.

16. Eric Gugler (landscape architect), Paul Manship (sculptor), *Theodore Roosevelt Island National Memorial*, dedicated 1967, Washington DC. Courtesy Bruce Glaser.

9

Theodore Roosevelt's Problematic Memorials

The two key memorials to Theodore Roosevelt celebrate his commitment to conservation, depict him as a heroic figure, and are by artists who were well-known and celebrated in their day. One has been removed while the other, his official national monument, is located in such a secluded spot that it is easily missed even by local residents.

James Earle Fraser's equestrian statue of Roosevelt, formerly in front of the American Museum of Natural History in New York, was removed in 2022 and placed on long-term loan to the Theodore Roosevelt Presidential Library in North Dakota, scheduled for completion in 2025. The statue was part of a larger design for the façade of the museum created by the architect John Russell Pope. In its entirety it was intended to celebrate Roosevelt's scientific and educational contributions as well as his outdoor activities and explorations, rather than his political and literary accomplishments. Many of the trophies he brought back from his hunting expeditions form part of the museum's collection.

Since Roosevelt was known for his love of the outdoors and hunting, James Earle Fraser portrayed him on horseback. He used a pose based on the well-known Renaissance statue of the Venetian condottiere, Bartolomeo

Colleoni by Andrea del Verrocchio, while following the general proportions of Roosevelt's horse, Man of War. It was not the equestrian statue per se that prompted the controversy. Rather, it was the fact that Roosevelt is on horseback while the flanking figures of a Native American and African are on foot. Even though this suggests a distinct (racial) hierarchy, their visual appearance is in no way abject. Nor was it Fraser's intent to denigrate Native American and African people.[1] Pope's instructions to him were clear: "In the center of the terrace, immediately in front of the great arch will arise a polished granite pedestal bearing an equestrian statue of Roosevelt with two accompanying figures on foot, one representing the American Indian and the other the primitive African. This heroic group will attain a height of thirty feet above the sidewalk and proceeding, as it were, in triumph from its lofty arch, will symbolize the fearless leadership, the explorer, benefactor and educator, a creation that should inspire the beholder with a feeling of the truly sublime in art and in history."[2]

For many years Fraser had been the chief assistant to Augustus Saint-Gaudens, the most prominent American sculptor at the time. A successful artist in his own right, Fraser was one of the most popular public sculptors during the early decades of the twentieth century until falling into relative obscurity.[3] According to Cécile Ganteaume, associate curator, National Museum of the American Indian, Fraser liked to work from photographs of Native peoples, creating a composite portrait rather than a representative of a specific tribe. For the Roosevelt memorial, "the type he wanted to create was that of the Noble Savage and Vanishing Indian, and the overwhelming majority of his viewers in 1936 would likely have regarded the sculpture as representing just that. . . . With the frontier closed, the country was moving on. Fraser's Native American is there to represent a major and defining chapter in the country's past."[4] More generally, Thayer Tolles, Marica F. Vilcek Curator of American Painting and Sculpture at the Metropolitan Museum of Art, observed, "Sculptors such as Cyrus Dallin, James Earle Fraser, and Hermon Atkins MacNeil created sensitive representations of Native Americans as noble savages diminished by White expansionist policies, in effect protesting their unjust treatment. Though dispossessed, they are presented as dignified, whether in poses of defiance or defeat."[5]

Pope described the African figure as "primitive," which generally has a negative connotation. While Fraser created a drawing and a bronze that fit this general description, the final work more closely resembles idealized classical sculpture. In all likelihood, the African figure, like the Native American, is a composite with some features specific to certain tribes or regions. James Green, curator of African Art, Yale Gallery of Art, noted that scarification is typically associated with some kind of status and is a sign of adulthood, an indicator that the figure has completed an initiation. There is, however, a disjuncture between the head, which is decidedly African, and the body that suggests classical or Renaissance sculpture. Indeed, the body bears a striking resemblance to the so-called Kritios Boy, an iconic example of an early classical Greek male nude. Although Fraser knew Native Americans and was therefore familiar with their body type and dress, that was not the case with Africans. An artist who had studied at the École des Beaux-Arts, as Fraser had, would typically use an idealized classical model for an allegorical figure.

Shortly before the unveiling of the Roosevelt memorial, Fraser wrote, "The two figures at his side are guides symbolizing the continents of Africa and America, and if you choose may stand for Roosevelt's friendliness to all races."[6] The figures stand in front of reliefs on the parapet depicting animals native to their respective continents. Symbolic sculptural representations of continents were common at the time. Prior to the Roosevelt commission Fraser had worked on Saint-Gaudens's (1903) monument to General Sherman, located at the southeast entrance to Central Park, depicting the general on horseback led by a female figure representing Victory. He would certainly have been thinking about this work when he designed the Roosevelt statue. Thayer Tolles noted the existence of photographs of Fraser in his studio with a model of Saint-Gaudens's Robert Gould Shaw Memorial (1897) in Boston, which depicted Shaw on horseback in front of a volunteer army of armed Black soldiers on foot. Tolles suggested that this was also a likely inspiration.[7]

Given the evidence of Fraser's own words and contemporary sculptural practice, in particular Saint-Gaudens's work, the standing figures can be understood both as allegories of continents and Roosevelt's gun bearers and guides. Fraser emphasized that Roosevelt was being celebrated here "not as the president of the United States, but as the naturalist, who has made a notable collection of animal specimens from Africa and America."[8] At the time, museums commissioned explorers to document and collect such examples for their collections.[9] Today serious concerns about animal extinction and preservation of the environment challenge the practice of hunting in this context. Yet, natural history museum collections provide important documentation of biodiversity as well as the history of the natural world. Somewhere a balance is called for.

In 2017 the New York City Mayoral Advisory Commission was charged with making recommendations about the fate of the controversial equestrian statue. Debates included a heated discussion about eugenics both in terms of Roosevelt's and the museum's ideology. Given the heinous expression of racist eugenics during World War II, this field of inquiry is now regarded with revulsion and rejection. During the early decades of the twentieth century, however, a focus on preserving the best in the human race (a loaded distinction to be sure) was common in scientific circles. Eugenics was closely linked with conservation and its focus on the natural world. The Progressive movement at that time saw eugenics and conservation as "contemporary social and political programs whose ideologies were not only compatible, but for those who adhered to them, mutually reinforcing."[10] This context is pertinent when considering the memorial today and is emblematic of the critical question of how past ideologies should be weighed in determining the fate of public art.

Nuanced complicated historical issues, however, rarely come to the fore in public controversies. The demonstrations calling for the removal of the Roosevelt statue, many organized by the protest group Decolonize This Place, were based on Roosevelt's imperialist policies. Those commission members in favor of keeping the statue in place felt that the only way to prevent its removal was to vote for further study, which is what was finally decided. Subsequently, Mayor Bill de Blasio determined that the work should stay, and the museum developed an exhibition intended to present the controversy surrounding the statue from various perspectives. Consisting largely of text and headshots with quotes, the exhibition also included a timeline for Roosevelt, various interpretations of the flanking figures, and different opinions on what the fate of the statue should be. On the online site for audience comments, roughly half supported maintaining the status quo, about 25 percent advocated for removal, and an additional 25 percent supported some sort of additional intervention, including moving the statue to another location or removing the standing figures. An exhibition is a useful public forum to consider controversies and the AMNH is to be commended for mounting it. The museum's position, however, was problematic. One of the wall texts stated categorically that the statue portrays a "racist hierarchy" that the museum "has long found disturbing," thereby closing off any other interpretation. Before the protests of 2020, however, the museum neither researched nor took any action to address this issue.

On 22 June 2020, in the wake of the protests over the murder of George Floyd by Minneapolis police, the museum officially asked the city to remove the work. Mayor de Blasio granted his approval; Roosevelt's great-grandson agreed; and the museum's president, Ellen Futter, announced that the Hall of Biodiversity would be renamed in Roosevelt's honor for his contribution to conservation. By spring 2021 the AMNH presented architect Rolando Kraeher's new design for the front of the museum to the local community board, the Landmarks Commission, and the Public Design Commission. At the Community Board 7 meeting on 13 May, Dan Slippen, AMNH's vice president of government affairs, emphasized that the hierarchical composition of the equestrian monument caused people to misinterpret it. This perceived racial content, he admitted, became more apparent after the George Floyd protests. Preservation consultant Bill Higgins emphasized that removal was in keeping with the museum's response to a changing world and that the statue now detracted from the overall memorial to Roosevelt. The Landmarks Commission approved removal on 15 June, and the Public Design Commission met on 21 June and agreed to this plan. At this time Slippen stated again that because the statue "appears to depict the superiority of the white race" its placement in front of the museum suggests "endorsement of this content . . . undermining the museum's mission."[11]

Kraeher's minimal redesigned entrance, intended to emphasize inclusivity, consists of an extended widened staircase stretching from the sidewalk up to the triumphal arch entrance. The arch, now the focus of the entry experience, is based on a definitively imperial Roman precedent. As a reminder of the missing statue, there will be a bronze plaque in the ground echoing the shape of the base engraved with a text explaining the removal of the statue.[12] Presumably, it could be overlooked and you could walk right over it, calling to mind the Stolpersteine (stumbling stones) in Berlin featuring the names and dates of those killed or persecuted by the Nazis.[13]

Regardless of the justifications now offered, it is clear that the Roosevelt statue was removed in response to ongoing public demonstrations. As in nearly all such protests, there is no evidence of how widely they are supported. Furthermore, there are no established guidelines or parameters for how decisions like this should be made, although some public art programs provide useful models.[14] The AMNH memorial was intended to celebrate Roosevelt for his work in conservation and his contributions to the museum collection, hence the reference to hunting, but protesters saw only a racial hierarchy and colonialism. A work of art in a public space is almost always understood literally (it looks like, therefore it must mean) and seen in an exclusively presentist frame, with contemporary values obscuring any (art) historical meaning or importance. Protestors raised issues that are pertinent to Roosevelt's legacy—but not in the context of this commission. A better solution might have been to move the statue inside the museum where a fuller history and various opinions could be displayed. In this setting it could be used for public programs that explore critical issues raised by this and other controversies as they evolve over time.

Theodore Roosevelt National Memorial

Although plans for a national memorial to honor Theodore Roosevelt began as early as 1919, one was not completed until 1967 on the 109th anniversary of his birth. Located on an eighty-eight-acre island in the Potomac River between Rosslyn, Virginia, and the Rock Creek waterfront in Washington DC, Theodore Roosevelt Island has had various uses during its long history.[15] Owners were documented as early as 1682. In 1711 explorers described the island as having a very good quality of soil and noted the presence of Native Americans. In 1790 it became part of the new federal capital, the District of Columbia. Two years later John Mason, a friend of Presidents Jefferson, Madison, and Monroe, inherited the island, living there and cultivating it until 1833; traces of artifacts from that time have been excavated. Subsequently it was rented as a site for recreation, a commercial garden, and athletic and boating clubs. From 1861–63 it was used as a military camp and occupied by the United States Army. By the time the Roosevelt Memorial Association (RMA) purchased the island in 1931 it was overgrown and Mason's home was in ruins.

The creation of the national memorial to Roosevelt was a prolonged process involving significant changes in planned location, protracted arguments about the placement of an access bridge to the island, delays caused by the Great Depression and World War II, and conflicts with the Roosevelt family.[16] In 1920, when the RMA initially petitioned to have the memorial located on the Tidal Basin, its goal was to build something comparable to the Washington Monument and Lincoln Memorial.[17] Locating the memorial to Roosevelt in the Tidal Basin, where the Jefferson Memorial was eventually installed, would have been seen as part of the presidential commemoration already present on the National Mall. Failing to obtain that site, the RMA purchased what was then called Analostan Island from the Washington Gas and Light Company and turned it over to the federal government. Initially renamed Roosevelt Island, "Theodore" was added to its appellation in 1933 to avoid confusion with the new president, Franklin Delano Roosevelt, his fifth cousin.

The RMA hired John Russell Pope, the architect who designed the façade of the AMNH memorial, to plan a memorial to complement the natural setting and a year later hired Frederick Law Olmsted Jr. to restore the original landscape as much as possible. Creating the sense of a primeval forest required considerable clearing; crews began the process in late 1934, developing trails and paths as well as planting native trees and shrubs. At that time the island was accessible only by boat, and ensuing debates regarding the location of a bridge—including a rejected plan to dig a tunnel under the Potomac—lasted for some six years. An official agreement was finally reached in 1958 for a bridge on the southern portion of the island.

Some three years earlier, Congress had created the Theodore Roosevelt Centennial Commission and allotted funds to both the Theodore Roosevelt memorial in DC and the Theodore Roosevelt National Memorial Park in North Dakota. The role of the RMA, however, remained paramount. Herbert Hagedorn, secretary and director since its inception, played a dominant role on the commission, writing most of its reports. Since the country was then in the midst of the Cold War, his focus was on Roosevelt's commitment to sound citizenship as evidenced by family life, the moral and spiritual foundations of free government, active participation in government, conservation of natural resources, and national defense.[18]

New York architect Eric Gugler and sculptor Paul Manship were hired to design a memorial for the island. There was an immediate controversy over whether a sculpture was needed at all, with many arguing that the landscape was enough. Roosevelt's daughter, Alice Longworth, supported the growing opposition to a planned giant astrolabe. Instead Manship proposed a seventeen-foot-high statue of Roosevelt standing on a thirteen-foot-high base with one arm outstretched evoking the president's style of speaking and suggesting precedents depicting Roman orators. This design was approved and sited in a two-acre formal plaza approached from a semi-secluded winding wooded path, barely visible from the entrance to the island. The open area containing the sculpture is punctuated on each side by a fountain and surrounded by a moat. Behind the statue there are four twenty-one-foot-high granite panels inscribed with quotes from Roosevelt's writings, dedicated to themes of Nature, Manhood, Youth and the State. Similar quotes with related murals appear in the lobby of the AMNH.

Nature reads in part, "There is delight in the hardy life of the open. . . . There are no words that can tell the hidden spirit of the wilderness, that can reveal its mystery, its melancholy, and its charm. . . . The nation behaves well if it treats the natural resources as assets which it must turn over to the next generation increased and not impaired in value. . . . Conservation means development as much as it does protection." *Youth* reads in part, "I want to see you game, boys: I want to see you brave and you gentle and tender. . . . Be practical as well as generous in your ideals. . . . Keep your eyes on the stars but remember to keep your feet on the ground . . . hard work self-mastery and intelligent effort are all essential to successful life. . . . Alike to the nation and the individual the one indispensable requisite is character." *Manhood* reads in part, "A man's usefulness depends upon his living up to his ideals in so far as he can. . . . It is hard to fail, but it is worse never to have tried to succeed. . . . All daring and courage all iron endurance of misfortune make for a finer and nobler type of manhood.... Only those are fit to live who do not fear to die and none are fit to die who have shrunk from the joy of life and the duty of life." *The State* reads in part, "Ours is a government of liberty by-through-and under the law.... A great democracy has got to be progressive or it will soon cease to be great or a democracy.... Order without liberty and liberty without order are equally destructive.... In popular government results worth having can be achieved only by men who combine worthy ideals with practical good sense.... If I must choose between righteousness and peace I choose righteousness." Taken together, these quotes convey a sense of Roosevelt's values and the way he was remembered at that time.

Nearly five decades had passed since the idea for a Roosevelt national memorial was proposed by the RMA and the world had changed. In 1920 the nation had just emerged from World War I and was soon to enter a major depression, followed shortly by World War II. At the time of the dedication in 1967, the United States was embroiled in the Vietnam War, splitting the country in two as nothing had since the Civil War. President Lyndon B. Johnson in his remarks at the dedication of the national Roosevelt memorial made a veiled reference to the current situation: "May our people always remember the generous, passionate spirit that is memorialized here. May it inform and strengthen all of us in our hours and our times of our greatest trials."[19] In this context, Roosevelt, with his boundless energy and commitment to nation and nature, seemed all the more relevant. The wooded island, open for the enjoyment of nature by any and all, is an appropriate memorial to Roosevelt's love of the outdoors and conservation legacy. That said, it remains the least accessible memorial in Washington, reachable only by boat or by foot from a parking lot on the Virginia shore.

Roosevelt contributed much more to the nation than his conservation efforts, flawed as they were by his seizure of some Native American lands. There are no memorials celebrating his opposition to big business monopolies, or the peace negotiations in the Russo-Japanese War for which he won a Nobel Prize in 1906.

10

Theodore Roosevelt's Contradictory Policies

Theodore Roosevelt's father was a New Englander, his mother a Southerner, and he had a Western connection from spending several years living on a ranch as a cowboy.[1] He had a privileged life but was a sickly child, stricken with frequent bronchial asthma attacks. He overcame his physical weakness by following a regime of bodybuilding made possible by professionals who were hired to work with him in the gym installed in his Manhattan town-house home.[2] He continued strenuous physical activities throughout his life, including fighting in the Spanish-American War, during which he led a troop that became known as the Rough Riders. He was eager to fight in World War I with a volunteer company but President Woodrow Wilson turned down his request, presumably because of Roosevelt's age.

Both conservationist and hunter, Roosevelt created a system of national parks and contributed many hunting trophies to the collection of the American Museum of Natural History in New York. His intellectual accomplishments are no less impressive. He graduated magna cum laude from Harvard; wrote a four-volume history titled *The Winning of the West*; a book about the Naval War of 1812; and additional books on natural history, politics, and literary criticism, including biographies of Senator Thomas Hart Benton (Democrat, Missouri, who championed westward expansion) and Oliver Cromwell (military leader and statesman, Lord Protector of Britain, and chancellor of Oxford University). He also wrote an extraordinary number of articles, including scholarly reviews and countless letters. He was invited to lecture at the Sorbonne, the University of Berlin, and Oxford; at the latter, he was asked to deliver the Romanes Lecture typically given by distinguished natural scientists.[3] It helped that he read widely and rapidly and apparently had a photographic memory.[4]

Roosevelt's political career began early. Elected to the New York State Assembly in 1881 at the age of twenty-three, he served three terms and worked to pass civil service reform and other bills benefiting New York City. From the start he was willing to challenge the powerful, including Governor Grover Cleveland and railroad mogul Jay Gould.[5] Subsequently, as head of the Civil Service Commission (1889–95), he attacked a rampant spoils system and advocated for a civil service law that would serve as the foundation of a merit-based system.[6] He continued his commitment to reform as the head of the Police Commission in New York City (1895–97): he reorganized the department, consolidating power in the central headquarters, published a manual of rules and regulations (an uncommon practice at the time), upgraded technical equipment, and mandated training in a range of critical skills. By instituting testing and screening practices, he made sure to recruit only qualified personnel; this resulted in the hiring of a number of women.[7]

After a brief stint as assistant secretary of the Navy (1897–98), Roosevelt volunteered to serve in the Spanish-American War and was eventually promoted to colonel of his regiment. Immediately thereafter he ran successfully for governor of New York, serving from 1898 to 1900. In this capacity, he continued to challenge corporate power and champion conservation. In 1900 he was elected vice president on the Republican ticket with William McKinley. After McKinley's assassination in 1901, Roosevelt at the age of forty-two became the youngest president in history. He was elected to a second term in 1904 and committed not to run again because he believed in a two-term limit. He later regretted this decision but was unsuccessful in obtaining the nomination in 1912. After the administrations of William Howard Taft and Woodrow Wilson, Roosevelt planned to run in 1919 and was widely anticipated to win. However, he died unexpectedly, at the age of sixty.

In each of his various and varied positions, Roosevelt expanded the powers of his office, instituting a range of much-admired reforms, as well as some policies that are criticized today. Doris Kearns Goodwin described his leadership style as "governed by a series of simple dictums and aphorisms: 'Hit the ground running; consolidate control; ask questions of everyone wherever you go; manage by wandering around; determine the basic problems of each organization and hit them head-on; when attacked, counterattack; stick to your guns; spend your political capital to reach your goals; and then when your work is stymied or done, find a way out.'"[8]

As president, Roosevelt's domestic reforms included making merit-based appointments, among them Secretary of State John Hay and Secretary of War Elihu Root.[9] Notably, he asserted the power of the federal government to regulate trusts at a time when the expansion of corporate mergers had increased exponentially. In 1903 Roosevelt created the Department of Commerce and Labor, headed by George B. Cortelyou, which was empowered to investigate corporations at all levels. The consolidation of the railroads was of particular concern because it resulted in corporate control of prices across broad areas of the country. In 1906 the Hepburn Act made it possible for shippers to file complaints against railroads for price gauging and allowed for the supervision and regulation of their practices.[10] Roosevelt's most publicized victory was the 1903 Supreme Court ruling in the *Northern Securities* case that dissolved the monopoly created by the merger of the Great Northern and Northern Pacific railroad companies.[11]

The president also made news with his settlement of the coal strike in 1902, an important win for labor that Roosevelt saw as a test of presidential authority.[12] Coal mines were controlled by coal-carrying railroads, the big business conglomerates that Roosevelt was determined to curtail if their practices were injurious to the general public. Up to this point, strikes had often been violent and strikers were dealt with as if they were simply an unruly mob. At the time of this strike the United Mine Workers of America, formed in 1890, had an effective leader in the person of John Mitchell. As the months-long coal strike headed into winter, public support for intervention increased and after a protracted and complicated process that required the utmost diplomacy, Roosevelt successfully managed the first-ever instance of binding federal arbitration.

Roosevelt is perhaps best known for his advocacy for conservation and preservation. Prompted by his love of the outdoors and concern with the exploitation of land and natural resources, he was the first president to express and support this policy.[13] The National Monuments Act (also known as the Antiquities Act) passed in 1906 and gave the president authority to restrict the use of any federally owned public lands that were deemed worthy of preserving. President Roosevelt established 150 national forests, fifty-one bird preserves, and four game preserves; during his presidency Congress established five national parks. He increased natural forest lands from 43 to 194 million acres.[14] This, however, involved seizing lands owned by Native Americans.[15]

Since his fighting days during the Spanish-American War, Roosevelt had been concerned with this country's military preparedness. Toward that end his secretary of war, Elihu Root, succeeded in getting the Militia Act passed in 1903, increasing the efficiency of the militia and giving the federal government greater supervision of some units of the National Guard.[16] Since his experience in the Naval Department Roosevelt was particularly concerned with building up the United States Navy. He campaigned steadily to increase the number of modern warships and eventually succeeded in making the American fleet second only to that of Great Britain.

Roosevelt was an ardent supporter of national expansion, considering it the responsibility of superior countries, defined by their race, to police practices of nations he considered inferior. In 1898, while Roosevelt was governor of New York, Rudyard Kipling, a personal friend, sent him his poem "The White Man's Burden." In doing so, the poet sought to convince the United States to take over the Philippines (which had been captured by Admiral Dewey during the Spanish-American War) and rule it accordingly.[17] In Roosevelt's acceptance speech of the nomination for vice president in 1900, he stated that he would find it preposterous to grant the Philippines self-government, comparing it to "granting self-government to an Apache reservation under some local chief."[18] Throughout his subsequent campaigns he consistently emphasized his support of U.S. imperialism.[19] In 1904, at a time when some European creditors of Latin American countries appeared to be threatening armed intervention to collect their debts, Roosevelt articulated what came to be known as the Roosevelt Corollary to the Monroe Doctrine. This posited that the United States had the right to intervene to address perceived chronic wrongdoing of another civilized nation; this was interpreted to mean anything thought detrimental to U.S. interests.[20] Roosevelt's corollary in effect asserted that the United States had the right, and implicitly the duty, to act as an international police force.[21]

Much of Roosevelt's foreign diplomacy was carried out on a personal level, without the involvement of Congress or the presence of the press. His most effective role was in helping to resolve the Russo-Japanese War, for which he received the Nobel Peace Prize in 1906. In a more public and aggressive way, Roosevelt regarded the successful building of the Panama Canal as one of the greatest accomplishments of his presidency, although his handling of the complex process prompted some criticism, as did his other expansionist policies both geographically and administratively.[22] Today charges of imperialism are among the strongest negative appraisals of his presidency, particularly his handling of the Philippines.

At the time of his death, however, Roosevelt was extremely popular, prompting an outpouring of mourning comparable only to that after Lincoln's assassination.[23] Michael Patrick Cullinane sees him as a "generic benign signifier for patriotism and national identity." Given the range of Roosevelt's interests and accomplishments, Cullinane notes that he was variously celebrated as a patriotic figure, an American cowboy, an American progressive, an ardent conservationist, a man of letter, and a preacher of righteousness.[24]

Theodore Roosevelt and Race

In Roosevelt's time, the concept of race was understood more broadly than it is today, encompassing what now would be called nationality and language.[25] It provided a baseline premise in generating ideas that today would certainly be considered racist.[26] Roosevelt grew up with assumptions of white supremacy. He rarely, if ever, came into contact with people of color until his college days at Harvard. His ideas about race appear in his early writings such as *The Winning of the West* and more emphatically in his later biography of Thomas Hart Benton, in which he linked white supremacy to nationalism, territorial expansion and imperialism.[27] Believing in a hierarchical view of the world's population, with Anglo-Americans of Scottish descent at the top, Roosevelt had a caste-based view of society.

At a time when ideas about evolution were just beginning to be accepted, Roosevelt's thinking was influenced primarily by the French naturalist Jean-Baptiste Lamarck. Preceding Darwin, Lamarck believed that new organisms came into existence through spontaneous generation, not an act of God, and that they evolved in part in response to changes in their environment.[28] Similarly, Roosevelt's pervasive commitment to reform was based on the premise that people would benefit from improvements to their surroundings.

Throughout his adult life Roosevelt, both before and after his presidency, was obsessed with the notion of "race suicide"—that the top echelon of the population would die out with insufficient reproduction. In his sixth annual message to Congress, he went so far as to propose considering a constitutional amendment rewarding larger families in a variety of ways.[29] His deeply held conviction in the existence of distinct racial categories and his fear of race suicide were at the root of his policies toward Native Americans and Black people, as well as his advocacy of imperialism.

Roosevelt's Native American Policies

Roosevelt's ideas and policies, like those of the other Mount Rushmore presidents, evolved with his experiences and political concerns. In 1886, early in his career at a time when he lived briefly in the West and his anti-Native American statements were the most extreme, he quipped, "I don't go so far as to think that the only good Indians are the dead Indians but I believe nine out of every ten are. And I shouldn't like to inquire too closely into the case of the tenth." In *Winning of the West* (1894), he defined settling the frontier as a contest between a superior white race and inferior natives, "a Darwinian theater where the fittest triumphed and the losers were subordinated or destroyed."[30]

Roosevelt fully supported the established national policy that Native Americans should be assimilated, advocating for intermarriage leading to their ultimate disappearance.[31] By seeing them as individuals rather than members of a tribe or sovereign nation, he dismissed their established way of life, aiming (as did his predecessors) to convert them to farming single plots of land, thereby making it easier for whites to obtain their property.[32] In his very first message to Congress as president he called the General Allotment

Act (1887) that legitimized this process "a mighty pulverizing engine to break up the tribal mass."[33] This treatment of Native Americans as errant individuals rather than members of tribal nations enabled representatives of the federal government to avoid meeting with them to address their claims.[34]

According to Roosevelt's beliefs, it was possible for races to improve their status, just as individuals might. The more that Native Americans emulated white ways, the higher his opinion of them. During his time at the United States Civil Service Commission he worked with Herbert Welsh, one of the founders of the Indian Rights Association, to prevent hiring unqualified candidates for positions in the Indian Service. They also made it possible to prosecute white murderers of Native Americans. Welsh went so far as to suggest that Roosevelt be made the head of the Indian Service.[35] However, his overall opinion of Native Americans hardly warranted this position; as president he recommended that their education remain basic and largely related to job training.[36]

Roosevelt's passionate commitment to westward expansion in the service of advancing white civilization led him to justify Native American genocide.[37] He even condoned the horrific brutality of the 1864 Sand Creek Massacre in which Colonel J. M. Chivington ordered the murder of peaceful Cheyenne and Arapaho men, women, and children who were living on land ceded to them by the 1851 Treaty of Fort Laramie.[38] Although Roosevelt's attitude softened somewhat over time, he always viewed Native Americans through a lens of racial superiority.[39]

Roosevelt's Policies toward Black People

In some ways Roosevelt was more concerned with the "Negro problem" than with the Native Americans, believing that Black people posed a bigger threat of race suicide to whites because they had larger families and could not be absorbed into the Anglo bloodline through assimilation and intermarriage.[40] Roosevelt came to power during the Jim Crow era, a time when the practice of lynching was widespread. As governor of New York from 1898 to 1900, he sought assistance from Booker T. Washington and other accomplished Black people on how to best address racist practices. When he invited Washington to dine at the White House two years later, the outcry was such that he acknowledged that this was political mistake.[41] Nevertheless, he continued to seek Washington's counsel.[42]

Ostensibly, Roosevelt's policies were guided by what he referred to as his "rule of righteousness," a policy of equal treatment based on merit: "The only wise and honorable and Christian thing to do is to treat every black man and every white man strictly on his merits as a man, giving him no more and no less than he shows himself worthy to have."[43] However, the few examples of his supporting or appointing persons of color to office (one as postmaster in Indianola, Mississippi, and another as head of the customhouse in Charleston, South Carolina) prompted such harsh backlash that protracted diplomacy was required to resolve the situation. Even so, it was deemed unsafe for the woman of color to retain her post office job.[44] In these instances political realities trumped Roosevelt's best intentions. Since he believed in the limited abilities of most Black people (similar to his view of Native Americans), he supported only industrial or technical education for them, something that Booker T. Washington had also supported.[45]

Roosevelt was, somewhat reluctantly, impressed with the performance of Native Americans and Black people as soldiers during the Spanish-American War. This prompted only some public acknowledgment but no changes in public policy or privately held prejudice.[46] When in 1906 a group of Black soldiers were (erroneously) charged with attacking white citizens in Brownsville, Texas, he dismissed all the troops "without honor," even though several were medaled officers and a grand jury could find no evidence bolstering the charge. He perceived this incident as the failure of Black people to police themselves, something he continued to advocate.[47]

Overall, Roosevelt's attitude toward both Native Americans and Black people was distinctly paternalistic. Considering them inferior races, he believed whites had a moral obligation to help uplift them. However, unlike his support of the intermarriage of whites and Native Americans, he was deeply opposed to miscegenation between white and Black people. He was appalled by Southern slave owners having sexual relations with their slaves and fathering their children.[48] Horrified by rape, he considered it a crime above nearly all else and frequently associated it with lynching.[49] Roosevelt's own prejudices ran deep. Although his early publications included criticism of slavery on moral and political grounds, this was framed by his overarching perspective of its effect on white society.[50] As a savvy and cautious politician, Roosevelt, like Lincoln, looked to public support before advocating for reform. Accordingly, his enforcement of the Fourteenth and Fifteenth Amendments was limited, as he himself admitted.[51] Although in private he constantly lamented the intransigence of Southern white support of slavery,[52] he also admonished Black people for not organizing themselves to protest their status. In spite of this, he considered his attitude to be moderate, in fact modeled after Abraham Lincoln's.[53]

Conclusion

All history is a conversation between the present and the past.

—KENAN MALIK

It is impossible for any figure from the past to reflect perfectly the
values of the present, particularly politicians who by the nature of
their jobs must engage in compromise.

—ALAN GREENBLATT

The giant heads depicted on Mount Rushmore—George Washington,
Thomas Jefferson, Abraham Lincoln, and Theodore Roosevelt—loom over
us like omnipresent gods presiding over a vast landscape. They embody the
vision of Manifest Destiny, a term coined in 1845 that held that the United
States must expand westward to the Pacific Ocean in order to fulfill a destiny
ordained by Providence.[1] This perceived God-given mission justified the
annexation of any land that stood in the way. Land in this capitalist context
was associated with monetary gain, which, in turn, is associated with the
Rushmore presidents, three of whose visages appear on bills and coins that
we use on a daily basis.[2]

Although the term Manifest Destiny was coined after the presidencies of Washington and Jefferson, they were motivated by the same drive for national expansion. The authority of the United States over all the land within its border was also supported by the Monroe Doctrine (1823), which was meant to prevent any European attempt to colonize the Western Hemisphere. Theodore Roosevelt in his corollary to that doctrine extended the limits of U.S. influence beyond the borders of this country. The belief that the United States had the right to act in its own interests was premised on the idea that its principles of freedom and democracy made it exceptional, placing it above other nations and even above criticism.[3] It also made it possible somehow to ignore the fact that Mount Rushmore is located on land that belonged to the Lakota Sioux.

Like the presidents depicted on Mount Rushmore, its sculptor, Gutzon Borglum, was passionate about American expansion. In selecting the presidents, he thought in terms of empire builders rather than champions of democracy. He felt that "the union of these four presidents carved on the face of the everlasting hills of South Dakota will constitute a distinctly national monument. It will be decidedly American in its conception, in its magnitude, in its meaning and altogether worthy of our country."[4] Borglum deemed colossal sculpture to be an appropriate way to express this.[5] He knew of the Colossus of Rhodes and the Great Sphinx in Giza, Egypt. Closer to home, he had heard of Senator Thomas Hart Benton's 1849 proposal for a gigantic statue of Columbus on a peak somewhere in the Rocky Mountains. Borglum also had direct experience with the Statue of Liberty; he designed new lights for its torch in 1913. His sculptural ambitions aligned perfectly with his vision of U.S. national identity.

For all the Mount Rushmore presidents, national identity was based on the primacy of a white male property-owning population. Their major concerns were preserving the Union as well as expansion. The Constitution allowed the importation of slaves (without explicitly naming them as such) to continue for another twenty years because they feared secession by some Southern states and the potential dissolution of the nation.[6] Washington and Jefferson, who were slave owners, shared that fear. They hoped that slavery would die out of its own accord or that future generations would be able to resolve this major issue. It fell to Lincoln to fight the Civil War and campaign for the passage of the Thirteenth Amendment. Expanding the country involved seizing Native American lands and enforcing a harsh policy of assimilation intended to convert Indigenous people to Western ways based on private property and farming. Theodore Roosevelt oversaw expansion in the Philippines, with similar disastrous results for the local population. The four Anglo Protestant presidents expressed racist opinions of Native Americans and Black people and enacted some policies accordingly. It is no exaggeration to say that enslavement of Black people and genocide of Native Americans were encoded into U.S. law. But so were the principles of (limited) democracy articulated in the Declaration of Independence: equality, life, liberty, and the pursuit of happiness. Over time these benefits were expanded beyond white males to women and people of other nationalities, such as Irish and Italians, who were considered white. Black people, Native Americans, and other people of color are still not treated equally.

Today the United States is no more united than it was at the time of its origin. Although definitions of whiteness have expanded over time to include once excluded groups such as Italians, Irish, and Jews, color divides still persist and now encompass Asians and Latinos.[7] Problems with embracing difference would appear to be part of national identity, but so too are recurrent attempts to reckon with and improve upon a racially biased history.

The presidency of Donald Trump (2016–20) was marked by consistent efforts to stoke dissension, culminating in the attack on the Capitol on 6 January 2021, just as the votes in the 2020 presidential election were being verified. Variously labeled an attempted coup, treason, or sedition, the attack was prompted by false claims (commonly referred to as the "Big Lie") that the election of Joe Biden as the forty-sixth president of the United States was not legitimate.[8] Not the first attack on the Capitol, it nevertheless was both shocking and alarming.[9] The flying of Confederate flags and the erection of a wooden cross reminiscent of Ku Klux Klan lynchings near a statue of Ulysses S. Grant clearly linked the insurrection to the toxic legacy of white supremacy. It echoed the 1876 attack on Hamburg, South Carolina, when white supremacists took control of the local government run by a Black mayor, sheriff, and many city officials.[10] The 2021 attack also featured Nazi flags and sweatshirts that read "Camp Auschwitz," as well as some royal-blue flags with

"AF" in white letters, the logo for the "America First" program hosted by a Holocaust denier and Trump supporter. The attack was well-planned; attackers wore tactical apparel and were variously armed.[11] Their MAGA (Make America Great Again) hats were closely associated with defeated president Trump. This attack on the foundational democratic principles of this country was intended to disrupt the process of a fairly conducted election and an orderly transition of power.[12]

Since his inauguration on 20 January 2021, President Joseph Biden has been trying to heal the deep rift stoked by Trump's rhetoric and disregard for the truth. In his first speech as president he called for the celebration of democracy while acknowledging its fragility.[13] He spoke of the need to confront "a rise in political extremism, white supremacy, domestic terrorism" and the "cry for racial justice." Biden's commitment to reflect a more inclusive country is evidenced in his major appointments, most significantly Vice President Kamala Harris, who is of Asian and Black ancestry and the first woman to hold national office, and Deb Haaland as the first Native American secretary of the Interior.

Native Americans Today

Deb Haaland, a Democratic representative from New Mexico, is the first Native American to become a cabinet secretary and head of the Department of the Interior, which includes the Bureau of Land Management, the National Parks Service, and the U.S. Fish and Wildlife Service, as well as the Bureaus of Indian Affairs, Indian Education, and Trust Funds.[14] The Department of the Interior manages nearly one-fifth of the land in the United States, overseeing 109 million acres of wilderness and 422 national park sites. It is charged with safeguarding more than one thousand endangered species and managing massive projects pertaining to clean and accessible water in the West. The department largely determines the way the federal government treats Native Americans. It is both significant and telling that only in 2021 was a Native American appointed to this post.

There is no way to undo the damage of the past treatment of Native Americans but there are some indications that the United States is beginning to reckon with some of the atrocities that were committed in the past. In June

2021 Haaland announced the Federal Indian Boarding School Initiative, which will undertake a search for the burial sites of children who were forced to attend these punitive institutions.[15] Haaland's own grandparents were taken to live at Carlisle Indian School from the age of eight to thirteen, but at least they made it home. She first learned about their experience when interviewing her grandmother for a college assignment. Haaland recalled, "It was an exercise in healing for her and a profound lesson for me about the resilience of our people, and even more about how important it is to reclaim what those schools tried to take from our people. . . . This attempt to wipe out Native identity, language and culture continues to manifest itself in the disparities our communities face, including long-standing intergenerational trauma, cycles of violence and abuse, disappearance, premature deaths, and additional undocumented physiological and psychological impacts." She concluded, "Though it is uncomfortable to learn that the country you love is capable of committing such acts, the first step to justice is acknowledging these painful truths and gaining a full understanding of their impacts so we can unravel the threads of trauma and injustice that linger."[16]

Of late there has been more publicity not only regarding past crimes against Native Americans and their current needs, but also their contributions, especially to worldwide conservation. Their cultural and spiritual beliefs regarding the land led them to protect both the lakes and the land, including the animals that inhabit it.[17] In January 2021 Gina McCarthy, Biden White House national climate advisor, announced an initiative called America the Beautiful acknowledging that "tribal nations have been serving as stewards of their land since time immemorial."[18]

Native Americans have also contributed to U.S. military actions. They have served in the U.S. armed forces in every major conflict since the Revolutionary War in greater per capita numbers than those of any other ethnic group.[19] These contributions were concretized in the National Native American Veterans Memorial, which opened on 11 November 2020. Although authorized in 1994, Congress only approved fundraising for this memorial in 2013. Competition guidelines specified that, among other things, "proposals reflect Native spirituality; honor American Indian, Alaska Native, and Native Hawaiians; and not include markers of specific tribal identification."[20] Installed outside the National Museum of the American Indian in Washington DC, the Warriors' Circle of Honor by Harvey Pratt (Cheyenne and Arapaho Tribes of Oklahoma) is centered around a water feature for sacred ceremonies. Benches line the inner perimeter of the surrounding circular wall, and there are four lances used for tying cloths for prayers and healing. An accompanying online exhibition is titled "Why We Serve: Native Americans in the United States Armed Forces."[21]

Finally, there is increasing recognition that we all live on land belonging to Native American tribes. If you text your zip code or your city and state to the phone number (907) 312-5085, a land acknowledgment program tells you whose land you occupy.[22] Finally, too, there are programs that present Native American life from their perspective. *Reservation Dogs*, a television series that began in 2021, is the first to be directed, written, and acted by Native Americans. Critics praised its naturalistic treatment of contemporary reservation life and Native culture. It represents a clear break with previous stereotypical depictions of Indigenous people in popular culture.[23]

Many Native Americans still live in impoverished conditions, plagued by social problems stemming from the way they were treated in the past. Greater recognition of traditional as well as contemporary Native American values and practices is required. Overall, however, there appears to be less opposition to reckoning with past treatment of Native Americans than confronting the enslavement of Black people and the history of slavery that is a central part of U.S. national identity. Attempts at reconfiguring the study of American history to include slavery, as well as protests against police treatment of Black people and other examples of institutional racism, have often been countered with virulent backlash. Even though slavery was a critical and central foundational element of U.S. history and the slave trade was sanctioned for an additional twenty years in the Constitution, these facts are not yet widely acknowledged, nor are they present in most school texts.[24] Nevertheless, there are also promising signs of acknowledging and incorporating this history as well.

Treatment of Black People

Sunday, 18 August 2019, was the four hundredth anniversary of the arrival of the first enslaved people from Africa to Virginia, where they were sold to colonists. On that day the *New York Times Magazine* published "The 1619 Project," whose goal was "to reframe American history, making explicit how slavery is the foundation on which this country is built."[25] The leader of the project, Nikole Hannah-Jones wrote the first essay, "The Idea of America," which began, "Our founding ideals of liberty and equality were false when they were written. Black Americans fought to make them true. Without this struggle, America would have no democracy at all."[26] Other essays addressed capitalism, inequities of the health care system, mass incarceration, and the wealth gap.[27] Although some of Hannah-Jones's pronouncements have been challenged, she succeeded in making the topic visible and a focus for discussions in academia and the general population. The *New York Times* published and distributed a high school curriculum based on the publication.

Hannah-Jones's claim that slavery was the primary cause of the Revolution is demonstrably false. This and her failure to acknowledge contributions of whites to the abolitionist cause have made it easy to discredit her important work.[28] The *Times* did not acknowledge the errors in their print editions, but one of their columnists, Bret Stephens, challenged a number of assertions in the essay. More importantly, he questioned the assertion by the paper's editors that they were now telling the true story even though they did not have input from intellectually diverse historians.[29] Subsequently the paper published a modest revision that did not go far enough in addressing these criticisms.[30]

Black history has also been acknowledged by the declaration of Juneteenth as a national holiday and the ongoing debate over critical race theory (CRT). Juneteenth is a contraction of June nineteenth, the date in 1865 that Union General Gordon Ganger officially granted "absolute equality of personal rights and rights of property between former masters and slaves" in Galveston, Texas.[31] This marked the end of slavery in Texas, the last Confederate state to free enslaved people, some two years after the Emancipation Proclamation. According to a 2021 Gallup poll, more than 60 percent of Americans know nothing at all or only a little bit about Juneteenth, while 37 percent were very or somewhat familiar with it.[32] Celebrated by Black Americans since the late nineteenth century, it is also known as Emancipation Day, Black Independence Day, or Jubilee Day. At the time the holiday was declared, Galveston, once the largest slave-trading port west of New Orleans, unveiled Reginald

Adams's large mural titled *Absolute Equality*.[33] President Biden commented, "Great nations don't ignore their most painful moments. They don't ignore those moments in the past; they embrace them. . . . And in remembering those moments, we begin to heal and grow stronger."[34] Juneteenth caught on rapidly. By June 2021 Walmart was selling Juneteenth T-shirts in a predominantly white area of Massachusetts.[35]

Unlike these signs of national recognition of a deeply problematic past, the intense antagonistic controversies over the teaching of CRT are ongoing. Based on the premise that racism is systemic, CRT emerged in the 1970s when legal scholars concluded that existing laws had not eliminated racial injustice. The first workshop on CRT was held in 1989. Subsequently it was codified in the 1995 publication *Critical Race Theory: The Key Writings That Formed the Movement*.[36] Today the phrase is used to refer to any number of subjects that some conservatives find objectionable; these include social justice and even critical self-reflection.[37] In September 2020 Donald Trump issued a ban prohibiting federal agencies from including CRT, white privilege, or other terms or references that he designated as propaganda in any of their programs. Later dismissed on First Amendment grounds, the ban was rescinded by President Biden. However, several states, including Arkansas, Idaho, Iowa, Oklahoma, Tennessee, and Texas, have prohibited teaching the subject in public schools and some public colleges and universities.[38] The American Civil Liberties Union criticized the bans as both curtailing the free speech of teachers and trying to erase a history of discrimination. Legal challenges are expected but for now widespread acrimonious controversies persist at the local level.

The efforts among Republicans to curtail voting rights are even more threatening to the foundations of democracy than the attempts to ban the teaching of CRT. As of June 2021, some four hundred such bills had been introduced in various states across the country by Republican lawmakers, specifically targeting Black people who tend to vote Democratic.[39] The proposals in Texas under Governor Greg Abbot were perceived to be so dire that Democratic state legislators physically left the state house en masse, thereby preventing the requisite quorum to vote on a measure that was one of the most restrictive voting bills in the country. Later they fled the state for Washington DC to seek support in their struggle, although they eventually returned and the bill passed. A particularly egregious feature allows a judge to overturn an election in response to any claim of fraudulent votes, even if there is no proof to back it up. While Republicans framed the bill as one of election integrity, it has been widely criticized as a racist attempt at intimidation.[40] President Biden defined opposing "this raw and sustained election subversion" as "the most significant test of our democracy since the Civil War."[41] He traced its source to Trump's false claims of voter fraud or the "Big Lie" leading to the January 6 attack on the Capitol.

Prior to the Civil War, voting was limited to male property owners. Slaves were counted as three-fifths of a person for congressional elections, thus skewing election results in favor of the South. Nine of the country's first twelve presidents, including Washington and Jefferson, were slave owners.[42] After World War I, in response to an influx of working-class immigrants, the presentation of citizenship papers was required for voting purposes, often accompanied by concomitant rationalizations of voter fraud.[43] Democracy has not been a stable element of the nation's history; it has been renegotiated over time. Lincoln concluded that the country would either have to be one thing another—a democracy according to the Declaration of Independence or a country defined by minority rule and pervasive unequal rights. That issue remains both critical and unresolved today.

Monumental Reckoning

There are indications in the cultural landscape that point toward the evolution of a more inclusive national narrative. The widespread removal of Confederate flags and statues on public property in response to the riots in Charlottesville in 2017 is one example. Arguably, the most publicized site of Confederate statues was the row of sculptures on Monument Avenue in Richmond, Virginia. Statues celebrating Robert E. Lee, Jeb Stuart, Jefferson Davis, Thomas "Stonewall" Jackson, and Matthew Fontaine Maury were originally erected as the centerpiece of an extended row of expensive new houses lining the grand boulevard.[44] Confederate heroes were considered status symbols for the inhabitants, whose wealth came from industry and development, rather than plantations.[45] In 2020 the Lee statue became the center of racial justice protests that covered it with graffiti in response to the murder of George Floyd. There were also protests and performances around the base of the monument. On 1 September 2021, the Virginia Supreme Court approved its removal, citing that the state had jurisdiction based on the terms under which private owners had ceded it. The other four statues had been removed previously. At present there are plans to leave the base of the statue, also covered in graffiti, in place. A commission organized by the Virginia Museum of Fine Arts will be created to develop a plan for the empty public spaces along Monument Avenue.[46]

Mitch Landrieu, mayor of New Orleans (once the site of America's largest slave market), felt that Confederate memorials in his city and elsewhere should be removed because they celebrated traitors who were "symbols of white supremacy, and of the systemic oppression of human beings." He concluded his widely publicized remarks by stating, "These monuments purposefully celebrate a fictional, sanitized Confederacy; ignoring the death, ignoring the enslavement, and the terror that it actually stood for." He also wondered why there were "no slave ship monuments, no prominent markers on public land to remember the lynchings or the slave blocks?"[47] More than 140 Confederate memorials were taken down in 2020 but hundreds still remain.[48] Not without controversy and, in some instances, fierce resistance, the removal of Confederate memorials prompted a review of other memorials. This included Mount Rushmore and some others dedicated to the four presidents.

To date, the National Memorial for Peace and Justice in Montgomery, Alabama, which opened in 2018, is the only major national monument in the United States focused on enslaved people.[49] The Equal Justice Initiative (EJI), directed by Bryan Stevenson, conceived the monument working with MASS Design Group. On the EJI website the multipart work is described as "a sacred space for truth-telling and reflection about racial terrorism and its legacy."[50] The central element of the six-acre site is an open structure with a roof. It contains over eight hundred rusty Corten steel slabs suspended from the ceiling—one for each county where a lynching took place. More than forty-four hundred Black people were lynched in the United States between 1877 and 1950. At this memorial the names of the victims and any known details about them are inscribed on the slabs, personalizing them, and in a sense implicating current viewers who didn't stop or have ignored the terrorism. At one end, a waterfall flows over a text acknowledging the thousands of unknown victims. There are duplicate slabs outside the central structure, intended to be planted at the sites where lynchings actually took place. The memorial also includes sculptures by Kwame Akoto-Bamfo, Dana King, and Hank Willis Thomas, as well as a wall inscribed with writings by Toni Morrison, Elizabeth Alexander, and Dr. Martin Luther King Jr. A separate space for reflection is dedicated to Ida B. Wells. A short distance away, the Legacy Museum is housed in a building that once held slaves before they were taken to auction. Together and separately, each element conveys a powerful and sobering experience. The location of the monument in Montgomery is fitting: the city was the site of the first White House of the Confederacy. Here the violence sanctioned in the name of white supremacy is made visible and gut wrenching.

On a more local level, the University of Virginia recently installed the Memorial to Enslaved Laborers by the design team of Höweler and Yoon. It honors the more than four thousand enslaved people who built and maintained the school. Designed as a forum for discussion, is it is both an acknowledgment of and a reckoning with history. It signals that the university's problematic past can be discussed and made to coexist with its accomplishments.

Other memorials to underrepresented groups are also significant in developing a more inclusive view of history. Meredith Bergmann's Boston Women's Memorial, dedicated in 2003, reconfigures memorials both conceptually and formally.[51] It honors three women, one white and two Black, that span history. Abigail Adams was the wife of the second president and mother of the sixth. Lucy Stone started the *Woman's Journal* and was one of the first women in Massachusetts to graduate from college and was also known as an abolitionist and orator. Phillis Wheatly, born in West Africa and sold as a slave from the ship *Phillis* in colonial Boston, wrote the 1773 volume *Poems on Various Subjects*. It was the first book by an African American writer published in the United States. None of the figures stand atop a base towering over the viewer. Instead two are seated on the ground resting against low blocks, while one stands next to a high block of stone.

Institutional Recognition

The National Museum of the American Indian was developed based on the private collection of Gustave Heye. Founded by Heye and a group of friends in 1916, and possibly based on the AMNH, it was initially installed at Broadway and 155th Street in Manhattan. The official opening was in 1922 and documents emphasize its purpose as scholarly and systematic collecting. The collection was refined after 1960 when Fredrick J. Dockstader became director. When it was transferred to the Smithsonian Institution in 1989, partnership with Native Americans on all aspects of the museum became important. The Gustav Heye Center in the old Alexander Hamilton Custom House in downtown New York City opened in 1994. Ten years later the NMAI building on the National Mall opened.[52] Both branches create a significant visible presence of Native American culture, one in the nation's cultural center, the other in the nation's capital.

The National Museum of African American History and Culture opened in Washington DC in 2016. Established by an act of Congress in 2003, it is, according to its website, "the only national museum devoted exclusively to the documentation of African American life, history, and culture." One of its four pillars relates the museum directly to national identity: "It explores what it means to be an American and share[s] how American values like resiliency, optimism, and spirituality are reflected in African American history and culture."[53] Not based on a private collection, it was funded by the Smithsonian, which supported construction of the museum, acquisitions, permanent installations, temporary exhibitions, and a range of public programs. According to Lonnie G. Bunch III, its founding director, "This Museum will tell the American story through the lens of African American history and culture. This is America's Story and this museum is for all Americans."[54]

The move toward inclusivity is also evident in the reinstallation of permanent collections in museums. The Metropolitan Museum of Art in New York now has an ongoing exhibition of Native American art from the donated Charles and Valerie Diker Collection that is integrated with artworks by other American artists and is located in the museum's American wing.[55] Previously, Native American art had been displayed in galleries featuring the art of Africa, Oceania, and the Americas. In 2020 the museum hired its first full-time Native American curator, Patricia Marroquin Norby, previously senior executive and assistant director at the NMAI in New York.[56] The Met has committed to buying more Native American art. The museum has also installed a plaque on the exterior of the building acknowledging that it is situated on the homeland of the Lenape people.

Elsewhere, new public programs in presidential homes of the Mount Rushmore presidents now more accurately reflect their histories. Mount Vernon and Monticello acknowledge the presence and role of slavery in plantation life. In 2016 Mount Vernon opened "Lives Bound Together: Slavery at George Washington's Mount Vernon," an exhibition focused on 19 of the 317 enslaved people who were housed there. It includes details intended to humanize these individuals.[57] An hour-long tour is advertised: "See where Mount Vernon's enslaved people worked and lived. Gain insights into enslaved individuals and their duties, what they ate, how they were clothed, how they established families, and the penalties for their resistance." The tour ends with a visit to the Mount Vernon Slave Memorial and Cemetery (opened in 1983) containing the unmarked graves of eighty-seven people.[58]

The Monticello website states that it "is committed to sharing an honest, inclusive history." It encourages actual or potential visitors to download a free application titled "Slavery at Monticello," inviting you to "meet the individuals who lived and worked on Mulberry Row, once the industrial hub and 'Main Street' of Thomas Jefferson's 5,000-acre plantation." There are additional programs on "Thomas Jefferson and Slavery," "People Enslaved at Monticello," and "Slavery FAQs." Outdoor tours focus on the experiences of the enslaved people who lived and worked on the plantation. A special exhibition, "The Life of Sally Hemings," defines her as "Daughter, mother, sister, aunt. Inherited as property. Seamstress. World traveler. Enslaved woman. Concubine. Negotiator. Liberator. Mystery." The text describes the status of women born to white slave owners and enslaved women. Details of Sally Hemings's life were provided by Madison Hemings, her son with Thomas Jefferson. In their efforts to present a more accurate history of plantation life, Washington's and Jefferson's homes now both acknowledge and particularize the enslaved people and their contributions.

Teaching an Inclusive History

Perhaps the most significant strategy for conveying more accurate narratives to a larger audience is to embed them in history textbooks and school curricula.[59] The predominant frame of American history books today was shaped by conservative Texas activists who tell history from a white supremacist perspective.[60] Over the past two decades, historian Alan Taylor published a series of books that present an alternative history: *American Colonies* (2001), *American Revolutions* (2016), and *American Republics* (2021). These books focus on what has been omitted and insist that American history cannot be encapsulated in a single narrative.[61] In the absence of more inclusive national standards, the organization Educating for American Democracy (EAD) has issued a report, *Excellence in History and Civics for All Learners*, which includes guidelines for addressing current shortcomings. They advocate Alexis de Tocqueville's concept of "reflective patriotism" defined as an "appreciation of the ideals of our political order, candid reckoning with the country's failures to live up to those ideals, motivation to take responsibility for self-government, and deliberative skill to debate the challenges that face us in the present and future."[62] The EAD report is intended "to help educate young Americans to participate in and sustain our constitutional democracy."[63] Toward that end they identify seven key themes, including "Civic Participation" and "Institutional and Social Transformation." Six core pedagogical principles emphasize "Inquiry as Primary Mode of Learning." Their purpose is to define an inheritance that can be acknowledged and embraced by all.

In July 2021 the NMAI held a three-day online program titled "The Power, Authority, and Governance of Native Nations: Understanding United States Federal Indian Policies." Prompted by a survey that found K–12 textbooks lacking in Native American perspectives, the course provided a lengthy list of resources, some general and some addressing specific topics such as boarding schools.[64] The Better Arguments Project, a collaboration by the Aspen Institute Citizen and American Identity Program, Facing History and Ourselves, and the Allstate Corporation, offers guidelines for middle and high school educators on how to prepare classes to tackle difficult and potentially contentious topics. Starting with neutral subjects such as "Cake is superior to pie," or "Cats make better pets than dogs," it moves on to more political issues such as "Immigration into this country should be limited," or "In times of crisis, personal liberties should be limited to give the government more power."[65] Among their five principles for better arguing are "Take Winning Off the Table," and "Prioritize Relationships and Listen Passionately."[66] Along similar lines, the Respect Project, defined as "a thought leadership forum based upon respectful conversations around the essential topics of our times," advocates respect, honesty, and celebration. This program offers "a master class in building respect across deep divides."[67]

In August 2021 the Smithsonian launched a new initiative intended "to help Americans deal with the history and legacy of racism."[68] The multiyear program, "Our Shared Future: Reckoning with Our Racial Past," will engage this complex history through conversations, community events, and digital media. Smithsonian secretary Lonnie G. Bunch III defined the goal of the project as finding a shared future. "Giving people the reality—here's the information, here's a way to contextualize the moment we are in—you can't build optimism unless you face the reality of the past, the reality of today," he notes. "But once you do that you can find ways to find common ground." This and all the above-mentioned resources provide strategies for getting from "or" to "and," thus generating a less divisive and more inclusive narrative.

Ingrained Either/Or Thinking

There are many ways in which an either/or way of thinking has become ingrained in our culture. Conservative media thrives on demonizing one party, while liberal outlets have tried to present even-handed reporting but often fail to identify outright lies or misinformation. The framing of any topic is usually absorbed without awareness. Since where and how we obtain news is determined by which media we follow, typically an either/or choice (Fox News or CNN), viewpoints are sharply divided.

Competition also embeds an either/or frame; there are either winners or losers. The widespread bipartisan audience of sports fans roots for their athlete, team, or country as if they were an extension of themselves. This holds true for the athletes who cut across racial and ethnic lines, united by their abilities and in team sports to their team.[69] In each case this creates a sense of unity, but when competitive feelings run high it can escalate to violence. Competition extends to many other arenas as well. In discussing U.S.-China relations, President Biden emphasized the need for this country to be competitive. Rivalry may be an excellent impetus for people to try to do better. Essentially, however, "winners or losers" is just another either/or way of thinking.

Tough Truths and Tougher Questions

Most controversies, including those pertaining to Mount Rushmore, are defined by either/or thinking—either the presidents were worthy of commemoration or they were not. Of course, in reality they were both. They made major contributions to the nation's history, but they also held racist ideas that were far from the democratic values this country has prided itself on since its foundation. There is more acknowledgment today than in the past that Native American genocide and the enslavement of Black people were intrinsic to the founding of the United States. That does not mean that the experiment of self-government and the concept for equality for all should be dismissed. Rather, it requires both reckoning with the past and a vigilant defense of those values that are threatened by those who deny the facts of history for the sake of political or economic gain. Washington, Jefferson, Lincoln, and Roosevelt were foundational to an American identity based on democratic values, and yet their personal prejudices and some of their policies reflected otherwise. How can we expand Mount Rushmore to include an acknowledgment of these facts? How can we build memorials that convey an inclusive narrative? How can we structure a society to make it more equitable and just? By even beginning to frame and consider these questions we are at the very least planting seeds for a better future, hopefully enabling us, in the words of Abraham Lincoln, "to form a more perfect union with malice toward none and charity for all."

Epilogue

March 2022

At the time of this writing, the belief that "a more perfect union" might be possible seems increasingly in question if not more remote than ever. We are still awaiting the findings of the House Select Committee to Investigate the January 6 attack on the U.S. Capitol, although it appears obvious that former President Trump was involved. On the first anniversary of the attack, a *New York Times* editorial titled "Every Day Is Jan. 6 Now" cautioned that "the Republic faces an existential threat from a movement that is openly contemptuous of democracy and has shown that it is willing to use violence to achieve its ends."[1]

In a research survey–based approach, David M. Rubenstein in *The American Experiment: Dialogues on a Dream* sought to define the essence of American national identity via thirteen key elements: democracy, voting rights, equality, freedom of speech, freedom of religion, the rule of law, separation of powers, civilian control of the military, peaceful transfer of power, capitalism and entrepreneurship, immigration, diversity, culture, and the American dream.[2] As many others have noted, he concluded that "the American Experiment is clearly still ongoing," because "the United States has still failed to live up to all of its founding ideals."[3]

The November 2021 report issued by the Stockholm-based International Institute for Democracy and Electoral Assistance (IDEA) began with the caveat: "Democracy is at risk." For the first time it found the United States backsliding because "the declines in civil liberties and checks on government indicate that there are serious problems with fundamentals of democracy." It noted, "A historic turning point came in 2020–21 when former president Donald Trump questioned the legitimacy of the 2020 [election] results in the United States." Kevin Casas-Zamora, secretary-general of the organization observed, "The visible deterioration of democracy in the United States as seen in the increasing tendency to contest credible election results, the efforts to suppress participation (in elections), and the runaway polarization . . . is one of the most concerning developments."[4] In the same vein, a Pew Research Center Global Attitudes Survey found that "few people in the United States or other developed nations view American democracy as an example for the rest of the world to follow."[5] Although democracy remains an ideal, it is clearly now and has always been an unstable condition.

Voting rights, considered the bedrock of a democratic government, were a long time in coming for many. The U.S. Constitution counted slaves as three-fifths of a free person for purposes of determining representation in the House of Representatives and Electoral College, thereby giving slaveholding states more power. Jim Crow legislation after the Civil War denied voting rights to Black people granted by the Fifteenth and Sixteenth Amendments to the Constitution. Women could not vote until 1920 when the Nineteenth Amendment was passed; Native Americans gained that right in 1924; and Chinese immigrants in 1943. Recently, attempts to ensure voting rights have failed. In January 2020 Senate Republicans and two Democrats succeeded in blocking both the Freedom to Vote Act that was designed to curtail voter suppression and the John Lewis Voting Rights Advancement Act that was intended to update and ensure the enforcement of the 1965 Voting Rights Act.[6]

The current electoral system does not guarantee majority rule and is open to manipulation. There have been frequent calls to reform or eliminate it in favor of majority votes not only for elected officials but also for amending the Constitution; this has met with strong opposition.[7] Any such systemic change will require demonstrable support from the voting public and, of course, will take time. Civic engagement is critical and must start early. The executive summary of *Educating for American Democracy: Excellence in History and Civics for All Learners* begins, "A healthy constitutional democracy always demands reflective patriotism."[8]

Washington and Jefferson were seriously concerned about the stability of the Union. The compromises in the Constitution regarding slavery reflect this as well as the fact that they were enslavers themselves. It fell to Lincoln to reassert the principles of the Declaration of Independence and fight a civil war to try to maintain a united country without slavery. All the Rushmore presidents were committed to a system of government based on the will of the people—a democratic vision, as far as it went. They each made major contributions but they were not perfect. We need an honest reckoning of their successes and their failures—"and" not "or." Without that, the American experiment is in real danger of falling far short of its idealistic founding principles.

August 2022 Update

The deep political divisions within the United States have grown much sharper during this past year, threatening the unity sought by the Rushmore presidents. A number of critical Supreme Court decisions pertaining to abortion, climate crisis, gun control, and religious freedom pitted the primarily Republican supporters of the conservative court against Democrats and liberals who saw its decisions as a threat to the very foundation of democracy. The court's six-member conservative block is comprised of judges appointed by some presidents who did not win the popular vote: three judges appointed by former President Donald J. Trump (Neil M. Gorsuch, Brett M. Kavanaugh, and Amy Coney Barrett), and two by President George W. Bush (Chief Justice John G. Roberts Jr. and Samuel A. Alito Jr.). President George Bush who won the popular vote appointed Clarence Thomas. Their votes all but guarantee the passage of legislation in line with their conservative views, or as some would argue, reactionary agenda.[9]

Reproductive Rights

Although there had been a leak in early May 2022 announcing the Supreme Court decision to overturn the 1973 *Roe v. Wade* ruling that codified a woman's right to terminate a pregnancy, it was nevertheless somehow shocking. The *Dobbs v. Jackson Women's Health Organization* (24 June 2022) ruling was a blow to women's rights comparable to the Dred Scott decision of 1857. That decision denied the citizenship of enslaved people, thereby depriving them of the right to protection from the federal government and the courts.[10] Justice Alito's majority opinion noted that abortion was not mentioned in the Constitution, but at the time it was written women were not entitled to any rights.[11] As it was with slavery, a major concern of the Rushmore presidents, the country is deeply divided about abortion. Recently historian Simon Schama observed that "when Roe v. Wade is overturned it will be time to find a different name for this country."[12]

The Supreme Court decision left it up to states to determine local abortion laws, creating widespread confusion as to access, prompting comparisons to the fugitive slave laws that resulted from distinct practices of enslavement in bordering states.[13] The negative effects of this decision are predicted to be dire, especially for women of color and those with lower incomes who cannot afford the costs of travel to states where abortion is legal. It remains to be seen what kind of aid, if any, will be available to the mothers who give birth unwillingly and the unwanted babies whose lives the Supreme Court is so anxious to protect.[14] For University of California, Davis law professor Mary Ziegler and many others, this decision makes clear that "rights can vanish." She concludes, "The justices seem to simply not care if this decision breaks the country in two."[15]

The issue of when life begins is at the heart of the majority decision that is based on the belief that it starts at conception.[16] It has been argued that this is a religious rather than a constitutional issue; in the first paragraph of the majority opinion, Justice Alito defined it as "a profound moral issue."[17] The Bible, however, says nothing about abortion, although it was written at a time when abortion was practiced.[18] There is also widespread evidence that at the time the Constitution was adopted abortion was considered a private matter and life was thought to start at quickening, when fetal movement was first detected, typically around sixteen to twenty-two weeks of pregnancy.[19] Thus, although constitutional precedent was cited as the basis for the majority opinion, it does not appear to pertain. Rather, it would seem that the right to abortion would have been protected by the Fourteenth Amendment, which in 1868 overturned the Dred Scott decision and gave the federal government the power to protect individual rights even in the face of state laws to the contrary. Section 1 of the amendment reads, "No State shall make or enforce any law which shall abridge the privileges or immunities of citizens of the United States; nor shall any State deprive any person of life, liberty, or property, without due process of law; nor deny to any person within its jurisdiction the equal protection of the laws." Section 5 concludes, "The Congress shall have the power to enforce, by appropriate legislation, the provisions of this article."[20]

Separation of Church and State

Two other recent Supreme Court decisions attack one of the basic elements of American democracy—the separation of church and state. *Kennedy v. Bremerton School District* (27 June 2022) ruled that a public high school football coach had a constitutional right to pray at the fifty-yard line after a game. It was deemed protected by the First Amendment, which states, "Congress shall make no law respecting an establishment of religion, or prohibiting the free exercise thereof; or abridging the freedom of speech, or of the press, or the right of the people peaceably to assemble, and to petition the Government for a redress of grievances." As quite a few legal scholars have pointed out, the so-called establishment clause has typically been invoked to prohibit enforced religious behavior, favoring one religion over another, or endorsing religion over atheism.[21] Ruling in favor of the coach's behavior clearly privileges one religion—Christianity—above all others.

The majority decision ruled that even though this was a public school function, the coach's prayer was private and personal, this in the face of images introduced by Justice Sonia M. Sotomayor in the minority opinion that clearly conveyed that this was a very public prayer meeting with many students participating.[22] The students at Bremerton, including those who practiced different religions or none at all, were thus obliged to participate in Christian prayer. High school athletes are sensitive to the unstated power of coaches, including among other things their ability to limit playing time.

In another decision, the Supreme Court in *Carson v. Makin* (21 June 2022) argued that Maine could not exempt religious schools from a tuition assistance program that allowed parents to use vouchers to send their children to public or private school because the practice discriminated against religion. Justice Stephen G. Breyer in the dissenting opinion argued for the necessity of government neutrality when it came to religion because there are at least one hundred different faiths in the United States.[23] Justice Sotomayor also noted, "Today the court leads us to a place where separation of church and state becomes a constitutional violation."[24]

The separation of church and state was of concern to the early Rushmore presidents. George Washington was very clear on the subject. Already at a time when he was commander of the Continental Army, he ordered ranking officers "to protect and support the free exercise . . . and undisturbed enjoyment of religious matters."[25] Like much else about Thomas Jefferson, his spiritual beliefs were complicated and evolving. Well-versed in various faiths and philosophies, toward the end of his life he assembled the so-called Jefferson Bible, a compilation of what he believed to be Jesus's essential teachings; it excluded miracles as well as resurrection. There was no question, however, that he was committed to religious freedom and the separation of church and state. His 1786 Virginia Statute of Religious Freedom is considered the forerunner of the First Amendment.[26]

Gun Control

Gun control has been a deeply divisive national issue for quite some time, largely linked to Second Amendment rights, which were enacted in 1791 when life in this country and types of available weapons were very different. The Second Amendment states, "A well regulated Militia, being necessary to the security of a free State, the right of the people to keep and bear Arms, shall not be infringed." Today, when mass shootings in the United States are increasing at an unprecedented and alarming rate, the Supreme Court in *New York State Rifle & Pistol Association, Inc. v. Bruen* (23 June 2022) struck down the state's law requiring demonstration of need for carrying a firearm outside the home.[27] Enacted more than a century ago, the law had already been weakened by a 2008 ruling in *District of Columbia v. Heller* that the Second Amendment gave individuals the right to keep guns at home for personal defense rather than for military purposes. Justice Clarence Thomas in the majority opinion wrote that "to confine the right to 'bear' arms to the home would nullify half of the Second Amendments operative protections." Noting that the Heller decision guaranteed individuals the right to carry weapons in case of confrontation, he argued that "confrontation can surely take place outside the home."[28] The ruling allowed that the right to bear arms could be limited from applying to sensitive places such as schools, polling places, courthouses, subways or, say, Times Square or Yankee Stadium. At the time of this writing, "sensitive places" have not been clearly designated and some justices indicated that this might be the subject of a future decision.[29] For Justice Breyer, "The primary difference between the court's view and mine is that I believe the [Second] Amendment allows States to take account of the serious problems posed by gun violence."[30]

The shooting on 4 July 2022 during an Independence Day parade in Highland Park, Illinois, linked the United States gun problem to national identity.[31] Illinois governor J. B. Pritzker lamented, "It is devastating that a celebration was ripped apart by our uniquely American plague. A day dedicated to freedom has put into stark relief the one freedom we, as a nation, refuse to uphold: The freedom of our fellow citizens to live without the daily fear of gun violence."[32] Although the primary focus was on the Highland Park shooting, in which seven people were killed and dozens of others wounded, at least 220 people were killed by guns and some other 570 wounded over the course of the July Fourth weekend.[33]

The Climate Crisis

Although climate concerns were not an issue to the Rushmore presidents, they represent a deep division in the country today. The *West Virginia v. EPA* (30 June 2022) ruling effectively cut back the environmental agency's ability to reduce carbon output of existing power plants.[34] Apparently favoring corporate over environmental interests, the court's decision hardened the split between big business and climate crisis skeptics and those concerned with environmental protection. In this, the court's bias might be compared to the Founding Fathers' protection of white male property owners. In the dissenting opinion, Justice Elena Kagan stated, "The Court appoints itself—instead of congress or the expert agency—the decision maker on climate policy. I cannot think of many things more frightening."[35] Her concern was reiterated by Harvard environmental law professor Richard Lazarus: "The court threatens to upend the national government's ability to safeguard the public health and welfare at the very moment when the United States, and all nations, are facing our greatest environmental challenge of all: climate change."[36]

National Unity Today?

The recent Supreme Court decisions have called into question the legitimacy of the court itself.[37] A major concern has been that it no longer reflects the opinions of the majority of the population.[38] The same applies to Republican senators who have consistently voted against the extension of voting and other individual rights. The country appears so divided that there has even been speculation over the likelihood of civil war.[39] All of this calls into question national unity and the future of democracy or, in other words, the ongoing viability of the American experiment.[40] As Abraham Lincoln famously observed, "A house divided against itself cannot stand." He was referring to slavery. Today the country is divided by many other issues, mostly along party lines driven by a pervasive national infrastructure of racism.

The recent hearings regarding the January 6 insurrection at the Capitol demonstrated the degree to which former president Donald Trump was prepared to go to hold on to power, including inciting and condoning violence. Extremist groups have continued to step up their activities and have infiltrated high levels of the Republican Party at state and local levels.[41] There are many civilians who still support Trump's lie that the election was stolen and support his running for president in 2024. Fears persisted that widespread gerrymandering as well as the partisan infiltration of the voting system will mean that the results of the 2022 midterm elections will not represent popular opinion and the threats to U.S. democracy will increase.

This book was prompted by the question of whether it is possible to move from an "or" to an "and" way of thinking about the Rushmore presidents and much else. Can we consider George Washington, Thomas Jefferson, Abraham Lincoln, and Theodore Roosevelt in terms of their accomplishments as well as their failings? Darren Walker, president of the Ford Foundation, makes a compelling argument that we value them for the tools they gave us, "with which to build a multiracial, multiethnic, pluralist democracy that extends the privilege of American identity to all."[42] Progress toward true democracy has always, in one way or another, been threatened, and the country today continues to be radically divided on numerous issues. The Rushmore presidents, each in their own way, believed in the ideal of democracy, and that important part of their legacy continues to be worth defending and upholding.

NOTES

INTRODUCTION

1. This passage is singled out by Boyd Matheson in "Unity Isn't Impossible. George Washington Showed the Way," *Deseret News*, 17 February 2021, https://www.deseret .com/opinion/2021/2/16/22285834/unity-is-essential-for-protection-safety-liberty -and-prosperity-george-washington-farewell.

2. See "Washington's Farewell Address," United States Senate, accessed 5 August 2022, https://www.senate.gov/about/traditions-symbols/washingtons-farewell-address .htm. This entry includes a copy of Washington's complete address, the history of the practice of reading it annually, and a list of all the readers since it became permanent in the Senate. See also Gillian Brockell, "On George Washington's Birthday, His Farewell Address Unites a Divided Senate," *Washington Post*, 22 February 2021, https://www.washingtonpost.com/history/2021/02/22/george-washington-farewell -address-senate/.

3. The campaign was so bitter that there were even rumors of the possibility of civil war. See "President Jefferson Seeks Unity and Reconciliation," *Monticello Newsletter* 12, no. 1 (Spring 2001).

4. These quotes are singled out in "Thomas Jefferson: A Plea for Unity," *New York Times*, reprinted 9 August 1974, https://www.nytimes.com/1974/08/09/archives /thomas-jefferson-a-plea-for-unity.html.

5. For a compendium of Lincoln's quote on the importance of maintaining the Union as well as many other subjects, see "Selected Quotations by Abraham Lincoln," Abraham Lincoln Online: Speeches & Writings, accessed 13 August 2022, http:// www.abrahamlincolnonline.org/lincoln/speeches/quotes.htm.

6. Edward N. Saveth, "Theodore Roosevelt: Image and Ideology," *New York History* 72, no. 1 (January 1991), 61–62.

7. "Excerpt from Address by Theodore Roosevelt at Everett, Washington," Theodore Roosevelt Center at Dickinson State University, accessed 6 August 2022, https:// www.theodorerooseveltcenter.org/Research/Digital-Library/Record?libID=o294233.

8. Roosevelt's inaugural address can be found at "Inaugural Address of Theodore Roosevelt," Avalon Project, Yale Law School, Lillian Goldman Law Library, accessed 5 August 2022, https://avalon.law.yale.edu/20th_century/troos.asp.

1. LAND OF THE LAKOTA SIOUX

Epigraphs: Alvin M. Josephy Jr., "Distortions of Indian History," in Dunbar-Ortiz, *Indigenous Peoples' History*, 56; Phillip Deere, "View from the Creek Nation" in Dunbar-Ortiz, *Great Sioux Nation*, 82.

1. Powell, "The Sacred Way," 62. Powell, who is also a Sun Dance priest, gives an excellent account of the main premises of Lakota religion and way of life.
2. Medicine, "Oral History," 121.
3. See, for example, Ortiz, "Indian Oral History," 14.
4. Alex Chasing Hawk in Dunbar-Ortiz, *Great Sioux Nation*, 136.
5. Later history written by academics may be skewed by Western theoretical premises. See Dunbar-Ortiz, "Oral History and Written History," 101, 103.
6. Jacobs, "Sioux Nation & the Treaty," 117; Deloria, "United States Has No Jurisdiction," 144.
7. Deere, "View from the Creek Nation," 77.
8. Dunbar-Ortiz, *Indigenous Peoples' History*, 55.
9. Larner, *Mount Rushmore*, 24. See also Patricia Albers's unpublished manuscript cited in Ostler, *Lakotas and the Black Hills*, 26.
10. For a discussion of the riches that were found in the Black Hills, see, for example, Ostler, *Lakotas and the Black Hills*, 14, 75.
11. Ostler, *Lakotas and the Black Hills*, 47.
12. Dunbar-Ortiz, "Oral History & Written History," 103.
13. Ostler, *Lakotas and the Black Hills*, 117–19, discusses the Ghost Dance in the context of the popular spiritual leader Wovoka, a Paiute living in Nevada.
14. Dunbar-Ortiz, *Indigenous Peoples' History*, 153.
15. Dennis Banks, in Dunbar-Ortiz, *Great Sioux Nation*, 179; Ostler, *Lakotas and the Black Hills*, 19.
16. See, for example, Dunbar-Ortiz, *Indigenous Peoples' History*, 25.
17. Powell, "The Sacred Way," 63.
18. Jacobs, "Indian-White Relations," 85.
19. Lakota concepts of punishment are discussed by the following authors in Dunbar-Ortiz, *Great Sioux Nation*: Powell, "The Sacred Treaty," 109; Jacobs, "The Sioux Nation and the Treaty," 117; Deloria, "United States Has No Jurisdiction," 145.
20. "Treaties and Other International Agreements," 1, states: "Treaties are a serious legal undertaking both in international and domestic law. Internationally, once in force, treaties are binding on the parties and become part of international law.

Domestically, treaties to which the United States is a party are equivalent in status to Federal legislation, forming part of what the Constitution calls 'the supreme Law of the Land.' However, the word treaty does not have the same meaning in the United States and in international law. Under international law, a 'treaty' is any legally binding agreement between nations. In the United States, the word treaty is reserved for an agreement that is made 'by and with the Advice and Consent of the Senate' (Article II, Section 2, Clause 2 of the Constitution). International agreements not submitted to the Senate are known as 'executive agreements' in the United States, but they are considered treaties and therefore binding under international law."

21. Deloria, "United States Has No Jurisdiction," 144.

22. DeMallie, "Treaties Are Made between Nations," 111. From 2014 to 2018 the National Museum of the American Indian held a sequence of exhibitions devoted to these treaties entitled "Nation to Nation." See National Museum of the American Indian, "'Nation to Nation' Exhibition," Media Fact Sheet, 19 September 2014, https://www.si.edu/newsdesk/factsheets/nation-nation-exhibition.

23. Ken Drexler, "Indian Removal Act: Primary Documents in American History," Library of Congress Research Guides, https://guides.loc.gov/indian-removal-act.

24. Kimbra Cutlip, "In 1868, Two Nations Made a Treaty, the U.S. Broke It and Plains Indian Tribes Are Still Seeking Justice," *Smithsonian Magazine*, 7 November 2018, https://www.smithsonianmag.com/smithsonian-institution/1868-two-nations-made -treaty-us-broke-it-and-plains-indian-tribes-are-still-seeking-justice-180970741/.

25. Ostler, *Lakotas and the Black Hills*, 66. He discusses the treaty in detail, 58–68.

26. Dunbar-Ortiz, *Indigenous Peoples' History*, 188.

27. Taliaferro, *Great White Fathers*, 34.

28. "Sioux Wars—1851–1890," Northern Plains Reservation Aid, accessed 18 April 2020, http://www.nativepartnership.org/site/PageServer?pagename=airc_hist_siouxwars.

29. See, for example, Medicine, "Oral History," 121; and DeLoria, "United States Has No Jurisdiction," 142–43. According to Ostler, *Lakotas and the Black Hills*, 100, this treaty elicited only 10 percent of the legally required signatures.

30. Ostler, *Lakotas and the Black Hills*, 102.

31. See, among others, Taliaferro, *Great White Fathers*, 23–35.

32. Treuer, *Heartbeat of Wounded Knee*, 134.

33. Means, "Those Who Left Are Returning," 181–82.

34. Dawes is quoted in Dunbar-Ortiz, "Dispossession," 162. The Dawes Act is also discussed in Ostler, *Lakotas and the Black Hills*, 115; Taliaferro, *Great White Fathers*, 43; Josephy, "Concise History," 26.

35. Treuer, *Heartbeat of Wounded Knee*, 113–14.

36. Ostler, *Lakotas and the Black Hills*, 120, called it "the largest military mobilization since the Civil War."

37. Treuer, *Heartbeat of Wounded Knee*, 96, 97.

38. Treuer, *Heartbeat of Wounded Knee*, 442–43, summarized the changes: "Of this ever-increasing population, in 2010 more than 70 percent lived in urban areas, continuing the trend begun in the years after World War II. . . . Between 1990 and 2000, the income of American Indians grew by 33 percent, and the poverty rate dropped by 7 percent. . . . Between 1990 and 1997 the number of Indian-owned businesses grew by 84 percent. And the number of Native kids enrolled in college has doubled in the past thirty. . . . Reservation people go to the city and bring the reservation with them, and city Indians go back to the reservation and bring the city with them."

39. Ostler, *Lakotas and the Black Hills*, 143.

40. Josephy, "Concise History," 26; Dunbar-Ortiz, *Indigenous Peoples' History*, 169.

41. Josephy, "Concise History," 26.

42. Taliaferro, *Great White Fathers*, 349.

43. Taliaferro, *Great White Fathers*, 354.

44. Larner, *Mount Rushmore*, 279–82; Ostler, *Lakotas and the Black Hills*, 167–69; Taliaferro, *Great White Fathers*, 350–56.

45. The changing status of Native Americans in the 1980s is summarized by Treuer, *Heartbeat of Wounded Knee*, 383.

46. Ostler, *Lakotas and the Black Hills*, xv, 158–65, 176, 188.

47. Taliaferro, *Great White Fathers*, 21. In 2002, two years before Baker's arrival, Taliaferro summarized the presentation as: "America loves the difficult task. The presidents on Mount Rushmore were extraordinary men who did extraordinary things. Gutzon Borglum and the workers who expended blood, sweat, and tears to create Mount Rushmore were extraordinary men who did extraordinary things. Finally, we as ordinary people have within us the potential to do extraordinary things. We too can achieve the American Dream."

48. Larner, *Mount Rushmore*, 15.

49. Bergman, "Can Patriotism Be Carved in Stone?," concluded that in addressing contemporary sociopolitical concerns, each inherently defined patriotism differently.

50. Information about Gerard Baker can be found at the following sites, all accessed 22 April 2020: "Gerard Baker," The Coalition to Protect America's National Parks, https://protectnps.org/centennial-biographies-2/gerard-baker/; Jesse Abernathy, "Gerard Baker Leaves Behind a Strong Legacy," *Native Sun News*, 23 September 2011, https://www.indianz.com/News/2011/003102.asp; Estella Claymore, "Gerard Baker, Top Indian Official at NPS, Retires," *Native Sun News*, 9 July 2010, https://www.indianz.com/News/2010/020636.asp. He also appeared in the PBS series on national parks by Ken Burns. See "The National Parks: America's Best Idea: People—Gerard Baker," www.pbs.org/nationalparks/people/nps/baker/.

51. Michelle Wheatley is quoted in an NPS release, "Michelle Wheatley Selected as Superintendent of Mount Rushmore National Memorial," 15 March 2021, https://www.nps.gov/moru/learn/news/michelle-wheatley-selected-as-superintendent-of-mount-rushmore-national-memorial.htm.

2. BORGLUM'S MOUNT RUSHMORE

1. Smith, *Carving of Mount Rushmore*, 22.
2. Fite, *Mount Rushmore*, 3. Doane Robinson's letter to Lorado Taft is reproduced in its entirely in Smith, *Carving of Mount Rushmore*, 25.
3. Smith, *Carving of Mount Rushmore*, 25.
4. Robinson's letter is quoted in Smith, *Carving of Mount Rushmore*, 26–27. Taft's *Big Injun* was part of his *Fountain of Time* (1920–22) in Washington Park in Chicago.
5. Email from Dana Pilson, curatorial researcher, Chesterwood, to the author, 20 November 2019. French was mentioned by Smith, *Carving of Mount Rushmore*, 27; Taliaferro, *Great White Fathers*, 52.
6. Robinson's letter is quoted in Taliaferro, *Great White Fathers*, 54.
7. Carter, *Gutzon Borglum*, 12–25 (the author is the daughter of Borglum's son, Lincoln); Larner, *Mount Rushmore*, 93–97; Smith, *Carving of Mount Rushmore*, 46–52; Taliaferro, *Great White Fathers*, 69–71.
8. Carter, *Gutzon Borglum*, 22.
9. Taliaferro, *Great White Fathers*, 118.
10. Larner, *Mount Rushmore*, 107, describes him as "one of the most prolific sculptors of his day."
11. Taliaferro, *Great White Fathers*, 102.
12. Carter, *Gutzon Borglum*, 28. See also, "Abraham Lincoln Bust," Architect of the Capitol, accessed 4 May 2021, https://www.aoc.gov/art/busts/abraham-lincoln-bust.
13. Schwartz, "Newark's Seated Lincoln," 22–39.
14. Charles Cummings, "Businessman Leaves Lasting Reminders of Leaders and Heroes," *Knowing Newark*, 4 September 1997, https://knowingnewark.npl.org/businessman-leaves-lasting-reminders-of-leaders-and-heroes/.
15. Roosevelt is quoted in Fite, *Mount Rushmore*, 21.
16. "Wars of America (Sculpture)," Smithsonian American Art Museum and its Renwick Gallery, accessed 5 May 2020, https://www.si.edu/object/siris_ari_2965. The photographer's perspective is discussed in "Gutzon Borglum: 'Wars of America,' a Monumental Bronze Sculpture in Newark," Artsology, accessed 5 May 2020, https://artsology.com/the-arts-adventurer/wars-of-america-newark.php.
17. "'Wars of America' by Gutzon Borglum," Military Park, accessed 5 May 2020, http://militarypark.com/monuments.

18. Benjamin Powers, "In the Shadow of Stone Mountain," *Smithsonian Magazine*, 4 May 2018, https://www.smithsonianmag.com/history/shadow-stone-mountain-180968956/.

19. Fite, *Mount Rushmore*, 45–55; Smith, *Carving of Mount Rushmore*, 17, 21, 59–76; Taliaferro, *Great White Fathers*, 54–56, 154–63.

20. Borglum is quoted in Smith, *Carving of Mount Rushmore*, 76.

21. Carter, *Gutzon Borglum*, 79.

22. Borglum is quoted in Fite, *Mount Rushmore*, 48.

23. Larner, *Mount Rushmore*, 194–238, delineates Borglum's complicated relationship to the Klan.

24. Taliaferro, *Great White Fathers*, 185–93, concluded that the KKK hardened Borglum's "already active prejudices. Careful review of his personal papers reveals that the shrillness and frequency of his long-festering anti-'isms' increased markedly once he embraced the Klan in 1923."

25. For a description of the various attractions at Stone Mountain, see Taliaferro, *Great White Fathers*, 159. For Stone Mountain as a site of contention, see, for example, Benjamin Fearnow, "Armed Black Militia Challenges White Nationalists at Georgia's Stone Mountain Park," *Newsweek*, 5 July 2020, https:www.newsweek.com/armed-black-demonstrations-challenge-white-supremacist-milital-georgia-stone-mountain-park-1515494.

26. See, for example, Smith, *Carving of Mount Rushmore*, 13–14.

27. Fite, *Mount Rushmore*, 63–64; Larner, *Mount Rushmore*, 89–90; Smith, *Carving of Mount Rushmore*, 103.

28. Borglum is quoted in Smith, *Carving of Mount Rushmore*, 131; he also discusses the choice of presidents, see 31, 90, 129–31.

29. Larner, *Mount Rushmore*, 6–7.

30. For details on the process of building of Mount Rushmore, see Smith, *Carving of Mount Rushmore*, 157–71; and Taliaferro, *Great White Fathers*, 228–40, 284–85.

31. Smith, *Carving of Mount Rushmore*, 110–11.

32. Smith, *Carving of Mount Rushmore*, 124–54, and Taliaferro, *Great White Fathers*, 222–26.

33. Coolidge is quoted in Smith, *Carving of Mount Rushmore*, 152–53.

34. Coolidge is quoted in Fite, *Mount Rushmore*, 2–3.

35. Coolidge is quoted in Smith, *Carving of Mount Rushmore*, 153.

36. Borglum is quoted in Smith, *Carving of Mount Rushmore*, 153–54.

37. Fite, *Mount Rushmore*, 125–26; Smith, *Carving of Mount Rushmore*, 211–14; Taliaferro, *Great White Fathers*, 238–40.

38. Fite, *Mount Rushmore*, 191–92; Smith, *Carving of Mount Rushmore*, 311–14; Taliaferro, *Great White Fathers*, 278–81.

39. Fite, *Mount Rushmore*, 207–9; Smith, *Carving of Mount Rushmore*, 330–35; Taliaferro, *Great White Fathers*, 282–85.

40. Borglum is quoted in Smith, *Carving of Mount Rushmore*, 334–35.

41. Borglum is quoted in Fite, *Mount Rushmore*, 208, and Smith, *Carving of Mount Rushmore*, 132.

42. Fite, *Mount Rushmore*, 231–32; Smith, *Carving of Mount Rushmore*, 369–72; Taliaferro, *Great White Fathers*, 297–99.

43. Borglum is quoted in Smith, *Carving of Mount Rushmore*, 242.

44. Fite, *Mount Rushmore*, 60, 116, 150–51, 174; Larner, *Mount Rushmore*, 117–20; Smith, *Carving of Mount Rushmore*, 132, 278–89; Taliaferro, *Great White Fathers*, 240–42, 276–77.

45. Smith, *Carving of Mount Rushmore*, 282–83.

46. Larner, *Mount Rushmore*, 117–18.

47. Fite, *Mount Rushmore*, 118.

48. Taliaferro, *Great White Fathers*, 277; Smith, *Carving of Mount Rushmore*, 287; John Andrews, "The Rushmore Essayist," *South Dakota Magazine*, 25 March 2014, https://www.southdakotamagazine.com/william-burkett.

49. Schama, *Landscape and Memory*, 393.

50. Larner, *Mount Rushmore*, 121.

51. Fite, *Mount Rushmore*, 18, 227; Smith, *Carving of Mount Rushmore*, 326, 354.

52. Taliaferro, *Great White Fathers*, 16.

53. Larner, *Mount Rushmore*, 306–7.

54. Tichi, *Embodiment of a Nation*, 10, concluded that Mount Rushmore, among other sites, "belong[s] to tourism and popular culture.... [They] have been socially constructed through promotional materials, television and motion pictures, journalistic accounts, scientific and pseudoscientific literature, narratives, tracts, fiction, and verse." See also Pomeroy, "Selections from Rushmore," 47.

55. "George H. W. Bush at Mount Rushmore, 1991," PBS (WNET), Season 5 Episode 5, aired 10 December 2018.

56. Clinton is quoted in Taliaferro, *Great White Fathers*, 34.

57. Katie Zezima, "As Obama Makes Rare Presidential Visit to Indian Reservation, Past U.S. Betrayals Loom," *Washington Post*, 14 June 2014, https://www.washingtonpost.com/politics/obama-to-make-rare-presidential-visit-to-indian-reservation-past-betrayals-loom-over-meeting/2014/06/13/70046890-f26f-11e3-9ebc-2ee6f81ed217_story.html; Pekka Mamalainen, "It Is Time to Recognize the Lakota, Like Other Groups, See Themselves as a Sovereign People. Can Indigenous Sovereignty Survive Colonization?" *Aeon*, January 2015, https://aeon.co/essays/in-the-north-american-interior-the-lakota-have-persevered.

58. Cheryl Schreier, "I Was in Charge of Mt. Rushmore. Trump's Plan for Fireworks Is a Terrible Idea," *Washington Post*, 1 July 2020, https://www.washingtonpost .com/opinions/2020/07/01/danger-fireworks-mount-rushmore/; David Naka- mura, Ashley Parker, Colby Itkowitz, and Maria Sacchetti, "At Mount Rushmore, Trump Exploits Social Divisions, Warns of 'Left-Wing Cultural Revolution' in Dark Speech Ahead of Independence Day," *Washington Post*, 4 July 2020, https://www .washingtonpost.com/politics/trump-mount-rushmore-fireworks/2020/07/03 /af2e84f6-bd25-11ea-bdaf-a129f921026f_story.html; Edward Helmore, "Donald Trump Should Stay Away from Mount Rushmore, Sioux Leader Says," *Guardian*, 1 July 2020, https://www.theguardian.com/us-news/2020/jul/01/mount-rushmore -donald-trump-sioux.

59. Robin Givhan, "Trump Got His Crowd and His Fireworks, and Peddled His Fiction," *Washington Post*, 4 July 2020, https://www.washingtonpost.com/lifestyle/2020/07 /04/trump-got-his-crowd-his-fireworks-peddled-his-fiction/, wrote, "If the president assured the country of anything on this night, with his buzzwords and generalities, with his *us* versus *those Americans* tone, it was that the monuments would be safe. He would defend the American fable, the mythology. The truth would go missing."

60. Smith, *Carving of Mount Rushmore*, 364–69; Taliaferro, *Great White Fathers*, 327–30.

61. Brooke Jarvis, "American Sphinx: What Does the Crazy Horse Memorial Really Stand For," *New Yorker*, 23 September 2019, 26. Unless otherwise noted, quotes are from this source.

62. "In History: First Blast on Crazy Horse Memorial, June 3, 1948," Rapid City South Dakota, 22 October 2020, https://www.visitrapidcity.com/blog/2020/10/history -first-blast-crazy-horse-memorial-june-3-1948.

63. "The Summer 2020 University Program at Crazy Horse Memorial," University of South Dakota, accessed 11 May 2020, https://www.usd.edu/summer-school/crazy-horse.

64. "Indian Museum of North America," AllTrips: Black Hills South Dakota, accessed 11 May 2020, https://www.allblackhills.com/history_museums/indian_museum _of_north_america.php.

65. See "The Native American Educational and Cultural Center," Crazy Horse Memo- rial, https://crazyhorsememorial.org/story/the-museums/the-native-american -educational-cultural-center; "Native Educational and Cultural Center," Purdue University, https://www.purdue.edu/naecc/, both accessed 11 May 2020. Purdue advertises tours in six different Native languages.

66. Lisa Friedman, "Standing Rock Sioux Tribe Wins a Victory in Dakota Access Pipe- line Case," *New York Times*, 25 March 2020, https://www.nytimes.com/2020/03 /25/climate/dakota-access-pipeline-sioux.html; Laurel Wamsley, "Court Rules Dakota Access Pipeline Must Be Emptied for Now," NPR, 6 July 2020, https://www .npr.org/2020/07/06/887593775/court-rules-that-dakota-access-pipeline-must-be

-emptied-for-now; Nick Martin, "The People Killed the Pipelines," *New Republic*, 6 July 2020, https://newrepublic.com/article/158368/people-killed=pipelines?utm _source=newsletter&utm_medium=eail&utm_campaign=tny_daily.

67. See, for example, Lisa Kaczke and Jonathan Ellis, "Mount Rushmore Should Be 'Removed,' Tribal President Says Ahead of Trump Visit," *Sioux Falls Argus Leader*, 25 June 2020, https://www.usatoday.com/story/news/nation/2020/06/25/mount -rushmore-oglala-sioux-leader-calls-removal-amid-trump-visit/3257166001/.

3. WASHINGTON IMAGINED

Epigraph: Garry Wills, *Cincinnatus: George Washington and the Enlightenment*, xxiv.

1. Taliaferro, *Great White Fathers*, 242, notes: "Popular prints, whiskey bottles, and tobacco cans bore his likeness. Even more conspicuous was Washington's name: 121 cities and towns, including the nation's capital, thirty-three counties, ten lakes, nine colleges, seven mountains, and one state are named after him, not to mention thousands of citizens. By 1900, forty-five states celebrated Washington's birthday as a legal holiday (compared to eight for Lincoln)."

2. Taliaferro, *Great White Fathers*, 242.

3. The sketch is illustrated and discussed in Fite, *Mount Rushmore*, 13, 33; and Smith, *Carving of Mount Rushmore*, 376–7.

4. Howard, *Painter's Chair*, 223, 226.

5. Borglum is quoted in Fite, *Mount Rushmore*, 124. The Peale and Stuart portraits of Washington are discussed in Howard, *Painter's Chair*, 210–16, 226–27, and 192–96.

6. Borglum is quoted in Taliaferro, *Great White Fathers*, 247.

7. The Houdon commission is widely discussed in the literature. See, for example, Howard, *Painter's Chair*, 90–106.

8. Howard, *Painter's Chair*, 103.

9. The terms of the commission are quoted and discussed in Webster, *Nation's First Monument*, 192–93. See also Craven, *Sculpture in America*, 168.

10. Hallam, "Houdon's Washington in Richmond," 72–80.

11. Washington is quoted in Howard, *Painter's Chair*, 104.

12. Jefferson is quoted in Hallam, "Houdon's Washington in Richmond," 76.

13. Clark, "An Icon Preserved," 42, noted that in the various busts over which the sculptor had control, he "evoked the classical past by depicting the figure as either toga-clad or undraped."

14. The various symbols in Houdon's statue have been widely analyzed. I rely here largely on Wills, *Cincinnatus*, 220–40. Schwartz, *George Washington*, 125, describes Washington as "suspended between public and domestic life" but finds an "essential ambiguity" in the placement of the plow behind the figure that might indicate a return to public life rather than the reverse.

15. Wills, *Cincinnatus*, 19, 25, observed, "Cincinnatus was an icon meant by the Enlighten-ment to *replace* churchly saints with a resolutely secular idea. . . . It was important to the success of the world's first truly secular state that its principal hero was glorified in Roman, not Christian, terms."

16. Clark, "An Icon Preserved," 39–42, observed that there was "almost universal depen-dence on Houdon's portent and accurate portrayals. . . . [The statue] enjoyed such wide publicity and acclaim, almost from that the moment it was unveiled in 1796, that it was hard for any aspiring sculptor of Washington to ignore."

17. Jefferson's letter is quoted in Salomon, Beltramini, and Guderzo, *Canova's George Washington*, 36.

18. Clark, "Icon Preserved," 42.

19. The popular response to Canova's statue is discussed in Fehl, "Thomas Appleton of Livorno and Canova's Statue of George Washington," 523.

20. Johns, "Proslavery Politics and Classical Authority," 140.

21. The plaster cast was the focus for an exhibition entitled "Canova's George Wash-ington," curated by Xavier F. Salomon with Guido Beltramini and Mario Guderzo at the Frick Museum, 22 May to 23 September 2018. Subsequently the exhibition traveled to the Gypsotheca e Museo Antonio Canova, Possagno, Italy. An image appeared on the front page of the *New York Times* on 22 June 2019, next to the coffin of a North Carolina soldier declared dead after the Korean War and now honored in a ceremony at the state Capitol. The caption under the Associated Press photo by Gerry Broome reads: "The Missing Returned," *New York Times*, 22 June 2019.

22. Craven, "Horatio Greenough's Statue of Washington," 429–40, establishes that Greenough knew of Phidias sculpture through a drawing by Quatremère de Quincy.

23. Johns, "Proslavery Politics and Classical Authority," 128.

24. Thayer Tolles, "Henry Kirke Brown and John Quincy Adams Ward, and Realism in American Sculpture," Heilbrunn Timeline of Art History, August 2016, https://www.metmuseum.org/toah/hd/reas/hd_reas.htm. Tolles notes that "together they redefined American sculpture in their choice of aesthetics, subjects, and materials."

25. Craven, *Sculpture in America*, 151–70, suggests that in 1851 the committee approached Greenough and sometime later also asked Brown, suggesting that he might have been asked to serve as an assistant. Clark, "Icon Preserved," 46, on the other hand, claims that the committee approached Greenough and Brown at the same time but when Greenough quarreled with the committee, the commission went to Brown.

26. "George Washington," NYC Parks, accessed 12 May 2020, https://www.nycgovparks.org/parks/union-square-park/monuments/1676.

27. Craven, *Sculpture in America*, 170.

28. Marling, *George Washington Slept Here*, 68. The first quote is from "Clark Mills's Statue of Washington," *Harpers Weekly*, 25 February 1860; the second is from "Monumental Celebrations," *New York Times*, 23 February 1860.

29. Catherine C. Lavoie, "Washington Monument (Baltimore)," Society of Architectural Historians Archipedia, accessed 6 June 2020, https://sah-archipedia.org/buildings/MD-01-510-0001.

30. A detailed account of the circumstances of the commission and evolution of the Baltimore Washington Monument can be found in Miller, "Designs for the Washington Monument," 19–28.

31. Godefroy's Battle Monument was subsequently placed in the location originally intended for the Washington Monument, which was moved to its present location. See Miller, "Designs for the Washington Monument," 25. See also Laurie Ossman, "Monument Square and the Battle Monument," Historic American Buildings Survey, May 2002, accessed 6 June 2020, https://www.nps.gov/hdp/exhibits/baltimore/B2L02.pdf.

32. The other entries were by J. Goldsborough Dugg, C. Seymour Dutton, Louis Stegagnini, and Montgomery C. Meigs. See "The Washington National Monument—A National Contest for a National Monument," 24 November 2020, https://unwritten-record.blogs.drupalme.net/2020/11/24/the-washington-national-monument-a-national-contest-for-a-national-monument/.

33. Mills is quoted in Miller, "Designs for the Washington Monument," 24.

34. Savage, "Self-Made Monument," 13.

35. Savage, "Self-Made Monument," 5–32, contextualizes the various design proposals. See also numerous references in Savage, *Monument Wars*.

36. Scott, "'Vast Empire,'" 36–58. For a summary history of the construction see "Washington Monument Construction Timeline," National Park Service, accessed 5 June 2020, https://www.nps.gov/wamo/learn/historyculture/monumentconstruction.htm. See also "Washington Monument: History and Culture," National Park Service, accessed 5 June 2020, https://www.nps.gov/wamo/learn/historyculture/index.htm.

37. Savage, "Self-Made Monument," 19.

38. Savage, *Monument Wars*, 108. In this work and in his earlier account in "Self-Made Monument" Savage presents a detailed analysis of Casey's role and accomplishments.

39. Savage, "Self-Made Monument," 26, observed, "It is not only ironic but also somehow troubling that a monument designed covertly, against enormous opposition, should so nearly reconcile so many competing ideals—ancient tradition and modern technology, republic values and national progress, communal harmony and individual enterprise. These are the conflicts of Washington's legacy . . . that had confused and divided earlier builders, campaigners, and critics."

40. The terms of the commission are cited in Clark, "Icon Preserved," 49.

41. Clark, "Icon Preserved," 49.

42. For a general overview of the Fair, see Appelbaum, *New York World's Fair 1939/1940*. For a discussion of the George Washington sculpture, see Greg Young, "George Washington's Inauguration and the 1939 World's Fair," Bowery Boys, 1 April 2019, https://www.boweryboyshistory.com/2019/04/george-washingtons-inauguration -and.html.

43. For background information on Arnautoff, see Cherny, *Victor Arnautoff and the Politics of Art*.

44. The mural controversy was widely covered in the daily media and general press. Among the best sources are Michele Bogart, "The Problem with Canceling the Arnautoff Murals," *New York Review of Books*, 16 September 2019, https://www.nybooks.com /daily/2019/09/16/the-problem-with-canceling-the-arnautoff-murals/; Jillian Caddell, "The George Washington Murals Are Meant to Make Viewers Uncomfortable," *Apollo*, 22 August 2019, https://www.apollo-magazine.com/life-of-washington -victor-arnautoff-san-francisco/; Mya Dosch, "Teaching Arnautoff: Public Art and Emotion in the Art History Classroom," *Public Art Dialogue Newsletter*, Fall 2019, https://publicartdialogue.org/newsletter/fall-2019; Robin D. G. Kelley, "We're Getting These Murals All Wrong," *Nation*, 10 September 2019, https://www.thenation .com/article/archive/arnautoff-mural-life-washington/.

45. Dosch, "Teaching Arnautoff," provides detailed examples of various ways to incorporate a discussion of the murals into classroom practice.

46. Dosch, "Teaching Arnautoff." In 2018 Sierra Rooney and I co-chaired a panel at the annual meeting of the College Art Association in Los Angeles titled "Teachable Monuments." This was subsequently expanded into an anthology coedited by Rooney and Wingate with my participation, *Teachable Monuments*.

47. Bogart, "Problem with Cancelling." The editorial board of the *LA Times* defined the controversy as "primarily among liberals—those who want the mural removed because they consider it a traumatically offensive reminder to Native American and African-American students of a horrible past, and those who defend the mural as an honest and anything-but-racist representation of the nation's history, including its less-than-admirable aspects." See "San Francisco Should Not Paint over the Mural about George Washington," *LA Times*, 24 July 2019, https://www.latimes.com /opinion/story/2019-07-23/san-francisco-mural-george-washington-slavery-native -americans.

48. Brown is quoted in Nancy Kenney, "African American Leaders Object to Erasure of Controversial School Mural in San Francisco," *Art Newspaper*, 7 August 2019, https://www.theartnewspaper.com/news/african-american-leaders-object-to-erasure -of-controversial-school-mural-in-san-francisco.

49. Crumpler discusses the evolution of his thinking and murals in Ben Davis, "This Artist Painted the Black Radical Response to the George Washington Salveholder Murals. Here's Why He Stands against Destroying Them," *Artnet*, 10 July 2019, https://news.artnet.com//art-world/san-francisco-mural-victor-arnautoff-dewey -cromplet-1596409. Crumpler feels strongly that "the point of art is to make you think, to make you see that the world is dynamic. Your confrontation with difficulty is the very thing you need . . . particularly in an educational environment, so you can learn how to deal with those difficulties that you are going to run into throughout your life. . . . You have to confront history. Art is a teaching tool."

50. Arnautoff is quoted in Gillian Brockell, "George Washington Owned Slaves and Ordered Indians Killed. Will a Mural of That History Be Hidden?" *Washington Post*, 25 August 2019, https://www.washingtonpost.com/history/2019/08/25/george -washington-owned-slaves-ordered-indians-killed-will-mural-that-history-be-hidden/.

4. WASHINGTON'S MIXED MESSAGES

1. Calloway, *Indian World of George Washington*, 7.

2. Calloway, *Indian World of George Washington*, 6–7. The Cherokee War (1759–61), a local southeastern phase of the French and Indian War, that broke out in response to border disputes between the Indians and European settlers in Virginia and North Carolina, as well as Pontiac's War, prompted the British to take this measure.

3. For Washington's work as a surveyor, see, for example, Calloway, *Indian World of George Washington*, 36–41; and Chernow, *Washington*, 18–24.

4. Chernow, *Washington*, 39–40.

5. Calloway, *Indian World of George Washington*, 327, observed, "Only the continued consumption of Indian land to make private property could sustain the American social order that combined inequality with opportunity."

6. The Fifth Amendment was based in part on principles defined by the British philosopher John Locke, who defined private property as "anything properly one's own." This would include life, liberty, and material possessions. Moulds, "Private Property in Locke's State of Nature," 179–88. Legal and philosophical arguments about exactly what Locke meant continue to this day. See, for example, Vaughn, "Locke on Property."

7. Washington's policies regarding trade are discussed in Nichols, "'Main Mean of Their Political Management,'" 145–61.

8. Washington is quoted in Ellis, *Founding Brothers*, 159.

9. Coe, *You Never Forget Your First*, 74–75, called it "a campaign of genocide."

10. Ragan, "Brother, Destroyer, Father," 133, summarized, "Washington sat at the Iroquois council fire as Brother, he fought with the Iroquois as warrior, he fought against

them as Destroyer, and as Father he set the precedent for future United States–Indian relations."

11. Washington is quoted in Chernow, *Washington*, 359.

12. Ragan, "Brother, Destroyer, Father," 137.

13. Ragan, "Brother, Destroyer, Father," 137.

14. Calloway, *Indian World of George Washington*, 372.

15. Wiencek, *Imperfect God*, 51, observed, "Indentured servitude was a colonial version of the American Dream: if you hated the squalor and stink of London or the tedium of your father's pig farm in Yorkshire, America beckoned. If you were too poor to buy passage to the New World you could get there by signing a contract selling your labor to a planter for seven years."

16. Morgan, *American Slavery, American Freedom*, 301.

17. Steinberg, "Presentism, George Washington and Slavery," 169–70.

18. Wiencek, *Imperfect God*, 78.

19. His father's death ended the possibility of obtaining an English education from which his older half-brothers had benefited. Washington was now the head of the household. See Wiencek, *Imperfect God*, 31, for more details.

20. Pogue, "George Washington and the Politics of Slavery," 3.

21. See, among others, Thompson, *"Only Unavoidable Subject of Regret,"* 13.

22. Wiencek, *Imperfect God*, 18, 29.

23. Chernow, *Washington*, 111.

24. For a discussion on Washington and farming, see, among others, Pogue, "George Washington and the Politics of Slavery," 3; Thompson, *"Only Unavoidable Subject of Regret,"* 7.

25. Riley, "George Washington's Last Will and Testament," 170.

26. Thompson, *"Only Unavoidable Subject of Regret,"* 2.

27. Thompson, *"Only Unavoidable Subject of Regret,"* 7.

28. Wiencek, *Imperfect God*, 119.

29. Wiencek, *Imperfect God*, 115, 122–23. Although Chernow presents Washington in the best possible light, he acknowledges that the design of Mount Vernon "made it arduous for slaves to maintain families." See Chernow, *Washington*, 112. Chernow, 113, disagrees with Wiencek on Washington's policy on whipping, stating that he believed it was counterproductive although his estate managers didn't always follow his instructions and he was away a lot of the time.

30. Wiencek, *Imperfect God*, 125, 132.

31. Wiencek, *Imperfect God*, 123–24.

32. Thompson, *"Only Unavoidable Subject of Regret,"* xiii.

33. Wiencek, *Imperfect God*, 179–82. Wiencek writes that, in April 1769, "Washington, acting as guardian for his stepchildren, had organized the raffle along with other

creditors. They could make more money with a lottery than with an auction because they could appeal to the sporting blood of Virginians. . . . The drawings took place in a tavern, amid the banging of dice boxes and tankards, and the inevitable bawdy songs. The majority of prizes, twenty-one, consisted of single men. There were six families, and five lots of women with a child or children. . . . The best male workers, appraised at the highest values, got to keep their wives and children . . . the less valuable families did not get to stay together." Chernow, *Washington*, 118, noted that Washington often bought tickets for lotteries.

34. Dunbar, *Never Caught.*
35. Chernow, *Washington*, 763.
36. Wiencek, *Imperfect God*, 197.
37. The complexities of the war with regard to Black and enslaved men serving in the army are discussed by Wiencek, *Imperfect God*, 199, 203–20. He notes that Jefferson estimated that some thirty thousand slaves (men, women, and children) fled their masters to take advantage of this offer.
38. This episode is discussed in Thompson, *"Only Unavoidable Subject of Regret,"* 65.
39. Wiencek, *Imperfect God*, 190, 243.
40. This initiative is discussed in detail by Wiencek, *Imperfect God*, 221–31. The summary here is largely based on this source.
41. Wiencek, *Imperfect God*, 254–59, discusses negotiations with the British on this issue in detail.
42. Abigail Adams is quoted in Wiencek, *Imperfect God*, 192. For an extensive summary of Washington's private statements on slavery see Twohig, "'That Species of Property,'" 114–38.
43. Pogue, "George Washington and the Politics of Slavery," 2–5.
44. Wiencek, *Imperfect God*, 68.
45. Wiencek, *Imperfect God*, 260.
46. For a detailed account of these debates, see Ellis, *Founding Brothers*, 91–96; Wiencek, *Imperfect God*, 266–71.
47. Ellis, *Founding Brothers*, 93.
48. Pogue, "George Washington and the Politics of Slavery," 5.
49. Pogue, "George Washington and the Politics of Slavery," 6.
50. Furstenberg, *In the Name of the Father*, 8–9.
51. Furstenberg, *In the Name of the Father*, 12.
52. This aspect of the speech is discussed by Chernow, *Washington*, 758; Wiencek, *Imperfect God*, 319.
53. Washington is quoted in Pogue, "George Washington and the Politics of Slavery," 6–7; Wiencek, *Imperfect God*, 217.
54. Chernow, *Washington*, 708.

55. Thompson, *"Only Unavoidable Subject of Regret,"* 303.

56. Chernow, *Washington*, 800.

57. Wiencek, *Imperfect God*, 5–6, emphasized, "The emancipation clause stands out from the rest of Washington's will in the unique forcefulness of its language ... [it] rings with the voice of command; it has the iron firmness of a field order. ... The force of his comments makes it clear that within his family Washington was entirely alone in his thinking about slavery."

58. Riley, "George Washington's Last Will and Testament," 168.

59. Thompson, *"Only Unavoidable Subject of Regret,"* 311, noted that that there had been an attempt to set fire to the main house and it was thought that slaves might have been involved.

60. Pogue, "George Washington and the Politics of Slavery," 8.

61. Wiencek, *Imperfect God*, 212, described Wheatley as "the most famous black person in America; indeed she was the *only* famous black person in America. She was the first black, the first slave, and only the third American woman to have a book of poems published."

62. Chernow, *Washington*, 802.

63. Wiencek, *Imperfect God*, 353. Chernow, *Washington*, 69, speculated that if Washington hadn't been farming tobacco, "he might never have become so enmeshed with a reprehensible system that he learned to loathe." Pogue, "George Washington and the Politics of Slavery," 3, compared Washington's changing views to his shift on the relationship of the colonies to Britain: "Just as Washington's misgivings with America's place in the British Empire initially were related to economic concerns, the basis for Washington's questioning of the viability of slavery first seems to have been related to financial considerations."

64. Chernow, *Washington*, 802, was perhaps the most euphoric: "By freeing his slaves, Washington accomplished something more glorious than any battlefield victory as a general or legislative act as president. He did what no other founding father dared to do, although all proclaimed a theoretical revulsion at slavery. He brought the American experience that much closer to the ideals of the American Revolution and brought his own behavior in line with his troubled conscience." Wiencek, *Imperfect God*, 358–59, concluded, "In the end George Washington did precisely what he had said was impossible: he freed his slaves all at once, not by imperceptible degrees ... [his] will was a blueprint for a future that did not come to pass ... the tragedy, for the nation, is that Washington did not act upon his convictions during his lifetime."

65. Pogue, "George Washington and the Politics of Slavery," 8, concluded, "Whatever the reason, the decision indicates that there was an upper limit that even George Washington placed on the value of his principles."

66. Furstenberg, *In the Name of the Father*, 85.

67. Furstenberg, *In the Name of the Father*, 100–103.

5. JEFFERSON'S MONUMENTS

1. A good summary of the various ways Jefferson was remembered is found in Stephenson, "Celebrating American Heroes," 217–18.

2. At the time there were two distinct political factions, the Federalists and the Republicans. The Republicans later became the Democratic-Republicans. These were more aligned groups rather than the organized political parties we have today. See Joseph J. Ellis, "Thomas Jefferson," *Encyclopedia Britannica*, 30 June 2021, https://www.britannica.com/biography/Thomas-Jefferson.

3. A succinct and useful summary of Jefferson's work and influence as an architect can be found in Richard Guy Wilson, "Thomas Jefferson and Architecture," *Encyclopedia of Virginia*, 2016, accessed 8 February 2021, https://www.encyclopediavirginia.org/Jefferson_Thomas_and_Architecture.

4. Many in the literature have made this observation. Among the most pointed are Peterson, *Jefferson Image in the American Mind*, 388: "In the contemporary imagination Jefferson and Monticello are two sides of the same coin . . . [and] a shrine to Jefferson's memory"; and Gordon-Reed and Onuf, *"Most Blessed of the Patriarchs,"* 157: "It would not be too much to say that he identified himself so closely with Monticello that the house and the man blended into a single image."

5. Gordon-Reed and Onuf, *"Most Blessed of the Patriarchs,"* 27, observed, "Home was a powerful idea for Thomas Jefferson, a fixed point in a sentimental geography formed from the melded associations of people, places, and events. When he was away from Monticello serving in the national government, he visualized his mountain as a paradise of domestic tranquility . . . his vision of his own family life carried out on cherished space merged with a broader dream of an enlightened republican society grounded in a fruitful attachment to the land."

6. The Enlightenment, sometimes referred to as the Age of Reason, is typically dated from 1685 to 1780, bracketed at its end by the American and French Revolutions. Expressed primarily in the writings of John Locke and Isaac Newton, this movement emphasized the questioning of authority and the primacy of rational thinking or reason. Jefferson acknowledged Locke, Newton, and Francis Bacon as the triumvirate upon which his thinking was based. See Pagden, *Enlightenment*, for an updated account on its ongoing influence.

7. Stein, *Worlds of Thomas Jefferson at Monticello*, 50, notes in particular, "a dome—the most conspicuous characteristic of the Hôtel de Salm—placed over the existing octagonal bow of the Parlor. Another attribute of the Hôtel de Salm that Jefferson admired was the outward appearance of a single story that cleverly concealed three stories. Jefferson's design for Monticello followed that model."

8. An excellent detailed description of this and other rooms in Monticello 2 is found in Stein, *Worlds of Thomas Jefferson at Monticello*, 70–114. Unless otherwise noted, my description is based on this source.

9. Ellis, *American Sphinx*, 16, considering the house as a whole, described: "Houdon busts next to Indian headdresses, mahogany tables brimming over with multiple sets of porcelain and silver candlesticks, wall-to-wall ports and prints and damask hangings and full-length gilt-framed mirrors. . . . By any measure, chockablock Monticello resembled a trophy case belonging to one of America's most self-indulgent and wildly eclectic collectors."

10. Jefferson's inclination to keep his slaves hidden as much as possible is also reflected in the overall placement of their quarters at Monticello. Known as Mulberry Row, these were constructed at a level below grade so as to make them invisible from the main house. This area also housed the woodworking and ironworking shops, a smokehouse, dairy, wash house, storehouses, and a stable—necessities of a large working plantation.

11. Stein, *Worlds of Thomas Jefferson at Monticello*, 12, notes that Jefferson's library was organized into three categories: "History, Philosophy, and the Fine Arts, intended to reflect Memory, Reason, and Imagination. As one of the Fine Arts, architecture was grouped with gardening, painting, sculpture, music, poetry, oratory, and criticism."

12. The evolution of Monticello and the role of the TJMF is described in Peterson, *Jefferson Image in the American Mind*, 380–88.

13. Lucian K. Truscott IV, "I'm a Direct Descendant of Thomas Jefferson. Take Down His Memorial," *New York Times*, 7 July 2020. Truscott suggested that his statue should be replaced by one of Harriet Tubman: "To see a 19-foot-tall bronze statue of a Black woman, who was a slave and also a patriot, in place of a white man who enslaved hundreds of men and women is not erasing history. It's telling the real history of America."

14. Peterson, *Jefferson Image in the American Mind*, 421–32, provides a detailed chronology of the evolution of the memorial.

15. Bedford, *John Russell Pope*, 216.

16. For examples of objections, see Bedford, *John Russell Pope*, 222.

17. See Peterson, *Jefferson Image in the American Mind*, 426, for various reasons for Congress's decision.

18. "Roosevelt Assails Dictator Rule, Hailing Way of 'Average Opinion,'" *New York Times*, 16 November 1939. Given the nature of FDR's remarks and his consistent support for the project, it is worth considering Joseph J. Ellis's speculation that "a good case can be made that Roosevelt championed the construction of the Jefferson Memorial primarily to provide the Democratic party with a symbolic counter to

the Lincoln Memorial, which the Republican party claimed as its own." See Ellis, *American Sphinx*, 350.

19. Peterson, *Jefferson Image in the American Mind*, 429, includes FDR's remarks: "Well, I don't suppose there is anybody in the world who loves trees quite as much as I do but I recognize that a cherry tree did not live forever . . . Jefferson did live forever. Let the enchained ladies be forewarned: they would be shoveled up bodily with the trees!"

20. For details of the modifications see Bedford, *John Russell Pope*, 222, who also observed that since the country was then at war with Japan there was no mention of the cherry trees.

21. Although the art jury appointed by the Jefferson Memorial Commission selected a different artist, they chose to override that in favor of Rudolph Evans, with FDR's support. See Peterson, *Jefferson Image in the American Mind*, 209.

22. The quotes are discussed and analyzed by Maier, *American Scripture*, 209–15; Peterson, *Jefferson Image in the American Mind*, 43.

23. Maier, *American Scripture*, 209–15; Wills, *Inventing America*, 306.

24. See especially Maier, *American Scripture*, 210–11.

25. See Wills, *Inventing America*, 306.

26. Fraser is quoted in Stephenson, "Celebrating American Heroes," 263.

27. Campbell, *Gateway Arch*, 11–29, includes a pertinent history of the Saint Louis riverfront. Unless otherwise noted, information in this section is taken from this source.

28. National Park Service site, accessed 1 February 2021, https://www.nps.gov/jeff/index.htm. Dred Scott, an enslaved Black man, sued for emancipation based on his residence on free soil. The 1857 seven-to-two Supreme Court decision written by Chief Justice Taney stated that the Constitution did not confer citizenship to Blacks even if they were free; that states no longer had to honor the "once free, always free rule"; and that Congress did not have the right to prohibit slavery in areas that weren't states.

29. Campbell, *Gateway Arch*, 28, suggests that Smith "seemed focused on the pioneer image."

30. Campbell, *Gateway Arch*, 4, observed that "by turning the memorial into a tribute to the founder of the Democratic Party, supporters of the riverfront development had finally found a strategy that could garner support from the White House."

31. Campbell, *Gateway Arch*, 4.

32. Graebner, "Gateway to Empire," 367.

33. Campbell, *Gateway Arch*, 55. The seven members of the committee are cited, see 56.

34. Campbell, *Gateway Arch*, 58, cites the requirement. The information in the twenty-four-page booklet sent to potential entrants is discussed on page 56.

35. Campbell, *Gateway Arch*, 23, 51.
36. Saarinen quoted in Campbell, *Gateway Arch*, 67.
37. The jury's instructions are noted in Campbell, *Gateway Arch*, 75.
38. The commission is quoted in Campbell, *Gateway Arch*, 175.
39. Claude Ricketts is quoted in Campbell, *Gateway Arch*, 35, summing up the situation: "The city's real estate and financial sector owned 109 properties in the district, representing 35% of its assessed value. Considering that the Jefferson National Expansion Memorial Association's Legal Committee was advised by 'experienced real estate men' that the compensation for a condemned property would be 25% more than the assessed value, it is no surprise that the city's realty interests saw the riverfront project as a source of immediate income. The clearing of the site to make way for the memorial would, in turn, immediately increase neighboring property values."
40. For more detailed information on this problematic issue, see Graebner, "Gateway to Empire," 368–87; Michael Z. Wise, "Walking Mussolini's Fascist Utopia," *New York Times*, 11 July 1999, https://www.nytimes.com/1999/07/11/travel/walking-mussolini-s-fascist-utopia.html.
41. "Rome's Most Famous Building That Never Was: The Arch for E 42," *Rome the Second Time*, 16 June 2015, https://romethesecondtime.blogspot.com/2015/06/romes-the-most-famous-building-that-never.html.
42. Graebner, "Gateway to Empire," 387.
43. Campbell, *Gateway Arch*, 5.

6. JEFFERSON'S LEGACY

1. These taxes, prompted by after the Seven Years' War with France left Britain with a huge debt, included the Stamp Act (1765), the Townshend Duties (1766), and the Tea Act (1773), and imposed the cry of "taxation without representation." See Monticello, "Thomas Jefferson and the Declaration of Independence," accessed 4 December 2020, https://www.monticello.org/thomas-jefferson/jefferson-s-three-greatest-achievements/the-declaration/jefferson-and-the-declaration/.
2. Jefferson's quote is cited in Wills, *Inventing America*, 56, and is taken from Julian P. Boyd et al., *Papers of Thomas Jefferson*, 1:242.
3. Maier, *American Scripture*, 8.
4. This aspect is discussed by Maier, *American Scripture*, 29–30, among others.
5. Wills, *Inventing America*, 32.
6. Maier, *American Scripture*, 48. Most of the states had their own declarations of independence.
7. Adopted on 12 June 1776, Section 1 states, "That all men are by nature equally free and independent and have certain inherent rights, of which, when they enter into a state of society, they cannot, by any compact, deprive or divest their posterity;

namely, the enjoyment of life and liberty, with the means of acquiring and possessing property, and pursuing and obtaining happiness and safety." For the full document see U.S. National Archives, "America's Founding Documents," accessed 5 December 2020, https://www.archives.gov/founding-docs/virginia-declaration-of-rights. Section 5 stipulated the separation of state legislative and executive power be separate from the judiciary. Other sections called for freedom of the press and freedom of religion.

8. The complete document can be found at "Locke's Political Philosophy," *Stanford Encyclopedia of Philosophy*, accessed 5 December 2020, https://plato.stanford.edu/entires/locke-political/. Wills, *Inventing America*, 49–55, argued the influence of Scottish Enlightenment philosophers, in particular Francis Hutcheson. In his introduction to the 2018 edition, he summarizes arguments against this influence and modifies his emphasis somewhat.

9. A useful diagram of the various sources, which Maier calls a "family tree," are found in Maier, *American Scripture*, 166. The Declaration of Independence, according to the Monticello website, was "spread by word of mouth, delivered on horseback and by ship, read aloud before troops in the Continental Army, published in newspapers from Vermont to Georgia, and dispatched to Europe." See the Monticello website, accessed 4 December 2020, https://www.monticello.org/thomas-jefferson/jeffersons-three-greatest-achievements/the-declaration/jefferson-and-the-declaration/.

10. "The Legacy of the Declaration," Monticello, accessed 4 December 2020, https://www.monticello.org/thomas-jefferson/jefferson-s-three-greatest-achievements/the-declaration/the-legacy-of-the-declaration/.

11. For a summary of congressional cuts see Wills, *Inventing America*, 310–19. Maier, *American Scripture*, 150, after discussing the various edits, concluded, "By exercising their intelligence, political good sense, and a discerning sense of language, the delegates managed to make the Declaration at once more accurate and more consonant with the convictions of their constituents, and to enhance both its power and its eloquence."

12. For a summary analysis of the cuts, see Wills, *Inventing America*, 310–19.

13. It read, "He has waged cruel war against human nature itself, violating its most sacred rights of life and liberty in the persons of a distant people who never offended him, captivating and carrying them into slavery in another hemisphere, or to incur miserable death in their transportation thither. This piratical warfare, the opprobrium of *infidel* powers is the warfare of the *Christian* king of Great Britain. Determined to keep open a market where MEN should be brought and sold, he has prostituted his negative for suppressing every legislative attempt to prohibit or to restrain this execrable commerce and that this assemblage of horrors might want no fact of

distinguished, die, he is now exciting those very people to rise in arms among us, and to purchase that liberty of which *he* has deprived them, by murdering the people upon whom *he* also obtruded them; thus paying off former crimes committed against the *liberties* of one people, with crimes which he urges them to commit against the *lives* of another."

14. Yohuru Williams, "Why Thomas Jefferson's Anti-Slavery Passage Was Removed from the Declaration of Independence," History.com, accessed 1 July 2020, https:// www.history.com/news/declaration-of-independence-deleted-anti-slavery-clause -jefferson, observed that at this time both the South and the North had financial stakes in slavery. The South "needed free labor to produce tobacco, cotton and other cash crops for export back to Europe. Northern shipping merchants, who also played a role in that economy, remained dependent on the triangle trade between Europe, Africa and the Americas that included the traffic in enslaved Africans." Jefferson was incensed at Congress's exclusion of his grievance about slavery from the Declaration of Independence. His notes on the Continental Congress state: "The clause . . . , reprobating the enslaving the inhabitants of Africa, was struck out in complaisance to South Carolina and Georgia, who never attempted to restrain the importation of slaves, and for who on the contrary still wished to continue it." See M. Andrew Holowchak, "What a Line Deleted from the Declaration of Independence Teaches Us about Thomas Jefferson," History News Network, accessed 30 December 2019, https://historynewsnetwork.org/article/173919.

15. Wills, *Inventing America*, xiv.

16. Wills, *Inventing America*, 225, 211.

17. Wills, *Inventing America*, 164, states, "When Jefferson spoke of pursuing happiness . . . he meant a public happiness which is measurable; which is, indeed, the test and justification of any government." See also 151, 240, 247, 254.

18. See Matthews, *Radical Politics of Thomas Jefferson*, 26–27.

19. Steele, "Jefferson's Legacy," 538, observes: "Although it can be argued that all reasonable men of that era assumed that property was a necessity (and perhaps sufficient) prerequisite to life, liberty, and the pursuit of happiness, that Jefferson did not use the word is historically novel. Moreover . . . property ownership per se was not considered by Jefferson to be an end in itself."

20. The First Amendment was introduced to Congress in 1789 and adopted 15 December 1791.

21. Jefferson is quoted in Ragosta, "Virginia Statute," 79. This section, unless otherwise noted, is based largely on this essay.

22. The entire statute is reproduced in Ragosta, "Virginia Statute," 87–88. Ragosta, 82, calls it "a foundation for American religious liberty."

23. Wood, "Trials and Tribulations," 401–2, 412–13.

24. Jefferson is quoted in Gordon-Reed and Onuf, *"Most Blessed of the Patriarchs,"* 278.

25. Ellis, *American Sphinx*, 355, observed that freedom of religion was "the one specific Jeffersonian idea that has negotiated the passage from the late eighteenth to the late twentieth century without any significant change in character of coloration."

26. A good summary of Jefferson's ongoing campaign for public education is found in National Park Service, "Thomas Jefferson's Plan for the University of Virginia: Lessons from the Lawn," 8–9, accessed 9 September 2020, https://www.nps.gov /articles/thomas-jefferson-s-plan-for-the-university-of-virginia-lessons-from-the -lawn-teaching-with-historic-places.htm#:~:text=By%20looking%20at%20thomas %20jefferson's,revolutionary%20new%20setting%20for%20higher.

27. Lipscomb and Bergh, *Writings of Thomas Jefferson*, 15, 326.

28. Jefferson is quoted in National Park Service, "Thomas Jefferson's Plan for the University of Virginia," 13.

29. See, Taylor, *Thomas Jefferson's Education*; McInnis and Nelson, *Educated in Tyranny*. Taylor is reviewed by Drew Faust, "How Slavery Warped Jefferson's Vision for the University of Virginia," *Washington Post*, 1 November 2019, https://www.washingtonpost .com/outlook/how-slavery-warped-jeffersons-vision-for-the-university-of-virginia /2019/11/01/c86974f0-cb57-11e9-a1fe-ca46e8d573c0_story.html; Gordon-Reed, "What Jefferson Couldn't Teach," *Atlantic*, 15 December 2019, 120–22; Alan Pell Crawford, "The Dream of a Better Society," *Wall Street Journal*, 28–29 September 2019. Crawford also reviews the edited volume.

30. Gordon-Reed and Onuf, *"Most Blessed of the Patriarchs,"* 20.

31. Finkelman, "Jefferson and Slavery," 181–82. The author portrays Jefferson in a very negative light.

32. For example, Stanton, "'Those Who Labor for My Happiness,'" 150, 155, 157, provides a good summary of the operations at Monticello. She observes that "the Monticello slaves were made more 'comfortable' in bondage than most of their fellows, even in Virginia" (164). On the other hand, Finkelman, "Jefferson and Slavery," 182, describes Jefferson's treatment of his slaves as harsh and almost barbaric, while Wood, "The Trials and Tribulations of Thomas Jefferson," 397, observed that "recent historians have emphasized, he bought, bred, and flogged his slaves, and hunted down fugitives in much the same way his fellow Virginia planters."

33. As late as 1814 he was railing against the practice: "Amalgamation with the other color produces a degradation to which no lover of his country, no love of excellence in the human character can innocently consent." See Wood, *Empire of Liberty*, 540.

34. "Thomas Jefferson and Sally Hemings: A Brief Account," Monticello, accessed 2 December 2020, https://www.monticello.org/thomas-jefferson/jefferson-slavery /thomas-jefferson-and-sally-hemings-a-brief-account/. This site provides a useful bibliography of primary and secondary sources.

35. See, for example, Gordon-Reed and Onuf, *"Most Blessed of the Patriarchs,"* 68, 129.

36. Wills, *Inventing America*, 297–98. Their children, with their seven-eighths white ancestry, were considered white according to Virginia law. Sally Hemings would have been considered a mulatto and therefore not Black; Jefferson had actually developed a detailed formula for precisely determining if someone could be defined as such.

37. Gordon-Reed and Onuf, *"Most Blessed of the Patriarchs,"* 61, observed, "Jefferson thought it possible to be a slaveholder and still have enslaved people's interests at heart . . . he believed that the enslaved actually could be made happy in their circumstances." He referred to this as amelioration, which the authors defined as "a way to make it emotionally easier for him to enslave people, given his professed values, and easier (in his mind) for the enslaved to endure their condition."

38. See, for example, Matthews, *Radical Politics of Thomas Jefferson*, 67. Subsequently Jefferson modified this unqualified emancipation with the proviso that freed slaves would have to leave the state within a year.

39. Jefferson is quoted in Matthews, *Radical Politics of Thomas Jefferson*, 69, among many other citations.

40. Wills, *Inventing America*, 219, relates these observations to the contemporary interest in crossbreeding.

41. Wilson, "Jefferson and the Republic of Letters," 51. A posthumous edition was published in 1853 by Jefferson's executor, Thomas Jefferson Randolph, that included Jefferson's notes and corrections.

42. In January 1821 Jefferson wrote in his autobiography, "Nothing is more certainly written in the book of fate than that [Black slaves] are to be free. Nor is it less certain that the two races, equally free, cannot live in the same government. Nature, habit, opinion has drawn indelible lines of distinction between them," quoted in Crawford, "Dream of a Better Society," 199.

43. Marienstras, "Common Man's Indian," observed that Jefferson was one of the first to consider "Negro removal" twenty years before he began to consider Indian Removal, and in his retirement continued to support such a program.

44. Wills, *Inventing America*, 297–306, presents an excellent summary of Jefferson's key thoughts on the subject. See also, Stanton, "'Those Who Labor for My Happiness,'" 167.

45. This provision is discussed by Wiencek, *Imperfect God*, 235.

46. Matthews, *Radical Politics of Thomas Jefferson*, 73.

47. Jefferson to John Holms, 22 April 1820, in Leicester, *The Works of Thomas Jefferson*, 12:159; reproduced "Famous Jefferson Quotes," Monticello, accessed 8 December 2020, https://www.monticello.org/site/research-and-collections/famous-jefferson -quotes. This quote is also the title of a book: Miller, *Wolf by the Ears*. Wiencek, *Imperfect God*, 276, observed that the work became "a philosophical pillar of the proslavery platform."

48. Drinnon, *Facing West*, 80, calls Jefferson "the slaveholding philosopher of free-dom." Steele, "Jefferson's Legacy," 534, observed Jefferson's dilemma as being "caught, throughout his public life, between the genuine revulsion at slavery on the one hand (it is difficult to think of a more emotionally powerful passage in his writing than the critique of slavery in Query 18 of the *Notes*) and his racism on the other (it is difficult to think of a more toe-curlingly racist statement in his writing than his passages in Query 14 of the *Notes*)."

49. This frequently quoted passage is found, for example, in Usner, "Iroquois Livelihood and Jeffersonian Agrarianism," 208.

50. For these and other examples, see Matthews, *Radical Politics of Thomas Jefferson*, 46–47.

51. See Wallace, *Jefferson and the Indians*, 203, 278. At the time Knox developed this policy Indian Affairs was under the jurisdiction of the secretary of war. Subsequently, in 1849 it was placed under the Department of the Interior.

52. Horseman, "The Indian Policy of an 'Empire of Liberty,'" 49, offers this explanation: "Immersed in Enlightenment optimism and ethnocentrism, Jefferson envisioned Indians willingly accepting a different way of life as white expansion confined them on smaller and smaller areas of land."

53. See, for example, Nichols in Cope, Pedersen, and Williams, *George Washington*, 158.

54. Horseman, "Indian Policy of an 'Empire of Liberty,'" 50–51. Jefferson felt "it con-sistent with our morality to lead them towards, to familiarize them to the idea that it is for their interest to cede lands at times to the United States, and for us thus to procure gratifications to our citizens, from time to time, by new acquisitions."

55. Wallace, *Jefferson and the Indians*, 21, notes that Jefferson began investing in western lands when in 1757 he inherited some of his father's share in the Loyal Land Company and subsequently made some investments of his own.

56. Wallace, *Jefferson and the Indians*, 161–67, 205.

57. Wallace, *Jefferson and the Indians*, 337, concluded, "The reservation world is the direct consequence of a general policy, maintained throughout the nineteenth century, of relentlessly removing Indians to ever-shrinking isolated enclaves, often far from their ancestral homelands. Jefferson was not alone in formulating this but he made it central to the federal system, and, by mourning the passing of the Indians into oblivion or civilized invisibility, gave moral justification to the seizure of lands he said they no longer needed."

58. Frymer, *Building an American Empire*, 74, 76, concluded that the Louisiana Purchase "changed the calculus of the young nation with regard to the position of Native Americans on the land. The fact that the nation was not yet ready to expand into much of the Louisiana Territory meant that President Jefferson and others began to move more swiftly toward the idea of removing Native Americans who lived east of

the Mississippi River to the lands to the West." Ultimately this resulted in the Indian Removal Act of 1830 permitting the scandalous Trail of Tears, in which some sixteen thousand Native Americans were forced to march over a rugged terrain, ultimately resulting in the death of some 25 percent either due to starvation or disease.

59. Jefferson quoted in Drinnon, *Facing West*, 89. Wallace, *Jefferson and the Indians*, 19, describes Jefferson's four-step plan for obtaining Native American lands including a four-stage threat of war tactics, concluding that "it was a process now known as 'ethnic cleansing.'"

60. Joseph A. Harriss, "How the Louisiana Purchase Changed the World," *Smithsonian Magazine*, April 2003, https://www.smithsonianmag.com/history/how-the-louisiana -purchase-changed-the-world-79715124, offers a useful account of the history of the territory and detailed account of the transaction. My account is largely based on this source.

61. Wood, *Empire of Liberty*, 357; Drinnon, *Facing West*, 88.

62. Jefferson's much quoted comment is included in Frymer, *Building an American Empire*, 206, among other sources. It formed the title of Gordon Wood's book, *Empire of Liberty*.

63. See, for example, Matthews, *Radical Politics of Thomas Jefferson*, 53; Drinnon, *Facing West*, 82; Wallace, *Jefferson and the Indians*, 96, 104, 144.

64. Matthews, *Radical Politics of Thomas Jefferson*, 53.

65. Matthews, *Radical Politics of Thomas Jefferson*, 64, 74, 124; Wills, *Inventing America*, 292.

66. Crawford, "Dream of a Better Society," 133, observed that "Jefferson's belief in an expanded role for local government is a more radical notion than it might first appear . . . to describe Jefferson during this period as an advocate of 'states' rights,' is to understate the case. What Jefferson proposed was a radical decentralization of government itself."

67. Onuf, *Jefferson's Empire*, 3, observed, "Jeffersonian ideals are so woven into the fabric of our national self-understanding that we have trouble distinguishing one from the other, Jefferson from America." Wood, *Empire of Liberty*, 277, concluded that "so long as there is a United States he will remain the supreme spokesman for the nation's noblest ideals and highest aspiration."

68. French and Ayers, "Strange Career of Thomas Jefferson," 418.

7. LINCOLN COMMEMORATED

1. A brief summary of the various fugitive slave acts and their ultimate repeal in 1864 can be found at History.com, "Fugitive Slave Acts," 11 February 2020, https://www .history.com/topics/black-history/fugitive-slave-acts.

2. Douglass is quoted in Stephenson, "Celebrating American Heroes," 44. David W. Blight, "'For Something beyond the Battlefield,'" 1165, suggested that Douglass's intention was "to assert an American national identity that included Blacks" and that "the monument was not only to Lincoln: rather, it was to the fact of emancipation."

3. Douglass quoted in Marie Fazio, "Boston Removes Statue of Formerly Enslaved Man Kneeling before Lincoln," *New York Times*, 29 December 2020, https://www.nytimes.com/2020/12/29/us/boston-abraham-lincoln-statue.html?smid=em-share.

4. An excellent detailed analysis of the Bethune memorial can be found in Woodley, "'Ma Is in the Park,'" 474–502. See also Jenny Woodley, "'No Longer Just Lincoln and a Slave': Consider Mary McLeod Bethune's Lincoln Park Statue," *History News Network*, 19 July 2020, https://historynewsnetwork.org/article/176409. For information on Robert Berks, see Erika Duncan, "Encounters: A Sculptor Whose Model Is History," *New York Times*, 14 April 1996, https://www.nytimes.com/1996/04/14/nyregion/encounters-a-sculptor-whose-model-is-history.html.

5. For Bethune's accomplishments see, Fiona Clem, "Mary McLeod Bethune," *DC Memorialist*, 2011–12, https://dcmemorialist.com/mary-mcleod-bethune/. A daughter of former slaves, Bethune founded the Daytona Normal and Industrial School for Negro Girls, in 1904. When it later became Bethune-Cookman College, she served as its president for forty years. In 1935 she founded the National Council of Negro Women. A year later she was appointed director of the Office of Negro Affairs under FDR's National Youth Administration.

6. The fundraising booklet is quoted in Woodley, "'Ma Is in the Park,'" 480–81.

7. Woodley, "'Ma Is in the Park,'" 485.

8. Elizabeth O'Gorek, "Fencing Comes Down Thursday in Lincoln Park," *HillRag*, 17 September 2020, https://www.hillrag.com/2020/09/17/fencing-comes-down-thursday-in-lincoln-park/. Subsequent attempts to remove the statue were not successful. See Christian Zapata, "D.C. Delegate Reintroduces Bill to Remove Emancipation Memorial from Lincoln Park," WAMU, 19 February 2021, https://www.npr.org//local/305/2021/02/19/969419030/d-c-delegate-reintroduces-bill-to-remove-emancipation-memorial-from-lincoln-park.

9. Bullock and Bessette were quoted in Cristela Guerra, "Boston to Remove Statue Depicting Abraham Lincoln with Freed Black Man at His Feet," NPR, 1 July 2020, https://www.npr.org/sections/live-updates-protests-for-racial-justice/2020/07/01/886445904/boston-to-remove-statue-depicting-abraham-lincoln-with-freed-black-man-at-his-fe.

10. Keith Winstead is quoted in David Harper, "A Controversial Boston Statue of Abraham Lincoln Standing over a Freed Slave Will Be Removed," *Artsy*, 1 July 2020, https:///www.artsy.net/news/artsy-editorial-controversial-boston-statue-abraham-lincoln-standing-freed-slave-will-removed.

11. The history of the monument is recounted in Pitcaithley, "A Splendid Hoax." See also Gloria Peterson, "An Administrative History of the Abraham Lincoln Birthplace National Historic Site Hodgenville Kentucky," National Park Service, 20 September 1968, updated 10 February 2003, https://www.nps.gov/parkhistory/online_books /abli/adhi/adhi.htm. See also "Abraham Lincoln Birthplace: Symbolic Birth Cabin," National Park Service, updated 14 April 2015, https://www.nps.gov/abli/planyourvisit /symbolic-cabin.htm.

12. Appleman is quoted in Peterson, *Administrative History*.

13. Pitcaithley, "Splendid Hoax," 21, concluded, "The public's perception of the Lincoln cabin is important to the nation's image and an indispensable part of the nation's ritualistic public tribute to its humble origins. It is symbolic of a need for an accessible past and a willingness to embrace myths that are too popular to be diminished by the truth."

14. The significance of the fasces is interpreted by Nathan King, "Secret Symbol of the Lincoln Memorial," *Ranger Journal*, 23 June 2013, https://www.nps.gov/nama/blogs /ranger-journal.htm?tagid=935b215c-1dd8-b71c-07360d8315e1a76c.

15. A detailed account of the various steps involved in creating the Lincoln Memorial is found in Stephenson, "Celebrating American Heroes."

16. Thomas, *Lincoln Memorial and American Life*, xxii, observed, "This portrayal served the goal of national reconciliation, a preoccupation of the governing American, especially Republican, elite of the period after Reconstruction."

17. Sandage, "Marble House Divided," 136–67, provides a definitive account of the how the content of the memorial was changed over this period through use.

18. Sandage, "Marble House Divided," 159, observed that "looking broadly from 1939 to the mid-1960s, then, the civil rights rituals at the Lincoln Memorial had repeatedly served two functions, uniting and invigorating activists and legitimating black political action."

19. Ed Hornick, "For Obama, Lincoln Was Model President," CNN, 17 January 2019, https://www.cnn.com/2009/politics/01/17/lincoln.obsession/index.html, includes examples of various presidents who came to the Lincoln Memorial for various reasons. He cites Eric Foner's observation: "Everybody finds themselves in Lincoln. Everybody finds what they want to find in Lincoln. There are dozens of Lincolns out there."

20. Philip Kennicott, "Forget the Tanks: Trump's Violation of the Lincoln Memorial Is the Real Offense," *Washington Post*, July 3, 2019, https://www.washingtonpost.com /lifestyle/style/forget-the-tanks-trumps-violation-of-the-lincoln-memorial-is-the -real-offense/2019/07/03/23c0894c-9da9-11e9-9ed4-c9089972ad5a_story.html.

21. Paul LeBlanc, "Famed DC Monuments Defaced after Night of Unrest," CNN, 31 May 2020, https://www.cnn.com/2020/05/31/politics/dc-monuments-lincoln -memorial-defaced/index.html.

1. Hofstadter, *American Political Tradition*, 124, concluded, "The clue to much that is vital in Lincoln's thought and character lies in the fact that he was thoroughly and completely the politician, by preference and by training. It is difficult to think of any man of comparable stature whose life was so fully absorbed into his political being." He quotes Lincoln's longtime law partner and friend, William Henry Herndon who saw Lincoln the same way: "It was in the world of politics that he lived. . . . Politics were his life, newspapers his food, and his great ambition his motive power."

2. Peterson, *Lincoln in American Memory*, 27. Goodwin, *Team of Rivals*, xvii, describes her book as "a story of Lincoln's political genius revealed through his extraordinary array of personal qualities that enabled him to form friendships with men who had previously opposed him; to repair injured feelings that, left untended, might have escalated into permanent hostility; to assume responsibility for the failures of subordinates; to share credit with ease; and to learn from mistakes."

3. Meir Soloveichik, "Painting the Tension at America's Founding Moment," *Wall Street Journal*, 3–4 July 2021, observed that "Lincoln came to combine his faith in the Declaration with a growing sense of the role of Providence. In his second inaugural address, he expressed an idea [that] . . . the Civil War was divine punishment for America's failure to live up to the Declaration's doctrine of equality."

4. These lines, quoted in most references to Lincoln, are taken from Thomas Gray's *Elegy Written in a Country Churchyard* (1742, published 1751) about the life of a plowman: "Let not Ambition mock their useful toil, / Their homely joys, and destiny obscure; / Nor Grandeur hear with a disdainful smile / The short and simple annals of the poor."

5. Hofstadter, *American Political Tradition*, 135, concluded, "For Lincoln the vital test of a democracy was economic—its ability to provide opportunities for social ascent to those born in its lower ranks. This belief in opportunity for the self-made man is the key to his entire career; it explains his public appeal; it is the core of his criticism of slavery."

6. See Foner, *Fiery Trial*, 12–13. Foner, 3, observed "Lincoln grew up in a world in which slavery was a living presence and where both deeply entrenched racism and various kinds of antislavery sentiment flourished."

7. Another oft quoted Lincoln remark is "with public sentiment, nothing can fail; without it nothing can succeed." He used it in the first of his famous debates with Stephen Douglas on 21 August 1858, reprinted in Balser, *Collected Works of Abraham Lincoln*, 3:251–52. Lincoln and Douglas held seven debates in Illinois, one in most of the state's congressional districts during the 1858 election campaign, which attracted national attention because of Douglas's stature. Although Douglas went on to defeat Lincoln and win his fourth term as senator, the debates were widely published and

discussed, establishing Lincoln's reputation as a politician with potential national credibility.

8. Lincoln's first speech to that effect was at the Illinois State Fair, followed shortly thereafter by speeches in Peoria, Illinois, and elsewhere. For Lincoln's evolving policy on slavery, see Hofstadter, *American Political Tradition*, 139–50; Goodwin, *Team of Rivals*, 91–92, 160–68.

9. Hofstadter, *American Political Tradition*, 145, expands on this argument. Hofstadter, on page 43, also quotes Lincoln's admission that he did not consider Blacks equal to whites in some basic ways: "Free them, and make them politically and socially our equals. *My own feelings will not admit of this*, and if mine would, we well know that those of the great mass of whites will not. Whether feeling accords with justice and sound judgment is not the sole question, if indeed it is any part of it. A universal feeling, whether well or ill founded, cannot be safely disregarded."

10. This frequently quoted statement is found in its entirely in Balser, *Collected Works of Abraham Lincoln*, 5:371–75. Lincoln even went so far as to apparently blame the presence of Blacks for the Civil War, but as Frederick Douglass rightly pointed out it was slavery that caused the war. See Foner, *Fiery Trial*, 224–25.

11. A useful documented history of colonization is found in Morgan Robinson, "The American Colonization Society," White House Historical Association, accessed 17 April 2021, https://www.whitehousehistory.org/the-american-colonization-society.

12. See, for example, Foner, *Fiery Trial*, 17. Foner observes that "for many white Americans, including Lincoln, colonization was part of a plan for ending slavery that represented a middle ground between abolitionist radicalism and the prospect of the United States existing forever half-slave and half-free" (127).

13. Foner, *Fiery Trial*, 254–57, 305–7.

14. Foner, *Fiery Trial*, 157–60. Goodwin, *Team of Rivals*, 324, observes that Lincoln's first inaugural was essentially based on "the constitution, Andrew Jackson's nullification proclamation, Daniel Webster's memorable 'Liberty and Union Forever' speech, Clay's address to the Senate arguing for the Compromise of 1850." Jackson's Nullification Proclamation prohibited states from nullifying federal law. Goodwin also notes the significance of William H. Seward's input in terms of editing and tone.

15. For a summary of the attack and its significance, see "Battle of Fort Sumter, April 1861," National Parks Service, accessed 18 April 2021, https://www.nps.gov/articles/battle-of-fort-sumter-april-1861.htm. For an analysis of Lincoln's strategy in provoking the attack, see Hofstadter, *American Political Tradition*, 155–56.

16. Goodwin, *Team of Rivals*, 462, lists as advantages the slaves provided the South as follows: "They labored on the home front, tilling fields, raising crops, and picking cotton, so their masters could go to war without fearing that their families would go hungry."

17. Louisiana and Virginia were added with some exemptions. The complete texts of both executive orders can be found at History Net, "Emancipation Proclamation," accessed 1 April 2021, https://www.historynet.com/emancipation-proclamation-text.

18. A good analysis of the border states is Amy Murrell Taylor, "The Border States," National Park Service, accessed 18 April 2021, https://www.nps.gov/articles/the-border-states.htm.

19. Foner, *Fiery Trial*, 24, observed that the Emancipation Proclamation "altered the nature of the Civil War, the relationship of the federal government to slavery, and the course of American history. It liquidated without compensation the largest concentration of property in the United States." By contrast, Hofstadter, *American Political Tradition*, 169, 170, opined that the Emancipation Proclamation added nothing to what previous acts of Congress had accomplished with the Confiscation Act of 1861, which permitted the Union to seize Confederate property and freed any slaves working with or for the Confederate army. Nevertheless, he felt that it "probably made genuine emancipation inevitable." Peterson, *Lincoln in American Memory*, 125, quotes Lincoln, "In giving freedom to the slave we assure freedom to the free." Emancipation was thus a profoundly national act.

20. Foner, *Fiery Trial*, 267–68, observed that Lincoln's language had taken on a new overtly biblical tone, and that he now called the country a nation rather than a union. Wills, *Lincoln at Gettysburg*, 37, observed that Lincoln "lifts the battle to a level of abstraction . . . Lincoln did for the whole Civil War what he accomplished for the single battlefield . . . he means to 'win' the whole Civil War in ideological terms as well as military ones." Peterson, *Lincoln in American Memory*, 361, linked the Gettysburg Address to the concept of American civil religion.

21. See, for example, Foner, *Fiery Trial*, 323–24. Goodwin, *Team of Rivals*, 699, observed that "more than any of his other speeches, the Second Inaugural fused spiritual faith with politics." Frederick Douglass, quoted on page 700, called the speech "a sacred effort."

22. For the full text of the speech, see, Balser, *Collected Works of Abraham Lincoln*, 7:333.

23. For a good capsule history of the Thirteenth Amendment, see "13th Amendment," History.com, 9 November 2009, updated 9 June 2020, https://www.history.com/topics/black-history/thirteenth-amendment.

24. See Foner, *Fiery Trial*, 261; Nichols, *Lincoln and the Indians*, 3.

25. Drinnon, *Facing West*, 123.

26. Nichols, *Lincoln and the Indians*, 3, cites his remarks that defined his main military accomplishments as having "bent a musket pretty badly on one occasion" and having had "a good many bloody struggles with the musquetoes [*sic*]." Lincoln's complete words are found in Balser, *Collected Works of Abraham Lincoln*, 1:455–56, 509–10, and 3:512.

27. Nichols, *Lincoln and the Indians*, 5–24, describes this patronage system in detail. It forms the basis of my summary.

28. Nichols, *Lincoln and the Indians*, 23–24, concluded that the system "had its roots in the growth of a white population and a dynamic, aggressive culture bent on the acquisition of material wealth . . . [that] mirrored the basic drive of American society—social mobility, the acquisition of wealth, unrestricted capitalism, and political activism."

29. On the cause of the war, see, for example, Dunbar-Ortiz, *Indigenous Peoples' History*, 136; Nichols, *Lincoln and the Indians*, xi.

30. Lincoln is quoted in numerous places. See, for example, Nichols, *Lincoln and the Indians*, xi, 80.

31. Lincoln had been warned that local residents might take matters into their own hands if there were no public hangings. For Lincoln's response, see Foner, *Fiery Trial*, 261; Nichols, *Lincoln and the Indians*, xiii.

32. Foner, *Fiery Trial*, 261.

33. See Nichols, *Lincoln and the Indians*, 117, 119, 123. After the hangings there were 329 prisoners at Mankato, including 49 who had been acquitted but never released. In total 52 more had died in prison than had been hanged.

34. Nichols, *Lincoln and the Indians*, 127–28, summed up Lincoln's actions in Minnesota: "His humaneness in this must be matched against what he did (or failed to do) following the executions. He made a bargain permitting the removal of tribes from Minnesota. . . . He ordered the permanent incarceration of the pardoned in conditions that led to more deaths than the hangings. His policies left the removed tribes in destitution, partly because of the corruption and mismanagement of officials in the Indian System. Lincoln sanctioned military missions designed to destroy as many Indians as possible in the region, and he acquiesced in sizable land grabs in Minnesota. He installed as secretary of the interior the man who cooperated so closely with the Minnesotans in all these matters. Lincoln dealt more with the politics of the executions than the welfare of the Indians. . . . But once the public outcry was over and the political threat gone, Lincoln seemed to lose interest. It was a 'disagreeable subject' he preferred to forget . . . the Minnesota Indians were left to languish by a Lincoln who had other things on his mind."

35. For a detailed study of Native Americans as slaveholders, see Abel, *Slaveholding Indians*. For a recent account, see Chris Cameron and Mark Walker, "Tribes Are Pressed to Confront Bias against Descendants of Enslaved People," *Wall Street Journal*, 30 May 2021.

36. For an analysis of Southern strategy and its implications, see Nichols, *Lincoln and the Indians*, 28–32.

37. Foner, *Fiery Trial*, 162, discusses how this action alienated Native American tribes thus abandoned. See also Nichols, *Lincoln and the Indians*, 28.

38. See Nichols, *Lincoln and the Indians*, 82.

39. See Foner, *Fiery Trial*, 130.

40. See Foner, *Fiery Trial*, 262. He concludes, on page 263, that "Lincoln's Indian policies are depressingly similar to those of virtually every nineteenth century president." (Critical portions of Lincoln's speech are reproduced in Nichols, *Lincoln and the Indians*, 187.)

41. Nichols, *Lincoln and the Indians*, 186, observed that "in three sentences, Lincoln managed to tie together the stereotype of the savage, nonfarming hunter with the inherently violent barbarian who was inferior to whites."

42. There are many examples. Nichols, *Lincoln and the Indians*, 67, 72, describes Dole's squelching such investigations in Minnesota.

43. Nichols, *Lincoln and the Indians*, 144, observed that "the proposal was made in a general way to the men who directly controlled Indian patronage."

44. Nichols, *Lincoln and the Indians*, 153–54, 158.

45. On the Sand Creek massacre, see Foner, *Fiery Trial*, 262; Nichols, *Lincoln and the Indians*, 21, 171, 174.

46. Nichols, *Lincoln and the Indians*, 164, concludes that Lincoln's priorities were "new territories, railroads, minerals, and finally Indians."

9. ROOSEVELT'S MEMORIALS

1. I became involved with this work as a member of the Mayoral Advisory Commission on City Art, Monuments, and Markers, which had been charged with making recommendations on the fate of this and three other controversial works. Initially I did some basic art historical research and shared my findings with the group. Subsequently, the AMNH hired me as the art history consultant for an exhibition addressing the controversy (discussed in this chapter). The content of this section on the Roosevelt memorial is drawn in part from that report and from my essay, "Addressing Monumental Controversies," 115–30.

2. New York State Roosevelt Memorial, Board of Trustees, "History, Plan and Design," 13. George N. Pindar is listed as secretary and therefore may have prepared this text, although that is not indicated.

3. In May 1951, when James Earle Fraser received the gold medal of the American Academy and National Institute of Arts and Letters, Aline Louchheim published an article titled "Most Famous Unknown Sculptor," *New York Times*, 13 May 1951, https://www.nytimes.com/1951/05/13/archives/most-famous-unknown-sculptor-james-earle-fraser-whose-statues-are.html. Today Fraser is probably best known for his sculpture of a Native American on horseback, *End of the Trail*, and the reliefs on the buffalo nickel.

4. Cécile Ganteaume, email to the author, 3 August 2018.

5. Tolles is quoted in Senie, "Report to the American Museum of Natural History, Theodore Roosevelt Memorial," internal document, 24 August 2018, 13.

6. Letter from Fraser to General McCoy, 9 October 1940, James Earle Fraser archives, Metropolitan Museum of Art.

7. Thayer Tolles, in-person conversation and email, 7 July 2021.

8. Senie, "Report," 11.

9. Lunde, *Naturalist*, 1–2, stated that Roosevelt was "an intrepid museum naturalist ... [who] studied animals by shooting them, stuffing them and preserving them.... He lived in an age when natural history museums commissioned scientists to explore and document uncharted terrain, collecting specimens for both study and exhibit.... Part scientist, part explorer, they collected animals by the thousand—and for such a naturalist, *collect* meant *kill and preserve*, a fact easily forgotten today."

10. Allen, "'Culling the Herd,'" 4.

11. Slippen is quoted in Valentina Di Liscia, "Why Is a Racist Roosevelt Statue Still Standing in New York City?," *Hyperallergic*, 21 June 2021, https://hyperallergic.com /657952/why-is-a-racist-statue-of-theodore-roosevelt-still-standing-in-new-york -city/. It includes a link to the proceedings of the meeting.

12. At the time of this writing, the planned text was not available. The plans exhibited at the Public Design Commission meeting featured text that was on display until 23 January 2022.

13. Stolpersteine in Berlin, https://www.stolpersteine-berlin.de/en, accessed 29 July 2021.

14. My thanks to Michele Cohen for pointing this out and providing the example of the deaccessioning policy for Arts and Humanities Council of Montgomery County (Maryland) program on which she worked.

15. A history of the island is found in Curry, "Theodore Roosevelt," 14–33. My summary is largely based on this source. Harrison, *Washington during Civil War and Reconstruction*, 46, provides a more detailed account of the use of what was then called Mason's Island during the Civil War. Alice Roosevelt Longworth, the president's daughter, remembered picnicking there as a child. See McManus, "Return of the Rough Rider," 18–21, 44.

16. A detailed account of the process is found in Heth, "Imagining TR," 237–88.

17. For a detailed account of the protracted process of creating the Roosevelt National Memorial, see Stephenson, "Celebrating American Heroes," 208–16.

18. See Heth, "Imagining TR," 260, for a summary of the RMA's new focus. According to Heth, page 261, "Theodore Roosevelt, in this context, became a symbol of the spirit, the integrity, and the righteousness of the American democratic cause."

19. Johnson is quoted in Willard Clopton, "Rough Rider 'Rides' Again," *Washington Post*, 28 October 1967.

1. For a useful description of his experiences in the West, see Budner, "Hunting, Ranching, and Writing," 161–70. Gould, *Presidency of Theodore Roosevelt*, 4, summarized his experience: "The gains in his physical well-being, emotional release, and political appeal lasted throughout his life."

2. For a discussion of Roosevelt's privileged upbringing, see, for example, Goodwin, *Leadership in Turbulent Times*, 24–29.

3. Dyer, *Theodore Roosevelt and the Idea of Race*, 19.

4. A good summary of Roosevelt's activities and interests is found in Morris, "Theodore Roosevelt, the Polygon," 25–32. See also, Naylor, "Introduction," 9–16.

5. Gould, *Presidency of Theodore Roosevelt*, 3.

6. Goodwin, *Leadership in Turbulent Times*, 132–35.

7. Roosevelt's accomplishments as police commissioner are enumerated by Berman, "Theodore Roosevelt as Police Commissioner," 171–88. See also Goodwin, *Leadership in Turbulent Times*, 136–40.

8. Goodwin, *Leadership in Turbulent Times*, 133.

9. On Roosevelt's appointments as President, see Gould, *Presidency of Theodore Roosevelt*, 15–21, 188–89.

10. Gould, *Presidency of Theodore Roosevelt*, 26–49, 102, 159.

11. On the Great Northern Securities case see Goodwin, *Leadership in Turbulent Times*, 253–54; Gould, *Presidency of Theodore Roosevelt*, 45, 204; Morris, "Theodore Roosevelt, the Polygon," 60–65, 89–94, 314–16.

12. The details of the strike are discussed by Goodwin, *Leadership in Turbulent Times*, 245–71; Gould, *Presidency of Theodore Roosevelt*, 63–67; Shaefer, "Theodore Roosevelt's Contribution," 201–20.

13. Roosevelt's conservation policies are discussed by Budner in "Hunting, Ranching, and Writing," 166–67; Gould, *Presidency of Theodore Roosevelt*, 38–40, 107, 193–99; Char Miller, "Keeper of His Conscience?," 231–44; Morris, "Theodore Roosevelt, the Polygon," 485–87; Shullery, "Theodore Roosevelt," 221–30.

14. Gary Scott, "The Presidents and the National Parks," *White House History* 28 (Fall 2010), www.whitehousehistory.org/the-presidents-and-the-national-parks.

15. Alysa Landry, "Theodore Roosevelt: The Only Good Indians are the Dead Indians," *Indian Country Today*, 28 June 2016, https://Indiancountrytoday.com/archive/theodore-roosevelt-the-only-good-indians-are-the-dead-indians-ON1cdfuEWO2kzOVVyrp7ig.

16. See for example, Gould, *Presidency of Theodore Roosevelt*, 117–18.

17. Brantlinger, "Kipling's 'The White Man's Burden' and Its Afterlives," 172–91. My thanks to Bruce Glaser for this reference.

18. Roosevelt is quoted in Drinnon, *Facing West*, 298. He continued to defend U.S. treatment of the local population throughout his presidency and after. For a good summary of U.S. policy regarding the Philippines, including those who protested American imperialism, see Kinzer, *True Flag*. Dunbar-Ortiz, *Indigenous Peoples' History*, 165–66, notes Roosevelt's statements to the effect that "Filipinos did not have the right to govern their country just because they happened to occupy it."

19. See, for example, Drinnon, *Facing West*, 288–91, 298–300, 460.

20. Dunbar-Ortiz, *Indigenous Peoples' History*, 166, interpreted the Roosevelt Corollary to mean "anything to threaten perceived United States economic or political interests."

21. Roosevelt's foreign policy is discussed in Gould, *Presidency of Theodore Roosevelt*, 11–12, 53–70, 167–82; Marks, "Theodore Roosevelt Foreign Policy," 391–410. For a concise summary of the Monroe Doctrine (1823), see Office of the Historian, United States Department of State, accessed 10 September 2022, https://history.state.gov/milestones/1801-1829/monroe. Roosevelt's Corollary to the Monroe Doctrine justified sending Marines into Santo Domingo (1904), Nicaragua (1911), and Haiti (1915).

22. For Roosevelt's handling of the creation of the Panama Canal Zone, see especially Gould, *Presidency of Theodore Roosevelt*, 56–58, 88–92. See also "Building the Panama Canal, 1903–1914," Office of the Historian, United States Department of State, accessed 17 June 2021, https://history.state.gov/milestones/1899-1913/panama-canal.

23. For the changing evaluations of Roosevelt see Dalton, "Bully Prophet," 559–76; Gable, "Man in the Arena of History," 613–44.

24. Cullinane, *Theodore Roosevelt's Ghost*, 10–18.

25. Dyer, *Theodore Roosevelt and the Idea of Race*, 29–30, identifies Roosevelt's various uses of the term "race" as defining "a broad designation, appropriate to employ when discussing nearly any human group which appeared to possess social, physical, or cultural traits in common"; "a national label"; "close ties of a racial nature" such as might exist between French and French Canadians; distinctions based on color; and "the principle ethnic divisions of mankind."

26. Dyer, *Theodore Roosevelt and the Idea of Race*, 21, observes, "Roosevelt, broadly acquainted with scientific and social scientific theories and possessing a penchant for intellectual orderliness, saw the concept of race as a cogent way to bring order, regularity, and consistency to human differences."

27. Dyer, *Theodore Roosevelt and the Idea of Race*, 9–17, summarizes the various sources of Roosevelt's thinking on race. For Roosevelt's expression of his racial philosophy in his writing, see the same volume at 50–56. Drinnon, *Facing West*, 230, refers to Roosevelt's "Manifest Destiny assumption that the West had to be won from the 'savage hordes' that 'infested' it."

28. See, for example, "Early Concepts of Evolution: Jean Baptiste Lamarck," U C Museum of Paleontology, Understanding Evolution, accessed 11 June 2021, https://evolution .berkeley.edu/evolibrary/article/history_09. Dyer, throughout emphasizes Roosevelt's following of Lamarckian thought.

29. Dyer, *Theodore Roosevelt and the Idea of Race*, 154, summarized his proposal as "apparently intended to promote childbearing by restricting divorce and by strengthening the institution of marriage. In effect Roosevelt seemed to suggest that it was necessary to legislate fecundity!"

30. Glenn, *Searchers*, 160. My thanks to Haitha Abdullah for this reference.

31. Dyer, *Theodore Roosevelt and the Idea of Race*, 83.

32. Gould, *Presidency of Theodore Roosevelt*, 43, 100, 200–201. He concludes that his policies and those of his commissioner of Indian Affairs, Francis E. Leupp, were "as debilitating and demoralizing as earlier abuses had been" (201).

33. Landry, "Theodore Roosevelt: The Only Good Indians are the Dead Indians."

34. Landry, "Theodore Roosevelt: The Only Good Indians are the Dead Indians," cites an example of a group of Sioux from Yankton, South Dakota, who traveled to Washington and tried to get assistance with settlers who had taken their lands and homes but neither Roosevelt and nor commissioner of Indian Affairs would see them.

35. Dyer, *Theodore Roosevelt and the Idea of Race*, 82.

36. See, for example, Landry, "Theodore Roosevelt: The Only Good Indians are the Dead Indians"; and Dyer, *Theodore Roosevelt and the Idea of Race*, 83.

37. Dyer, *Theodore Roosevelt and the Idea of Race*, 74. Dyer concluded that "in Roosevelt's view, the pioneers had accomplished a task of great 'race-importance' in killing off the Indians, a weaker and inferior race. . . . Because of the great racial importance he attached to the winning of the West, Roosevelt had early reached the conclusion that the extermination of Indians must be approached with little regard for traditional morality" (76).

38. Dyer, *Theodore Roosevelt and the Idea of Race*, 79.

39. Dyer, *Theodore Roosevelt and the Idea of Race*, 88, concluded, "For Theodore Roosevelt the Indian would always remain a victim of White racial destiny."

40. Dyer, *Theodore Roosevelt and the Idea of Race*, 89.

41. Dyer, *Theodore Roosevelt and the Idea of Race*, 105; Sinkler, "Theodore Roosevelt and the Black American," 370–72.

42. Sinkler, "Theodore Roosevelt and the Black American," 342, observed that "history may yet record that Roosevelt had more conferences at the White House on the race question than any other President."

43. Sinkler, "Theodore Roosevelt and the Black American," 341–42. The prevalence of deep-seated racism during this period led Dyer, *Theodore Roosevelt and the Idea of Race*, 91, to conclude that "nearly all Americans deduced that the future of blacks in

the United States could not measurably improve and that Afro-Americans should either be removed from the population or forced to conform to a caste system."

44. Dyer, *Theodore Roosevelt and the Idea of Race*, 102–5. In spite of Roosevelt's commitment to meritocracy the number of Black appointments declined during his presidency. See also Sinkler, "Theodore Roosevelt and the Black American," 362–68. Sinkler, "Theodore Roosevelt and the Black American," 365, notes that Roosevelt was proud of the fact that he had raised the quality of his Black appointments even if not the number.

45. Dyer, *Theodore Roosevelt and the Idea of Race*, 111, summarized Roosevelt's assumptions for this policy. "First, he assumed that technical education would well serve both whites and blacks in the 'New South' and provide a source of skilled labor for white industry. Second, he concluded that in a changing and thoroughly hostile region, skilled blacks would fare better than unskilled. Third, he argued that education would decrease the extent of black lawlessness and thus of much white violence." Significantly, he ignored "environmental factors and the existence of a double standard for blacks." See also Sinkler, "Theodore Roosevelt and the Black American," 351.

46. Sinkler, "Theodore Roosevelt and the Black American," 352–53.

47. Dyer, *Theodore Roosevelt and the Idea of Race*, 115–16; Sinkler, "Theodore Roosevelt and the Black American," 359.

48. Dyer, *Theodore Roosevelt and the Idea of Race*, 107.

49. Dyer, *Theodore Roosevelt and the Idea of Race*, 102, notes that during his presidency the number of lynchings reached an all-time high. See also Dyer, *Theodore Roosevelt and the Idea of Race*, 113–14; Sinkler, "Theodore Roosevelt and the Black American," 354–58.

50. Dyer, *Theodore Roosevelt and the Idea of Race*, 94, describes Roosevelt's attitude as one of "racial self-centeredness."

51. Sinkler, "Theodore Roosevelt and the Black American," 348.

52. Sinkler, "Theodore Roosevelt and the Black American," 342, 345, 349, 362, 369, 371.

53. Sinkler, "Theodore Roosevelt and the Black American," 348. Sinkler observed that "like Abraham Lincoln, Roosevelt found himself being accused of being both too liberal and too conservative on the race question" (349).

CONCLUSION

Epigraphs: Kenan Malik, "When Monuments Fall," *New York Review of Books*, 8 September 2020; Alan Greenblatt, "History Matters: Debates about Monuments Reflect Current Divisions," *Governing*, 8 March 2021.

1. The term Manifest Destiny first appeared in an editorial published in the July–August 1845 issue of the *Democratic Review*. The writer, in criticizing opposition to annexing

Texas, insisted that national unity depended on "the fulfillment of our manifest destiny to overspread the continent allotted by Providence for the free development of our yearly multiplying million." See "Manifest Destiny," History.com, updated 15 November 2019, https://history.com/topics.westward-expansion/manifest-destiny.

2. Washington appears on the dollar bill and the quarter. Jefferson appears on the nickel. Lincoln appears on the penny.

3. Larner, *Mount Rushmore*, 11, observed, "Manifest Destiny may be only a phrase, yet it allowed the American belief in American exceptionalism, American virtue, to coexist with the conquest of land occupied by others."

4. Borglum is quoted in Fite, *Mount Rushmore*, 3.

5. For a summary of colossal sculpture and Borglum's attraction to it, see, Taliaferro, *Great White Fathers*, 147–53. See also Blair and Michel, "The Rushmore Effect," 166. The authors analyze Mount Rushmore "both figuratively and literally, as constituting a dwelling place of national character, [and] a construction of national *ethos*" (159).

6. For a discussion of the Slave Trade Clause (Article 1, Section 9, Clause 1 of the Constitution), see Gordon Lloyd and Jenny S. Martinez, "The Slave Trade Clause," National Constitution Center, accessed 14 August 2022, https://constitutioncenter .org/interactive-constitution/interpretation/article-1/clauses/761.

7. Justin Gest, "What the 'Majority Minority' Shift Really Means for America," *New York Times*, 24 August 2021, https://www.nytimes.com/2021/08/24/opinion/us -census-majority-minority.html?smd=em-share. Gest cites Theodore Roosevelt as an exception in that, in spite of his personal prejudices, he defined national identity in terms of civic criteria. For him this was determined by "their encounters with the wilderness and their cultivation of strength, individualism and democratic community."

8. See, for example, Fiona Hill, "Yes, It Was a Coup. Here's Why," *Politico*, 11 January 2021, https://www.politico.com/news/magazine/2021/01/11/capitol-riot-self-coup -trump-fiona-hill-457549; Jennifer Schuessler, "'Sedition': A Complicated History," *New York Times*, 7 January 2021, https://www.nytimes.com/2021/01/07/arts/what -are-sedition-charges.html.

9. Becky Little, "A History of Attacks at the US Capitol," History.com, 11 March 2021, https:///www.history.com/news/us-capitol-building-violence-fires, provides a useful summary. Among the most notable are the following: In 1814, during the War of 1812, the British stormed and burned the Capitol after American troops set fire to a capital in colonial Canada. In 1856 pro-slavery representative Preston Brooks nearly beat the abolitionist Charles Sumner to death on the Senate floor. In 1915 a German Harvard professor planted three sticks of dynamite in the Capitol at night when it was not in session in protest to U.S. wartime aid to Britain. In 1954 four Puerto Rican Americans shot and injured five congressmen in the House of Representatives

in their demand for independence. In 1971 a bomb exploded at night in the Senate, placed there by the Weather Underground in protest of the U.S.-supported bombing of Laos, and in 1983 the Armed Resistance Unit set off a bomb also at night in retaliation for military actions in Grenada and Lebanon.

10. Lois Beckett, "'The Past Is So Present': How White Mobs Once Killed American Democracy," *Guardian*, 22 February 2021, https://www.theguardian.com/us-news /2021/feb/22/us-white-supremacy-democracy-capitol-attack, notes that "mobs of white Americans unwilling to accept multi-racial democracy have successfully overturned or stolen elections before: in Wilmington, North Carolina, in 1898, in Colfax, Louisiana, in 1873 and New Orleans in 1874, and, in Hamburg, South Carolina, in 1876." The Hamburg attack in particular was compared to the January 6 attack on the Capitol. Historians Rhae Lynn Barnes and Keri Leigh Merritt, "A Confederate Flag at the Capitol Summons America's Demons," CNN Opinion, 7 January 2021, https://www.cnn.com/2021/01/07/opinions/capitol-riot-confederacy -reconstruction-birth-of-a-nation-merritt-barnes/index.html, concluded, "The lineage between slaveholding secessionists and the modern insurrectionists could not have been more clear: Both groups were willing to destroy the union and both used violence to deflect their own racial fantasies of power and privilege slipping away." The authors refer to the attack as treason.

11. Luke Mogelson, "Chronicle of an Attack Foretold," *New Yorker*, 15 January 2021, https://www.newyorker.com/magazine/2021/01/25/among-the-insurrectionists, offers a detailed first-person account of the January 6 attack. He observed that "the Capitol siege was so violent and chaotic that it has been hard to discern the specific political agendas of its various participants."

12. Peggy Noonan, "Why We Can't Move on from Jan. 6," *Wall Street Journal*, 12–13 June 2021, commented, "If you weren't appalled by what happened that day, you have given up on American democracy." Annette Gordon-Reed in Chauncey Devega, "Historian Annette Gordon-Reed: Jan. 6 Was a 'Turning Point' in American History," *Salon*, 12 July 2021, https://www.salon.com/2021/07/12/historian-annette-gordon-reed-jan-6-was -a-turning-point-in-american-history/, warned, "Historians cannot predict the future, but Jan. 6 is going to be looked at as potentially a turning point in the country's history. If there is no proper reckoning, then the United States is facing serious problems. The whole concept of democracy and the republic are at stake." Heather Cox Richardson, "July 6, 2021," *Letters from an American*, 6 July 2021, https://heathercoxrichardson .substack.com/p/july-6-2021, observed, "In American history, the attempt to overturn our election procedures for one man, based on a lie, is unprecedented."

13. The full text of Biden's speech can be found at CNN, "Joe Biden's Inaugural Address," 20 January 2021, https://www.cnn.com/2021/01/20/politics/joe-biden-speech -transcript/index.html.

14. Haaland previously served as vice-chair of the House Committee on Natural Resources and also was chairwoman of the Laguna Development Corporation, New Mexico's second largest tribal gaming business, an important source of their income. For more on Deb Haaland, see, for example, Juliet Eilperin and Dino Grandoni, "Biden Picks Rep. Deb Haaland (D-NM) to Be First Native American Interior Secretary," *Washington Post*, 17 December 2020, https://www.washingtonpost .com/climate-environment/2020/12/17/deb-haaland-interior-secretary-biden/; Nick Martin, "Deb Haaland's Ascent and the Complicated Legacy of Native Representation," *New Republic*, 22 February 2021, https://newrepublic.com /article/161195/deb-haaland-department-of-i . . . ion?utm_source=newsletter& utm_medium=email&utm_campaign=tnr_daily; Michael Leroy Oberg and Joel Helfrich, "Why Deb Haaland Matters," History News Network, 2 March 2021, https://historynewsnetwork.org/article/179633, who conclude that "her confirmation was a signal event for those who value the environment and appreciate the 172-year long historic relationship between Interior and America's Native Nations." See also Olivia B. Waxman, "The Historical Significance of Deb Haaland Becoming the First Native American Cabinet Secretary," *Time*, 15 March 2021, https:// time.com/5933398/deb-haaland-first-native-american-cabinet-secretary-history/; Elizabeth Williamson, "How the 1st Native American Cabinet Member Carries the Weight," *New York Times*, 3 June 2021. The subheading reads, "Haaland Is Charged with Running an Agency That Once Targeted Indigenous People with Genocide."

15. See, for example, Hallie Golden, "'Suddenly I'm Breathing': Hope as Haaland Takes on Crisis of Missing and Murdered Native Americans," *Guardian*, 3 April 2021, https://www.theguardian.com/us-news/2021/apr/11/deb-haaland-interior -missing-murdered-native-americans-unit; Christine Hauer and Isabella Grullon Pax, "Search for Burial Sites in U.S. Is to Be Conducted at Former 'Indian Schools,'" *New York Times*, 25 June 2021; Nick Martin, "Is America Ready to Face the Truth about the Atrocities against Indigenous Children?," *New Republic*, 24 June 2021, https://newrepublic.com/article/162821/america-ready-face-truth-at . . . dren?utm _source=newsletter&utm_medium=email&utm_campaign=tnr_daily. On 20 July 2021 there was an article on the front page of the *New York Times* acknowledging this history: Rukmini Callimachi, "Lost Lives, Lost Culture: The Brutal Legacy of Indigenous Schools," *New York Times*, 20 July 2021.

16. Haaland discussed her family history in the context of the larger practice of Indigenous boarding schools in "Opinion: Deb Haaland: My Grandparents Were Stolen from Their Families as Children. We Must Learn about this History," *Washington Post*, 11 June 2021, https://www.washingtonpost.com/opinions/2021/06/11/deb -haaland-indigenous-boarding-schools/.

17. Benji Jones, "Indigenous People Are the World's Biggest Conservationists, but They Rarely Get Credit for It," *Vox*, 11 June 2021, https://www.vox.com/22518592 /indigenous-peop;e-conserve-nature-icca, discussed the previously unacknowledged significant additions of Indigenous people worldwide to conservation, concluding that "indigenous peoples and local communities conserve far more of the Earth than, say national parks and forests." Furthermore, although different cultures have different practices, "they tend to share a holistic and human-inclusive view of nature that's imbued with cultural or spiritual value. It's this view, in part, that forms the basis for Indigenous land management, which often includes protecting sacred lakes or forests, or creating rules against exploiting certain species."

18. Gina McCarthy is quoted in Jones, "Indigenous People Are the World's Biggest Conservationists."

19. "The Visual Culture of Memorials for Indigenous Communities: Properly Recognizing Native Contributions to War," Migration Memorials Project, Duke University, accessed 19 July 2021, https://migrationmemorials.trinity.duke.edu/visual-culture -memorials-indigenous-communities-properly-recognizing-native-contributions-war.

20. Details about the competition and the five finalists' designs can be found in Claire Voon, "See the Finalists for the National Mall's First Memorial to Native American Veterans," *Hyperallergic*, 7 February 2018, https://hyperallergic.com/423110/see -the-finalists-for-the-national-malls-first memorial-to-native-american-veterans/. Voon described Pratt's proposal as "a minimal but striking memorial in the form of a large loop that represents a sacred circle, rooted in symbolic elements of water and fire."

21. For visitor information about the memorial and the artist, see "National Native American Veterans Memorial: Honoring the Military Service of Native Americans," National Museum of the American Indian, accessed 19 July 2021, https:// americanindian.si.edu/visit/washinton/navm.

22. Valentina Di Liscia, "Text This Number in the US to Find Out which Native Land You're Living On," *Hyperallergic*, 20 August 2020, https://hyperallergic.com/583503 /code-for-anchorage-sms-bot/.

23. See, for example, Stuart Millar, "Reservation Dogs Uses Humor, Not Magic to Conjure Native Culture," *New York Times*, 6 August 2021, https://www.nytimes.com/2021 /08/06/arts/television/reservation-dogs.html. Millar describes the show as "an often gritty, often dark look at life on a modern-day Native American reservation," and praises its "nuanced and comic realism." See also, Kelly Boutsales, "The Indigenous Creatives Feel the Wind at Their Backs," *New York Times*, 10 August 2021. She cites *Rutherford Falls* as well as *Reservation Dogs* as evidence of "new opportunities for Hollywood's small but growing community of Native creators and performers."

24. Alan J. Singer, "Defending the 1619 Project in the Context of History Education Today," History News Network, 20 December 2020, https://historynewsnetwork

.org/article/178586, argued that "the roles that slavery, race and racism ... are fundamental to understanding the history of this country and need to be highlighted in secondary school curricula."

25. "The 1619 Project," *New York Times Magazine*, 18 August 2019.

26. Nikole Hannah-Jones, "Idea of America," in "1619 Project," 14.

27. The full table of contents read as follows: Matthew Desmond, "Capitalism"; Jeneen Interlandi, "A Broken Health Care System"; Kevin M. Kruse, "Traffic"; Jamelle Bouie, "Undemocratic Democracy"; Linda Villarosa, "Medical Inequality"; Wesley Morris, "American Popular Music"; Khalil Gibran Muhammad, "Sugar"; Bryan Stevenson, "Mass Incarceration"; Trymaine Lee, "The Wealth Gap"; Djeneba Aduayom, "Hope, a Photo Essay."

28. The most measured and informative critique of the Hannah-Jones essay is Leslie M. Harris, "I Helped Fact-Check the 1619 Project. The Times Ignored Me," *Politico*, 3 June 2020, https://www.politico.com/news/magazine/2020/03/06/1619-project -new-york-times-mistake-122248. Harris had informed the fact checker that since Britain would not end slavery in its Caribbean colonies for another sixty years, this would not have been a reason for the Revolution. Additionally, Lord Dunmore's proclamation discussed earlier in this book actually disrupted the practice since it led to Blacks being allowed to fight on the side of the colonists. Harris concludes, "It is easy to correct facts; it is much harder to correct a worldview that consistently ignores and distorts the role of African Americans and race in our history in order to present white people as all powerful and solely in possession to the keys of equality, freedom and democracy. At least that is the corrective history toward which the 1619 Project is moving, if imperfectly." See also, Matthew Karp, "History as End: 1619, 1776, and the Politics of the Past," *Harpers*, July 2021, https://harpers.org/archive/2021/07 /history-as-end-politics-of-the-past-matthew-karp/. Karp argues against considering the country's origin as the only determining actor: "History is not the end; it is only one more battleground where we must meet the vast demands of the ever-living now."

29. Bret Stephens, "The 1619 Chronicles," *New York Times*, 9 October 2020, https:// www.nytimes.com/2020/10/09/opinion/nyt-1619-project-criticisms.html. Stephens asserts, "It should have been enough to make strong and nuanced claims about the role of slavery and racism in American history. Instead, it issued categorical and totalizing assertions that are difficult to defend on close examination." For the *Times* defense of the project see Jake Silverstein, "On Recent Criticism of the 1619 Project," *New York Times*, 16 October 2020, https://www.nytimes.com/2020/10 /16/magazine/criticism-1619-project.html.

30. Peter Wood, "The New York Times Revises the 1619 Project, Barely," *National Association of Scholars*, 16 March 2020, https://www.nas.org/blogs/article/the-new -york-times-revises-the-1619-project-barel. Editor-in-chief Jake Silverstein stated,

"We recognize that our original language could be read to suggest that protecting slavery was a primary motivation for *all* the colonists. The passage has been changed to make clear that this was a primary motivation for *some* of the colonists. A note has been appended to the story as well." Although Silverstein also noted that the paper was "grateful to the many scholars whose insightful advice has helped us decide to make this change," Wood observed that this list did not include the established scholars who rallied against the project. Hannah-Jones tweeted, "Yesterday, we made an important clarification to my #1619Project essay about the colonists' motivations during the American Revolution. In attempting to summarize and streamline, journalists can sometimes lose important context and nuance. I did that here."

31. Gordon-Reed, *On Juneteenth*, 124.

32. Isabella Grullon Paz, "Poll Finds Many Know Little or Nothing about It," *New York Times*, 19 June 2021.

33. See absoluteequality.org, accessed 11 August 2022.

34. Biden is quoted in Grullon Paz, "Polls Find." Kevin Young, Andrew W. Mellon director of the National Museum of African American History and Culture, quoted in Janelle Ross, "What Juneteenth Means," *Time*, 16 June 2021, https://time.com /6073043/who-made-juneteenth/, stated, "When we know and accept the unvarnished truth—in all of its complexity, conflict and context—it can change how we view things, including ourselves." He sees the holiday as commemorating "both the promise of freedom and its delay." Put more stringently, Vann R. Newkirk quoted in Derrick Bryson Taylor, "Juneteenth, a Celebration of Freedom and Family," *New York Times*, 19 June 2021, referred to Juneteenth as "the purest distillation of the evils that still plague America, and a celebration of the good people who fought those evils." Gordon-Reed, in *On Juneteenth*, contextualizes the holiday both from personal experience and a historical perspective.

35. Kaitlyn Greenidge, "Emancipation Goes Corporate," *New York Times*, 20 June 2021. Greenidge worries that "the lessons of Juneteenth will become lost because we have seen the promising visions of Black freedom-dreaming co-opted before. . . . You can lose sight of the possibility that exists in marginalized histories, which is the space to imagine another, better world."

36. See Marisa Iati, "What Is Critical Race Theory, and Why Do Republicans Want to Ban It in Schools," *Washington Post*, 29 May 2021, https://www.washingtonpost .com/education/2021/05/29/critical-race-theory-bans-schools/, for an excellent summary of the key premises and controversies. See also Chelsea Sheasley, "Critical Race Theory: Who Gets to Decide What Is History," *Christian Science Monitor*, 4 June 2021, https:///www.csmonitor.com/usa/Education/2021/0604/Critical-race -theory-Who-gets-to-decide-what-is-history.

37. These are part of a longer list of objectionable words created by a Utah school board member considered euphemisms for critical race theory cited in Iati, "What Is Critical Race Theory."

38. Kmele Foster, David French, Jason Stanley, and Thomas Chatterton Williams, "The Misguided Bans on Critical Race Theory," *New York Times*, 6 July 2021, cite specific provisions in the various state legislations. They conclude that "they are speech codes. They seek to change public education by banning the expression of ideas. Even if this censorship is legal in the narrow context of public primary and secondary education, it is antithetical to educating students in the culture of American free expression." See also Clyde W. Ford, "The History of Systemic Racism That CRT Opponents Prefer to Hide," History News Network, 18 July 2021, https://historynewsnetwork .org/article/180750.

39. Fredreka Schouten, "Eighteen States Have Enacted New Laws That Make It Harder to Vote," CNN Politics, 22 July 2021, https://www.cnn.com/2021/07/22/politics /voting-restrictions-state-laws/index.html.

40. Sue Halpern, "The Republicans' Wild Assault on Voting Rights in Texas and Arizona," *New Yorker*, 6 June 2021, https://www.newyorker.com/magazine/2021/06 /14/the-republicans-wild-assault-on-voting-rights-in-texas-and-arizona.

41. President Biden is quoted in Katie Rogers, "'Have You No Shame?' Biden Frames Voting Rights as a Moral Reckoning," *New York Times*, 13 July 2021, https://www .nytimes.com/2021/07/13/us/politics/biden-voting-philadelphia.html.

42. Matt Ford, "Our 250-Year Fight for Multiracial Democracy," *New Republic*, 17 May 2021, https://newrepublic.com/article/162250/250-year-fight-majority-rule -multiracial-democracy. After reviewing the history of challenges to voting rights, Ford concluded that the current one was "arguably the most concerted attack in our history."

43. Jamelle Bouie, "Republicans Now Threaten Elections in Two Ways," *New York Times*, 17 July 2021.

44. Driggs, Wilson, and Winthrop, *Richmond's Monument Avenue*. See also Savage, "Politics of Memory," 127–49. The statue of Arthur Ashe was added in 1996.

45. Philip Kennicott, "On Richmond's Evolving Monument Avenue, Myth and Ugly Lies Run Deep," *Washington Post*, 29 July 2020, https://www.washingtonpost.com /entertainment/museums/on-richmonds-evolving-monument-avenue-myth-and -ugly-lies-run-deep/2020/07/28/03a2084a-d032-11ea-9038-af089b63ac21_story .html, suggested that "the creators of Monument Avenue appropriated the Lost Cause pantheon to lay claim to their own social legitimacy."

46. Gregory S. Schneider, "Virginia Supreme Court Clears Way for Lee Statue in Richmond to Come Down," *Washington Post*, 2 September 2021, https://www

.washingtonpost.com/local/virginia-politics/lee-statue-richmond-court-removal
/2021/09/02/4a2ee794-0bee-11ec-a6dd-296ba7fb2dce_story.html.

47. Jack Holmes, "New Orleans Mayor Mitch Landrieu's Remarkable Speech about Removing Confederate Monuments," *Esquire*, 23 May 2017, http://www.esquire .com/news-politics/a55218/new-orleans-mayor=speech-confederate-monuments/.

48. Bonnie Berkowitz and Adrian Blanco, "A Record Number of Confederate Monuments Fell in 2020," *Washington Post*, 12 March 2021, https://www.washingtonpost .com/graphics/2020/national/confederate-monuments/.

49. Equal Justice Initiative, "The National Memorial for Peace and Justice," accessed 11 September 2020, https://museumandmemorial.eji.org/memorial.

50. The website for the Equal Justice Initiative is eji.org, accessed 26 July 2021.

51. City of Boston, "*Boston Women's Memorial*," updated 10 August 2020, https://www .boston.gov/departments/womens-advancement/boston-womens-memorial.

52. "History of the Collections," National Museum of the American Indian, accessed 2 September 2021, https://americanindian.si.edu/explore/collections/history.

53. "About the Museum," National Museum of African American History and Culture, accessed 2 September 2021, https://nmaahc.si.edu/about/museum.

54. Lonnie G. Bunch III is quoted on the NMAAH home page, "About the Museum," accessed 8 September 2021, https://nmaahc.si.edu/about/museum.

55. Erin Blakemore, "The Met Will Finally Integrate Some Native American Art into Its American Wing," *Smithsonian Magazine*, 11 April 2017, https://www.smithsonianmag .com/smart-news/met-will-finally-integrate-some-native-american-art-its-american -wing-180962860/.

56. Sarah Bahr, "The Met Hires Its First Full-Time Native American Curator," *New York Times*, 9 September 2020; https://www.nytimes.com/2020/09/09/arts/design/met -museum-native-american-curator.html.

57. Sara Georgini, "In a Groundbreaking Exhibit at Mount Vernon, Slaves Speak and History Listens," *Smithsonian Magazine*, 12 October 2016, https://www.smithsonianmag .com/history/groundbreaking-exhibit-mount-vernon-slaves-speak-and-history-listens -180960747/.

58. "The Enslaved People of Mount Vernon Tour," George Washington's Mount Vernon, accessed 27 July 2021, https://www.mountvernon.org/plan-your-visit/calendar /events/the-enslaved-people-of-mount-vernon-tour/.

59. Joe Heim, "Massive Investment in Social Studies and Civics Education Proposed to Address Eroding Trust in Democratic Institutions," *Washington Post*, 1 March 2021, https://www.washingtonpost.com/education/civics-social-studies-education-plan /2021/03/01/e245e34a-747f-11eb-9537-496158cc5fd9_story.html, began, "It has been a bad 12 months for the practice of civics in America." The focus of his article

was the "long-standing failure to adequately teach American government, history and civic responsibility."

60. Rob Alex Fitt, "Conservative Activists in Texas Have Shaped the History All American Children Learn," *Washington Post*, 19 October 2020, https://www.washingtonpost .com/outlook/2020/10/19/conservative-activists-texas-have-shaped-history-all -american-children-learn/. See also Rebecca Klein, "These Textbooks in Thousands of K-12 Schools Echo Trump's Talking Points," *Huffpost*, 15 January 2021, https://www.huffpost.com/entry/christian-textbooks-trump-capitol-riot_n _6000bce3c5b62c0057bb711f.

61. Taylor, *American Colonies*; *American Revolutions*; *American Republics*. For a review of all three see, Osita Nwanevu, "The Incoherence of American History," *New Republic*, 24 August 2021, https://newrepublic.com/article/163096/incoherence-us-history -ame . . . iew?utm_source=newsletter&utm_medium=email&utm_campaign= tnr_daily.

62. Alexis de Tocqueville's "On Public Spirit in the United States" from his *Democracy in America* is highlighted in Educating for American Democracy Initiative, *Excellence in History and Civics for All Learners* (2021), 12, https://www .educatingforamericandemocracy.org/wp-content/uploads/2021/02/Educating-for -American-Democracy-Report-Excellence-in-History-and-Civics-for-All-Learners .pdf.

63. Educating for American Democracy Initiative, *Excellence in History and Civics*, 25.

64. Maria Marable-Bunch, "Transforming Teaching and Learning about Native Americans," *Smithsonian Magazine*, 28 December 2020, https://www.smithsonianmag.com /blogs/smithsonian-education/2020/12/28/transforming-teaching-and-learning -about-native-americans/. See also Michel Martin, "How Children's Books Grapple with the Native American Experience," History News Network, 3 January 2021, https://historynewsnetwork.org/article/178663.

65. *How to Have a Better Argument in School*, The Better Arguments Project, accessed 10 September 2022, https://betterarguments.org/. See also James Brewer Stewart, "Re-Animating the 1619 Project: Teachable Moments Not Turf Wars," History News Network, 9 February 2020, https://historynewsnetwork.org/article/174256.

66. "Our Approach," The Better Arguments Project, accessed 17 July 2021, https:// betterarguments.org/our-approach/.

67. "Respect. Honesty. Celebration," The Respect Project, accessed 17 July 2021, https:// /www.therespectproject.org/. See also Gary Abernathy, "Stop Insulting Trump Voters and Their Concerns. Talk to Them," *Washington Post*, 22 July 2021, https://www .washingtonpost.com/opinions/2021/07/22/stop-insulting-trump-voters-their -concerns-talk-them/.

68. Peggy McGlone, "Ambitious New Smithsonian Initiative Aims to Help American Deal with the History and Legacy of Racism," *Washington Post*, 24 August 2021, https://www.washingtonpost.com/entertainment/museums/smithsonian-race-initiative/2021/08/23/80eeabe6-041b-11ec-a654-900a78538242_story.html.

69. Walter G. Moss, "Can Sports Realize Frederick Douglass's Ideal of the Composite Nation?" History News Network, 18 July 2021, https://historynewsnetwork.org./article/180751.

EPILOGUE

1. The Editorial Board, "Every Day Is Jan. 6 Now," *New York Times*, 2 January 2022.

2. Rubinstein, *American Experiment*, 6–12.

3. Rubinstein, *American Experiment*, 2, 15.

4. Agence France-Presse in Stockholm, "US Added to List of 'Backsliding' Democracies for First Time," 22 November 2021, https://www.theguardian.com/us-news/2021/nov/22/us-list-backsliding-democracies-civil-liberties-international. See also Jason Stanley, "America Is Now in Fascism's Legal Phase," *Guardian*, 22 December 2021, https://www.theguardian.com/world/2021/dec/22/america-fascism-legal-phase.

5. Annabelle Timsit, "'Very Few' Believe U.S. Democracy Sets a Good Example, Global Survey Finds," *Washington Post*, 2 November 2021, https://www.washingtonpost.com/world/2021/11/02/pew-us-democracy-poll/. The survey was conducted after Trump's false claims that the 2020 election was stolen and the January 6 riots at the Capitol. In March 2021, "Freedom House, a democracy-watchdog group, ranked the state of democracy in the United States well below that in Chile, Costa Rica, and Slovakia, citing gerrymandering, the influence of money in politics, and the disenfranchisement of people of color among the reasons." Quoted in Sue Halpern, "Biden's Global Democracy Summit Raises an Awkward Question: Can Ours Endure?," *New Yorker*, 30 November 2021, https://www.newyorker.com/news/daily-comment/bidens-global-democracy-summit-raises-an-awkward-question-can-ours-endure.

6. See, for example, Carl Hulse, "After Fiery Debate, Voting Bill Dies in the Senate," *New York Times*, 20 January 2022; Sam Levine, "Democrats Fail to Advance Voting Rights Law as Senate Holdouts Defend Filibuster," *Guardian*, 20 January 2022, https://www.theguardian.com/us-news/2022/jan/19/voting-rights-senate-democrats-filibuster; Grace Segers, "Hope and Despair on Capitol Hill as Democrats' Voting Reforms Die by Republican Filibuster (and Manchinema)," 20 January 2022, https://newrepublic.com/article/165075/voting-rights-manchin-sinema-filibuster.

7. See, for example, Jedediah Britton-Purdy, "We're Not a Real Democracy," *New York Times*, 6 January 2022. In this context it is important to note that even though he was elected, Trump lost the popular vote in 2016 by some three million. In 2020 he lost the election and the popular vote by over seven million.

8. EAD is authored by an executive committee consisting of Danielle Allen, Paul Carrese, Louise Dubé, Michelle M. Herczog, Emma Humphries, Jane Kamensky, Kei Kawashima-Ginsberg, Peter Levine, Adam Seagrave, and Tammy Waller. "Educating for America Democracy: Excellence in History and Civics for All Learners," iCivics, 2 March 2021, www.educatingforamericandemocracy.org. It cites five challenges: "Motivating Agency, Sustaining the Republic; America's Plural Yet Shared Story; Simultaneously Celebrating and Critiquing Compromise; Civic Honesty, Reflective Patriotism; Balancing the Concrete and the Abstract."

9. See, for example, Ruth Marcus, "The Rule of Six: A Newly Radicalized Supreme Court Is Poised to Reshape the Nation," *Washington Post*, 2 December 2021, https://www.washingtonpost.com/opinions/2021/11/28/supreme-court-decisions-abortion-guns-religious-freedom-loom/.

10. "Dred Scott v. Sandford (1857)," National Archives, https://www.archives.gov/milestone-documents/dred-scott-v-sandford. The Dred Scott decision was overridden by the Thirteenth and Fourteenth Amendments, which abolished slavery and declared all persons born in the United States to be citizens. The court's three liberal justices wrote in a joint dissent of *Dobbs v. Jackson Women's Health Organization*: "One result of today's decision is certain, the curtailment of women's rights, and of their status as free and equal citizens." See Ariane de Vogue, "Supreme Court Makes It Clear There's a Red and a Blue America," CNN, 2 July 2022, https://www.cnn.com/2022/07/02/politics/supreme-court-red-blue-america-abortion-guns-climate-change/index.html.

11. See, for example Jill Lepore, "Of Course the Constitution Has Nothing to Say about Abortion," *New Yorker*, 4 May 2002, https://www.newyorker.com/news/daily-comment/why-there-are-no-women-in-the-constitution. See also Jill Elaine Hasday, "On Roe, Alito Cites a Judge Who Treated Women as Witches and Property," *Washington Post*, 9 May 2002, https://www.washingtonpost.com/opinions/2022/05/09/alito-roe-sir-matthew-hale-misogynist/; Philip Cohen, "Overturning Roe Is an Attack on the Modern Family," *New Republic*, 3 May 2022, https://newrepublic.com/article/166285/overturning-roe-attack-modern-family. Cohen remarked that the ruling was "about denying the essential humanity of women . . . Like voting rights, abortion rights are a cornerstone on which the structure of modern democracy rests." For a good summary of the changing laws regarding abortion, see Deepa Shivaram, "The Movement against Abortion Rights Is Nearing Its Apex. But It Began Way before Roe," NPR, *Morning Edition*, 4 May 2022; https://www.npr.org/2022/05/04/1096154028/the-movement-against-abortion-rights-is-nearing-its apex-but-it-began-way-before.

12. Simon Schama is quoted in David Smith, "Divided States of America: Roe v Wade Is 'Precursor to Larger Struggles,'" *Guardian*, 10 May 2022, https://www.theguardian.com/us-news/2022/may/10/divided-america-roe-v-wade-supreme-court-cold-civil

-war. Smith called the ruling "a milestone in America's seemingly inexorable journey from United States to divided states."

13. A detailed analysis of the similarities is provided by Kate Masur, "What Pre-Civil War History Tells Us about the Coming Abortion Battle," *Washington Post*, 14 July 2022, https://www.washingtonpost.com/made-by-history/2022/07/14/what -pre-civil-war-history-tells-us-about-coming-abortion-battle/. Masur sees this as a reminder of "the corrosive impact of interstate conflict and of the importance of federal protections for freedom and individual rights."

14. Peggy Noonan, "The End of Roe Will Be Good for America," *Wall Street Journal*, 5 May 2022, https://www.wsj.com/articles/the-end-of-roe-will-be-good-for -america-supreme-court-draft-leak-decision-abortion-pro-life-choice-justices-alito -11651787057. Noonan, who is against abortion, calls on Republicans to "use the moment to come forward as human beings who care about women and want to give families the help they need. Align with national legislation that helps single mothers to survive. Support women, including with child-care credits that come in cash and don't immediately go to child care, to help mothers stay at home with babies. Shelters, classes in parenting skills and life skills. All these exist in various forms: make them better, broader, bigger." See also Robin Morgan, "Compulsory Pregnancy, Forced Birth," *Robin Morgan*, 9 May 2022, https://www.robinmorgan.net/blog/compulsory -pregnancy-forced-birth/. Activist and novelist Robin Morgan points out: "American women have the highest maternal-mortality rates in the developed, industrialized world . . . that sixteen per cent of its children live in poverty, that it spends something like two percent of what some Scandinavian countries do on day care per toddler. In other words, America cares passionately about life—but only in the fetal form."

15. Mary Ziegler, "If the Supreme Court Can Reverse *Roe*, It Can Reverse Anything," *Atlantic*, 24 June 2022, https://www.theatlantic.com/ideas/archive/2022/06/roe -overturned-dobbs-abortion-supreme-court/661363. Indeed, Clarence Thomas's concurring decision suggested that the court should reconsider the right to use birth control and the legitimacy of gay relationships and marriage.

16. Eliott C. McLaughlin, "How the Supreme Court Recalibrated the Abortion Debate in Just 3 Words," CNN, July 17, 2022, https://www.cnn.com/2022/07/17/us/abortion -religion-dobbs-roe/indes.html. McLaughlin noted that Justice Alito replaced the wording of *Roe v. Wade* of "potential life" with "unborn human being." He quotes religious studies professor Rebecca Todd Peters's observation that this was a veiled "religious narrative" that "erases whole groups of people who have different religious beliefs." The article includes a breakdown by religion and agnostics or atheists of the varied beliefs regarding abortion. See also Jeannie Suk Gersen, "The Supreme Court's Conservatives Have Asserted Their Power," *New Yorker*, 3 July 2022, https://www .newyorker.com/magazine/2022/07/11/the-supreme-courts-conservatives-have

-asserted-their-power. Gersen notes that a synagogue in Florida is challenging the state's constitution that criminalizes abortions after conception because Jewish law stipulates that life begins at birth and requires an abortion if the mother's health or emotional well-being is at risk.

17. Linda Greenhouse makes a strong case for the religious basis of the decision in "Religious Doctrine, Not the Constitution, Drove the Dobbs Decision," *New York Times*, 22 July 2022, https://www.nytimes.com/2022/07/22/opinion/abortion -religion-supreme-court.html. She quotes Congregational minister John Nelson, who observed that the justices in their "'concern for the lives of fetuses,' overlooked the 'lived experience' of women. 'To show no regard for a lived experience is immoral.'" See also Madeleine Carlisle, "Fetal Personhood Laws Are a New Frontier in the Battle over Reproductive Rights," *Time*, 28 June 2022, https://time.com/6191886 /fetal-personhood-laws-roe-abortion/?utm . . . &utm_content=+++20220706+ ++body&et_rid=206179207&lctg=206179207.

18. For a detailed discussion of abortion and the Bible, see Melanie A. Howard, "What the Bible Actually Says about Abortion May Surprise You," *Conversation*, 20 July 2022, https://theconversation.com/what-the-bible-actually-says-about-abortion -may-surprise-you-186983.

19. Sarah Hougen Poggi and Cynthia A. Kierner, "A 1792 Case Reveals That Key Founders Saw Abortion as a Private Matter," *Washington Post*, 19 July 2022; https://www .washingtonpost.com/made-by-history/2022/07/19/1792-case-reveals-that-key -founders-saw-abortion-private-matter/. The authors discuss a case where Thomas Jefferson's daughter Martha Jefferson provided abortion-inducing herbs to eighteen-year-old Nancy Randolph who had been impregnated by her twenty-two-year-old brother-in-law and cousin, Richard Randolph. The authors also cite Justice Harry A. Blackmun's majority opinion in *Roe v. Wade*, that "at the time of the adoption of our constitution, and throughout the majority of the 19th century, abortion was viewed with less disfavor than under most American statues currently in effect. Phrasing it another way, a woman enjoyed a substantially broader right to terminate a pregnancy than she does in most States today."

20. The Fourteenth Amendment has been used in many landmark cases pertaining to discrimination, including *Brown v. Board of Education* (1954) as well as *Roe v. Wade*. See, for example, "14th Amendment," Cornell Law School Legal Information Institute, https://www.law.cornell.edu/constitution/amendmentxiv. It is worth noting in this context that the Equal Rights Amendment, which stated, "Equality of rights under the law shall not be denied or abridged by the United States or by any States on account of sex" and would also have given Congress the power of enforcement, was never passed. However, with this Supreme Court, I doubt that it would have made a difference.

21. See, for example, Fabio Bertoni, "Justice Neil Gorsuch's Radical Reinterpretation of the First Amendment," *New Yorker*, 20 July 2022; https://www.newyorker.com /news/daily-comment/justice-neil-gorsuchs-radical-reinterpretation-of-the-first -amendment. The author's detailed analysis thoroughly eviscerates Justice Gorsuch's majority opinion. See also Pamela Paul, "In the Face of Fact, the Supreme Court Chose Faith," *New York Times*, 17 July 2022, https://www.nytimes.com/2022/07 /17/opinion/kennedy-bremerton-supreme-court.html. Paul points out that participation in Kennedy's prayers was expected and the "ruling curtailed the liberty of those whose prayers take other forms. . . . Kitsap County is home to a variety of religions including Judaism, Islam, Sikhism, Hinduism and Baha'ism. A coach-led Christian prayer on the playing field is necessarily exclusionary."

22. Justice Sotomayor called the ruling "a disservice to schools" and a "perilous path in forcing States to entangle themselves with religion." She is quoted in de Vogue, "Supreme Court Makes It Clear." Lindsay Langholz, director of Policy and Program at the American Constitution Society, observed that Sotomayor's inclusion of images struck her "as using whatever tool was available to her to really underline just how egregious the manipulation of the facts was in that case." Langholz is quoted in Joan E. Greve, "What the Liberal Justices' Scorching Dissent Reveals about the US Supreme Court," *Guardian*, 11 July 2022, https://www.theguardian.com/law/2022 /jul/11/us-supreme-court-liberal-justices-dissenting-opinions.

23. Justice Breyer stated: "The Religion Clauses give Maine the right to honor that neutrality by choosing not to fund schools as part of its public school tuition program." He is quoted in de Vogue, "Supreme Court Makes It Clear."

24. Justice Sotomayor is quoted in Nina Totenberg, "Supreme Court Rules Maine's Tuition Assistance Program Must Cover Religious Schools," NPR, 21 June 2022.

25. Washington is quoted in Harlow Giles Unger, "The U.S a Christian Nation? Not According to the Founders!" History News Network, 11 July 2022, https:// historynewsnetwork.org/article/172973. Unger noted that Thomas Paine, author of the widely read and influential *Common Sense* (1776), did not believe in any church and called the "connection of church and state adulterous . . . Mingling religion with politics [should be] disavowed and reprobated by every inhabitant of America." Benjamin Franklin, Thomas Jefferson, James Madison, and John Adams agreed.

26. For an annotated summary of Jefferson's religious beliefs, see Rose Campion, "Jefferson's Religious Beliefs," Thomas Jefferson Monticello: Thomas Jefferson Encyclopedia, https://www.monticello.org/site/reserach-and-collections/jeffersons-religious-beliefs. For a discussion of his Virginia Statute, see "Thomas Jefferson and the Virginia Statute for Religious Freedom," Virginia Museum of History & Culture, https:// virginiahistory.org/learn/thomas-jefferson-and-virginia-statute-religious-freedom.

Among other things, it clearly states that "an individual is free to worship as he pleases with no discrimination."

27. On the increase of mass and other shootings, see, for example, Mark Berman, Lenny Bernstein, Dan Keating, Andrew Ba Tran, and Artur Galocha, "The Staggering Scope of U.S. Gun Deaths Goes Far beyond Mass Shootings," *Washington Post*, 8 July 2022, https://www.washingtonpost.com/nation/interactive/2022/gun-deaths-per -year-usa/. There are many more than those that make headlines. See, for example, Shaila Dewan, Mitch Smith, Gray Beltran, and Troy Closson, "A Month of Shootings, One on Top of Another," 7 July 2022; https://nytimes.com/interactive/2022 /07/07/us/mass-shootings-us.html.

28. Justice Thomas is quoted in Robert Barnes and Ann E. Marimow, "Supreme Court Finds N.Y. Law violates Right to Carry Guns Outside Home," *Washington Post*, 23 June 2022; https://washingtonpost.com/politics/2022/06/23/supreme-court-gun -control/. The authors noted that the ruling was "a stark reminder that the nation's divide over guns remains, in some circumstances, insurmountable."

29. Herb Pinder, "Supreme Court Strikes Down New York's Tough Concealed-Carry Handgun Law: What We Know Now," *Gothamist*, 23 June 2022; https://gothamist .com/news/supreme-court-strikes-down-new-yorks-tough-concealed-carry-handgun -law-what-we-know-now.

30. Justice Breyer is quoted in de Vogue, "Supreme Court Makes It Clear."

31. See, for example, Christine Emba, "A New Symbol for the Fourth of July: The Active Shooter," *Washington Post*, 5 July 2022; https://www.washingtonpost.com/opinions /2022/07/05/highland-park-july-fourth-active-shooter/. Emba concludes, "Thanks to our gun regime, that ever-present fear is now as American as apple pie."

32. Governor Pritzker was quoted in Stephen Collinson, "July 4 Parade Slaughter Again Shows Nowhere Is Safe *from* America's Mass Killing Contagion," CNN, 5 July 2022, https://www.cnn.com/2022/07/05/politics/illinois-parade-mass-shooting-gun -violence-analysis/index.html.

33. These statistics provided by the Gun Violence Archive are discussed by Emily Mae Czachor, "More than 220 Shot and Killed in U.S. Gun Violence over July 4 Holiday Weekend," CBS News, 5 July 2022, https://www.cbsnews.com/news/us-gun-violence -shootings-220-killed-july-4-weekend/. The archive listed 315 mass shootings in the country since the start of the year and around 22,500 deaths and a roughly equal number of injuries caused by gun violence.

34. The court opted to consider the Clean Power Plan proposed during the Obama era, which aimed to cut power emissions by one-third by 2030, although the Biden administration had taken it off the table in order to develop new guidelines. Biden's solicitor general, Elizabeth B. Prelogar, urged the court not to hear the case because "the Question whether the Clean Power Plan was lawful has no continuing practical

significance since that Plan is no longer in effect and the EPA does not intend to resurrect it." Prelogar is quoted in Marcus, "The Rule of Six."

35. Justice Elena Kagan is quoted in Robert Barnes and Dino Grandoni, "Supreme Court Limits EPA's Power to Combat Climate Change," *Washington Post*, 30 June 2022; https://washingtonpost.com/politics/2022/06/30/supreme-court-epa-climate-change/.

36. Professor Richard Lazarus is quoted in Robert Barnes and Dino Grandoni, "Supreme Court Limits EPA's Power."

37. For an incisive analysis of the legal vagaries and worse of recent Supreme Court decisions, see David Cole, "Egregiously Wrong: The Supreme Court's Unprecedented Turn," *New York Review of Books*, 18 August 2022; https://www.nybooks.com/articles/2022/08/18/egregiously-wrong-the-supreme-courts-unprecedented-turn-david-cole/?utm_medium=email. For example, Cole concluded: "Dobbs will almost certainly be included among the Court's worst decisions in history. Never has the Court eliminated a constitutional right so central to the equality and autonomy of half the nation. And never has the Court overturned precedent on such a transparently thin basis."

38. Nick Ehli and Robert Barnes, "Kagan Says Question of Legitimacy Risky for Supreme Court," *Washington Post*, 21 July 2022, https://www.washingtonpost.com/politics/2022/07/21/elena-kagan-supreme-court-legitimacy/. Her concern was that overturning long-standing precedents would be perceived as political and would weaken the public's confidence in the court. See also Christine Adams, "The Dictatorship of the Supreme Court," History News Network, 8 July 2022, https://historynewsnetwork.org/article/183453. The historian argues that "the United States is governed now to an alarming degree by six unelected Supreme Court justices with lifetime tenure who have arrogated to themselves the power to make and break laws with impunity.... Since attaining its 6–3 majority, the right-wing court has moved aggressively to impose its revanchist vision on a country that opposes its ideological bent."

39. See, for example, K. K. Ottesen, "'They Are Preparing for War': An Expert on Civil Wars Discusses Where Political Extremists Are Taking This Country," 8 March 2022, https://www.washingtonpost.com/magazine/2022/03/08/they-are-preparing-war-an-expert-civil-wars-discusses-where-political-extremists-are-taking-this-country/

40. There is considerable evidence that voters are ready to change the system. See, for example, Reid J. Epstein, "As Faith Flags in U.S. Government, Many Voters Want to Upend the System," *New York Times*, 13 July 2022, https://www.nytimes.com/2022/07/13/us/politics/government-trust-voting-poll.html.

41. On the current dangers to U.S. democracy and the infiltration of the Florida Republican Party, see Ed Pilkington, "'US Democracy Will Not Survive for Long': How January 6 Hearings Plot a Roadmap to Autocracy," *Guardian*, 24 July 2022; https://

www.theguardian.com/us-news/2022/jul/23/january-6-hearings-us-democracy
-roadmap-autocracy/. See also Sam Levine, "January 6 Panel: Shining a Light on
American Democracy's Nose Dive," *Guardian* 22 July 2022; https://www.theguardian
.com/us-news/2022/jul/22/january-6-panel-american-democracy-nose-dive. Levine
observed that "even though Trump's effort didn't succeed in overturning the election in 2020, he unleashed a movement of election deniers that is now trying to set
its hooks deep into the machinery of America's elections systems." See also Charles
Homans, "How 'Stop the Steal' Captured the American Right," *New York Times
Magazine*, 19 July 2022, https://www.nytimes.com/2022/07/19/magazine/stop
-the-steal.html/.

42. Darren Walker, "America Is Worth Saving," *New York Times*, 4 July 2022, A18.
Walker concluded that acknowledging "the callous cruelty of our founders—at least
34 of the 56 men who signed the declaration also enslaved human beings—is less
remarkable than what they set in motion, however contradictory. They initiated a
grand, complicated experiment with self-government that made possible abolition
and suffrage, workers' rights and civil rights and women's rights, however slowly
and unevenly."

BIBLIOGRAPHY

Abel, Annie Heloise. *The Slaveholding Indians*. Cleveland: Arthur H. Clark Company, 1915.

Abrams, Dan, and David Fisher. *Theodore Roosevelt for the Defense: The Courtroom Battle to Save His Legacy*. Toronto: Hanover Square Press, 2019.

Adams, William Howard, ed. *The Eye of Thomas Jefferson*. Columbia: University of Missouri Press, 1976.

Allen, Garland E. "'Culling the Herd': Eugenics and the Conservation Movement in the United States, 1900–1940." *Journal of the History of Biology* 46, no. 1 (February 2013): 31–72.

Anderson, Christopher. "Native Americans and the Origin of Abraham Lincoln's Views on Race." *Journal of the Abraham Lincoln Association* 37, no. 1 (Winter 2016): 11–29.

Appelbaum, Stanley. *The New York World's Fair 1939/1940*. New York: Dover, 1977.

Balser, Roy P., ed. *The Collected Works of Abraham Lincoln*. 9 volumes. New Brunswick NJ: Rutgers University Press, 1953.

Baruch, Mildred C., and Ellen J. Beckman. *Civil War Union Monuments*. Washington DC: Daughters of Union Veterans of the Civil War, 1978.

Bedford, Steven McLeod. *John Russell Pope: Architect of Empire*. New York: Rizzoli International, 1998.

Berger, Stefan, and Bill Niven, eds. *Writing the History of Memory*. London: Bloomsbury, 2014.

Bergman, Teresa. "Can Patriotism Be Carved in Stone? A Critical Analysis of Mt. Rushmore's Orientation Films," *Rhetoric and Public Affairs* 11, no. 1 (Spring 2008): 89–112.

Berman, Jay. "Theodore Roosevelt as Police Commissioner of New York: The Birth of Modern American Police Administration." In Naylor, Brinkley, and Gable, *Theodore Roosevelt*, 171–88.

Blair, Carole, and Neil Michel. "The Rushmore Effect: Ethos and National Collective Memory." In *The Ethos of Rhetoric*, edited by Michael Hyde, 156–96. Columbia: University of South Carolina Press, 2004.

Blight, David W. "'For Something beyond the Battlefield': Frederick Douglass and the Struggle for the Memory of the Civil War." *Journal of American History* 75, no. 4 (March 1989): 1156–78.

Blumenthal, Sidney. *A Self-Made Man: The Political Life of Abraham Lincoln Vol. I–III, 1809–1849*. New York: Simon and Schuster, 2016, 2017, 2019.

Bodnar, John. *Remaking America: Public Memory, Commemoration, and Patriotism in the Twentieth Century*. Princeton NJ: Princeton University Press, 1992.

Boyd, Julian P., et al., eds. *The Papers of Thomas Jefferson*. Princeton NJ: Princeton University Press, 1950–74.

Brantlinger, Patrick. "Kipling's 'The White Man's Burden' and Its Afterlives." *English Literature in Transition, 1880–1920* 50, no. 2 (2007): 172–91.

Brinkley, Douglas. *The Wilderness Warrior: Theodore Roosevelt and the Crusade for America*. New York: Harper, 2009.

Brown, Dee. *Bury My Heart at Wounded Knee*. New York: Henry Holt, 1970.

Brown, Thomas J. *The Public Art of Civil War Commemoration: A Brief History with Documents*. Boston: St. Martin's, 2004.

Budner, Lawrence H. "Hunting, Ranching, and Writing." In Naylor, Brinkley, and Gable, *Theodore Roosevelt*, 161–70.

Calloway, Colin G. *The Indian World of George Washington*. New York: Oxford University Press, 2018.

Campbell, Tracy. *The Gateway Arch: A Biography*. New Haven: Yale University Press, 2013.

Carter, Robin Borglum. *Gutzon Borglum: His Life and Work*. Austin TX: Eakin Press, 1998.

Chernow, Ron. *Washington: A Life*. New York: Penguin, 2010.

Cherny, Robert W. *Victor Arnautoff and the Politics of Art*. Champaign: University of Illinois Press, 2017.

Clark, H. Nichols B. "An Icon Preserved: Continuity in the Sculptural Images of Washington." In Mitnick, *George Washington*, 39–54.

Coe, Alexis. *You Never Forget Your First: A Biography of George Washington*. New York: Viking, 2020.

Cogliano, Francis D., ed. *A Companion to Thomas Jefferson*. Oxford: Blackwell, 2012.

Cook, Robert J. *Civil War Memories: Contesting the Past in the United States since 1865*. Baltimore: Johns Hopkins University Press, 2017.

Cooper, James Fenimore. *The Last of the Mohicans*. New York: Penguin, 1986 [1826].

Cooper, Wendy A. *Classical Taste in America 1800–1840*. New York: Baltimore Museum of Art and Abbeville Press, 1993.

Cope, Kevin L., with William S. Pederson, and the Honorable Frank Williams, eds. *George Washington in and as Culture*. New York: AMS Press, 2001.

Craven, Wayne. "Horatio Greenough's Statue of Washington and Phidias' Olympian Zeus." *Art Quarterly* 36, no. 4 (1963): 429–40.

———. *Sculpture in America*. Newark: University of Delaware Press, 1984 [1968].

Crawford, Alan Pell. *The Final Years of Thomas Jefferson*. New York: Random House, 2008.

Cullinane, Michael Patrick. *Theodore Roosevelt's Ghost: The History and Memory of an American Icon*. Baton Rouge: Louisiana State University Press, 2017.

Curry, Mary E. "Theodore Roosevelt: A Broken Link to Early Washington, D.C. History." *Records of the Columbia Historical Society, Washington, D.C.*, 71/72 (1971/1972): 14–33.

Dalton, Kathleen M. "The Bully Prophet: Theodore Roosevelt and American Memory." In Naylor, Brinkley, and Gable, *Theodore Roosevelt*, 559–76.

Davies, William. *Nervous States: Democracy and the Decline of Reason*. New York: W. W. Norton, 2018.

Deere, Phillip. "View from the Creek Nation." In Dunbar-Ortiz, *Great Sioux Nation*, 74–78.

Deloria, Vine, Jr. *Behind the Trail of Broken Treaties*. New York: Dell, 1974.

———. *Custer Died for Your Sins*. London: Collier-Macmillan, 1969.

———. "The United States Has No Jurisdiction in Sioux Territory." In Dunbar-Ortiz, *Great Sioux Nation*, 141–46.

Deloria, Vine, Jr., and Clifford M. Lytle. *American Indians, American Justice*. Austin: University of Texas Press, 1983.

DeMallie, Raymond J., Jr. "Treaties Are Made Between Nations." In Dunbar-Ortiz, *Great Sioux Nation*, 110–15.

Drexler, Ken. "Indian Removal Act: Primary Documents in American History." Library of Congress Research Guides. Accessed 12 April 2020. https://guides.loc.gov/indian -removal-act.

Driggs, Sarah Shield, Richard Guy Wilson, and Robert W. Winthrop. *Richmond's Monument Avenue*. Chapel Hill: University of North Carolina Press, 2001.

Drinnon, Richard. *Facing West: The Metaphysics of Indian-Hating and Empire-Building*. Norman: University of Oklahoma Press, 1997.

Dunbar, Erica Armstrong. *Never Caught: Washington's Relentless Pursuit of Their Runaway Slave, Ona Judge*. New York: Simon and Schuster, 2017.

Dunbar-Ortiz, Roxanne. "Dispossession." In Dunbar-Ortiz, *Great Sioux Nation*, 162–63.

———, ed. *The Great Sioux Nation: Sitting in Judgment on America*. Lincoln: University of Nebraska Press, 2013 [1977].

———. *An Indigenous Peoples' History of the United States*. Boston: Beacon Press, 2014.

———. "Oral History and Written History." In Dunbar-Ortiz, *Great Sioux Nation*, 100–104.

Dupres, Judith. *Monuments: America's History in Art and Memory*. New York: Random House, 2007.

Dyer, Thomas G. *Theodore Roosevelt and the Idea of Race*. Baton Rouge: Louisiana State University Press, 1980.

Eadie, John W., ed. *Classical Traditions in Early America*. Ann Arbor: University of Michigan / Center for Coordination of Ancient and Modern Studies, 1976.

Ellis, Joseph J. *American Sphinx: The Character of Thomas Jefferson*. New York: Random House, 1996.

———. *Founding Brothers: The Revolutionary Generation*. New York: Alfred A. Knopf, 2001.

Fehl, Philip. "Thomas Appleton of Livorno and Canova's Statue of George Washington." *Festschrift Ulrich Middeldorf*, 523–52. Berlin: Walter De Gruyter, 1968.

Fine-Dare, Kathleen S. *Grave Injustice: The American Indian Repatriation Movement and NAGPRA*. Lincoln: University of Nebraska Press, 2002.

Finkelman, Paul. "Jefferson and Slavery: 'Treason against the Hopes of the World.'" In Onuf, *Jeffersonian Legacies*, 181–224.

Fite, Gilbert C. *Mount Rushmore*. Keystone SD: Mount Rushmore History Association, 1952.

Flores, Richard R. "The Alamo: Myth, Public History, and the Politics of Inclusion." In *Contested Histories in Public Space: Memory, Race, and Nation*, edited by Daniel J. Walkowitz and Lisa Maya Knauer, 122–35. Durham NC: Duke University Press, 2009.

Foner, Eric. *The Fiery Trial: Abraham Lincoln and American Slavery*. New York: W. W. Norton, 2010.

Freeman, David B. *Carved in Stone: The History of Stone Mountain*. Macon GA: Mercer University Press, 1997.

French, Scot A., and Edward L. Ayers. "The Strange Career of Thomas Jefferson: Race and Slavery in American Memory, 1943–1993." In Onuf, *Jeffersonian Legacies*, 418–56.

Freundlich, A. L. *The Sculpture of James Earle Fraser*. Irvine CA: Universal Publishers, 2001.

Fryd, Vivien Green. "Horatio Greenough's George Washington: A President in Apotheosis." *Augustan Age*, Occasional Papers, no. 1 (1987): 70–86.

Frymer, Paul. *Building an American Empire*. Princeton NJ: Princeton University Press, 2017.

Furstenberg, Francois. *In the Name of the Father: Washington's Legacy, Slavery, and the Making of a Nation*. New York: Penguin, 2006.

Gable, John Allen. "The Man in the Arena of History: The Historiography of Theodore Roosevelt." In Naylor, Brinkley, and Gable, *Theodore Roosevelt*, 613–44.

Gallagher, Gary W. *Causes Won, Lost, and Forgotten: How Hollywood and Popular Art Shape What We Know about the Civil War*. Chapel Hill: University of North Carolina Press, 2008.

Glazer, Nathan, and Cynthia R. Field, eds. *The National Mall: Rethinking Washington's Monumental Core*. Baltimore: Johns Hopkins University Press, 2008.

Glenn, Frankel. *The Searchers: The Making of an American Legend*. New York: Bloomsbury, 2013.

Gonzalez, Mario, and Elizabeth Cook-Lynn, eds. *The Politics of Hallowed Ground: Wounded Knee and the Struggle for Indian Sovereignty.* Urbana: University of Illinois Press, 1999.

Goodwin, Doris Kearns. *Leadership in Turbulent Times.* New York: Simon and Schuster, 2018.

———. *Team of Rivals: The Political Genius of Abraham Lincoln.* New York: Simon and Schuster, 2005.

Gordon-Reed, Annette. *On Juneteenth.* New York: Liveright Publishing, 2021.

Gordon-Reed, Annette, and Peter S. Onuf, *"Most Blessed of the Patriarchs": Thomas Jefferson and the Empire of the Imagination.* New York: Norton, 2016.

Gould, Lewis L. *The Presidency of Theodore Roosevelt.* 2nd ed. Lawrence: University Press of Kansas, 2011.

Graebner, William. "Gateway to Empire: An Interpretation of Eero Saarinen's 1948 Design for the St. Louis Arch." *Prospectus: An Annual of American Cultural Studies* 18 (1993): 367–99.

Grandin, Greg. *The End of the Myth: From the Frontier to the Border Wall in the Mind of America.* New York: Henry Holt, 2019.

Hallam, John S. "Houdon's Washington in Richmond: Some New Observations," *American Art Journal* 10, no. 2 (November 1978): 72–80.

Harjo, Suzan Shown, ed. *Nation to Nation: Treaties between the United States and American Indian Nations.* Washington DC: National Museum of the American Indian with Smithsonian Books, 2014.

Harrison, Robert. *Washington during Civil War and Reconstruction: Race and Radicalism.* Cambridge, UK: Cambridge University Press, 2011.

Heth, Jennifer. "Imagining TR: Commemorations and Representations of Theodore Roosevelt in Twentieth-Century America." PhD diss., Texas A&M, 2014.

Higginbotham, Don, ed. *George Washington Reconsidered.* Charlottesville: University of Virginia Press, 2001.

Hilburn, Dorothy K., and Steven L. Walker. *Mount Rushmore: Monument to America's Democracy.* Bellemont AZ: Camelback/Canyonlands, 1997.

Hofstadter, Richard. *The American Political Tradition and the Men Who Made It.* New York: Random House, 1989 [1948].

Horseman, Reginald. "The Indian Policy of an 'Empire of Liberty.'" In Hoxie, Hoffman, and Albert, *Native Americans and the Early Republic,* 37–61.

Howard, Hugh. *The Painter's Chair: George Washington and the Making of American Art.* New York: Bloomsbury, 2009.

Howe, Daniel Walker. *Making the American Self: Jonathan Edwards to Abraham Lincoln.* Cambridge MA: Harvard University Press, 1997.

Hoxie, E. Frederick, Ronald Hoffman, and Peter J. Albert, eds. *Native Americans and the Early Republic.* Charlottesville: University Press of Virginia, 1993.

Jacobs, Wilbur. "Indian-White Relations." In Dunbar-Ortiz, *Great Sioux Nation*, 79–88.

———. "The Sioux Nation & the Treaty." In Dunbar-Ortiz, *Great Sioux Nation*, 116–18.

James Earle Fraser Archives, Metropolitan Museum of Art, New York.

Johns, Christopher M. S. "Proslavery Politics and Classical Authority: Antonio Canova's George Washington." *Memoirs of the American Academy in Rome* 47 (2002): 119–50.

Josephy, Alvin M., Jr. "Concise History of United States–Sioux Relations." In Dunbar-Ortiz, *Great Sioux Nation*, 19–28.

———. "Distortions of Indian History." In Dunbar-Ortiz, *Indigenous Peoples' History*, 55–57.

Kaplan, Amy, and Donald E. Pease, eds. *Cultures of United States Imperialism*. Durham NC: Duke University Press, 1993.

Kettl, Donald. *The Divided States of America*. Princeton NJ: Princeton University Press, 2020.

Kinzer, Stephen. *The True Flag: Theodore Roosevelt, Mark Twain, and the Birth of American Empire*. New York: Henry Holt, 2017.

Kunhardt, Philip B., III, Peter W. Kunhardt, and Peter W. Kunhardt Jr. *Looking for Lincoln: The Making of an American Icon*. New York: Alfred A. Knopf, 2008.

Larner, Jesse. *Mount Rushmore: An Icon Reconsidered*. New York: Thunder House Press, 2002.

Lazarus, Edward. *Black Hills/White Justice: The Sioux Nation versus the United States, 1775 to the Present*. New York: Harper Collins, 1991.

Leicester, Paul, ed. *The Works of Thomas Jefferson*. 12 volumes. New York: G. P. Putnam's Sons, 1905.

Levinson, Sanford. *Written in Stone: Public Monuments in Changing Societies*. Durham NC: Duke University Press, 2018.

Lipscomb, Andrew, and Albert Bergh, eds. *The Writings of Thomas Jefferson*. Washington DC: Thomas Jefferson Memorial Association of the United States, 1903–4.

Loewen, James W. *Lies across America: What Our Historic Sites Get Wrong*. New York: New Press, 1999.

Longmore, Paul K. *The Invention of George Washington*. Berkeley: University of California Press, 1988.

Lunde, Darrin. *The Naturalist: Theodore Roosevelt, a Lifetime of Exploration, and the Triumph of American Natural History*. New York: Broadway Books, 2016.

Maier, Pauline. *American Scripture: Making the Declaration of Independence*. New York: Random House, 1977.

Manning, Susan, and Francis D. Cogliano, eds. *The Atlantic Enlightenment*. Hampshire, UK: Ashgate, 2008.

Marienstras, Elise. "The Common Man's Indian: The Image of the Indian as a Promoter of National Identity in the Early National Era." In Hoxie, Hoffman, and Albert, *Native Americans and the Early Republic*, 261–96.

Marks, Frederick W., III. "Theodore Roosevelt Foreign Policy, and the Lessons of History." In Naylor, Brinkley, and Gable, *Theodore Roosevelt*, 391–410.

Marling, Karal Ann. *George Washington Slept Here: Colonial Revivals and American Culture, 1876–1986*. Cambridge MA: Harvard University Press, 1988.

Matthews, Richard K. *The Radical Politics of Thomas Jefferson: A Revisionist View*. Lawrence: University Press of Kansas, 1984.

McInnis, Maurie D., and Louis P. Nelson, eds. *Educated in Tyranny: Slavery at Thomas Jefferson's University*. Charlottesville: University of Virginia Press, 2019.

McManus, Irene. "Return of the Rough Rider." *American Forests* 73 (October 1967): 18–21; 44.

Means, Ted. "Those Who Left Are Returning." In Dunbar-Ortiz, *Great Sioux Nation*, 181–82.

Medicine, Beatrice. "Oral History." In Dunbar-Ortiz, *Great Sioux Nation*, 121–38.

Miller, Char. "Keeper of His Conscience? Pinchot, Roosevelt, and the Politics of Conservation." In Naylor, Brinkley, and Gable, *Theodore Roosevelt*, 231–44.

Miller, John Chester. *The Wolf by the Ears: Thomas Jefferson and Slavery*. Charlottesville: University Press of Virginia, 1991.

Miller, Lillian B. *Patrons and Patriotism: The Encouragement of the Fine Arts in the United States, 1790–1860*. Chicago: University of Chicago Press, 1966.

Miller, T. Jefferson, II. "The Designs for the Washington Monument in Baltimore." *Journal of the Society of Architectural Historians* 23, no. 1 (March 1964): 19–28.

Mitnick, Barbara J., ed. *George Washington: American Symbol*. New York: Hudson Hills Press, 1999.

Morgan, Edmund S. *American Slavery, American Freedom*. New York: W. W. Norton, 1975.

Morris, Edmund. *Theodore Rex*. New York: Random House, 2001.

———. "Theodore Roosevelt, the Polygon." In Naylor, Brinkley, and Gable, *Theodore Roosevelt*, 25–32.

Moulds, Henry. "Private Property in Locke's State of Nature." *American Journal of Economics and Sociology* 23, no. 2 (April 1964): 179–88.

Mowry, George E. *The Era of Theodore Roosevelt and the Birth of Modern America, 1900–1912*. New York: Harper and Row, 1958.

Naylor, Natalie A. "Introduction." In Naylor, Brinkley, and Gable, *Theodore Roosevelt*, 9–16.

Naylor, Natalie A., Douglas Brinkley, and John Allen Gable, eds. *Theodore Roosevelt: Many-Sided American*. Interlaken NY: Heart of the Lakes, 1992.

New York State Roosevelt Memorial, Board of Trustees. "History, Plan and Design of the New York State Memorial." Albany: J. B. Lyon, 1928.

Nichols, David A. *Lincoln and the Indians: Civil War Policy and Politics*. St. Paul: Minnesota Historical Society Press, 1978, 2000, 2012.

————. "'The Main Mean of Their Political Management': George Washington and the Practice of Indian Trade in the Early Republic." In Cope, Pederson, and Williams, *George Washington*, 145–61.

————. "The Other Civil War: Lincoln and the Indians." *Minnesota History* 44, no. 1 (Spring 1974): 3–15.

Onuf, Peter S., ed. *Jeffersonian Legacies*. Charlottesville: University Press of Virginia, 1993.

————. *Jefferson's Empire: The Language of American Nationhood*. Charlottesville: University Press of Virginia, 2000.

Onuf, Peter S., and Nicholas P. Cole, eds. *Thomas Jefferson, the Classical World, and Early America*. Charlottesville: University Press of Virginia.

Ortiz, Simon. "Indian Oral History: A Sacred Responsibility." In Dunbar-Ortiz, *Great Sioux Nation*, 14–15.

Ostler, Jeffrey. *The Lakotas and the Black Hills: The Struggle for Sacred Ground*. New York: Penguin, 2020.

Pagden, Anthony. *The Enlightenment and Why It Still Matters*. New York: Random House, 2013.

Peterson, Gloria. *An Administrative History of Abraham Lincoln Birthplace National Historic Site, Hodgenville, Kentucky*. Division of History, Office of Archaeology and Historic Preservation, National Park Service, U.S. Department of the Interior, 20 September 1968. https://www.nps.gov/parkhistory/online_books/abli/adhi/adhi.htm.

Peterson, Merrill, D. *The Jefferson Image in the American Mind*. New York: Oxford University Press, 1960.

————. *Lincoln in American Memory*. New York. Oxford University Press, 1994.

Pitcaithley, Dwight. "A Splendid Hoax: The Strange Case of Abraham Lincoln's Birthplace Cabin." Paper presented at the Annual Meeting of the Organization of American Historians, Louisville KY, 1991.

Pogue, Dennis J. "George Washington and the Politics of Slavery," *Historic Alexandria Quarterly* (Spring/Summer 2003): 1–10.

Pomeroy, Jim. "Selections from Rushmore—Another Look." In Senie and Webster, *Critical Issues in Public Art*, 44–56.

Powell, Peter. "The Sacred Way." In Dunbar-Ortiz, *Great Sioux Nation*, 62–66.

Ragan, Edward D. "Brother, Destroyer, Father: George Washington's Legacy in Iroquois." In Cope, Pederson, and Williams, *George Washington*.

Ragosta, John A. "The Virginia Statute for Establishing Religious Freedom." In Cogliano, *Companion to Thomas Jefferson*, 75–90.

Riley, John P. "George Washington's Last Will and Testament." *Virginia Cavalcade* (Autumn 1999): 168–78.

Rooney, Sierra, Jennifer Wingate, and Harriet F. Senie, eds. *Teachable Monuments: Using Public Art to Spark Dialogue and Confront Controversy*. New York: Bloomsbury Visual Arts, 2021.

Rubinstein, David M. *The American Experiment: Dialogues on a Dream*. New York: Simon and Schuster, 2021.

Salomon, Xavier F., with Guido Beltramini and Mario Guderzo. *Canova's George Washington*. New York: Frick Collection, 2018.

Sandage, Scott A. "A Marble House Divided: The Lincoln Memorial, the Civil Rights Movement, and the Politics of Memory, 1939–1963." *Journal of American History* 80, no. 1 (June 1993): 136–67.

Savage, Kirk. *Monument Wars: Washington, D.C., the National Mall, and the Transformation of the Memorial Landscape*. Berkeley: University of California Press, 2009.

——— . "The Politics of Memory: Black Emancipation and the Civil War Monument." In *The Politics of National Identity*, edited by John R. Gills, 127–49. Princeton NJ: Princeton University Press, 1994.

——— . "The Self-Made Monument: George Washington and the Fight to Erect a National Memorial." In Senie and Webster, *Critical Issues in Public Art*, 5–32.

——— . *Standing Soldiers, Kneeling Slaves: Race, War, and Monument in Nineteenth-Century America*. Princeton NJ: Princeton University Press, 1997.

Schama, Simon. *Landscape and Memory*. New York: Alfred A. Knopf, 1995.

Schwartz, Barry. *Abraham Lincoln and the Forge of National Memory*. Chicago: University of Chicago Press, 2009.

——— . *Abraham Lincoln in the Post-Heroic Era: History and Memory in Late Twentieth-Century America*. Chicago: University of Chicago Press, 2008.

——— . *George Washington: The Making of an American Symbol*. New York: Free Press, 1987.

——— . "Newark's Seated Lincoln," *New Jersey History* 113, nos. 3–4 (Fall/Winter 1995): 22–39.

Scott, Pamela. "'The Vast Empire': The Iconography of the Mall, 1791–1848." *Studies in the History of Art* 30 (1991): 36–58.

Senie, Harriet F. "Addressing Monumental Controversies in New York City Post Charlottesville." In Rooney, Wingate, and Senie, *Teachable Monuments*, 115–30.

Senie, Harriet F., and Sally Webster, eds. *Critical Issues in Public Art*. New York: Harper Collins, 1992.

Shaefer, Arthur M. "Theodore Roosevelt's Contribution to the Concept of Presidential Intervention in Labor Disputes: Antecedents and the 1902 Coal Strike." In Naylor, Brinkley, and Gable, *Theodore Roosevelt*, 201–20.

Shaff, Howard, and Audrey Karl Shaff. *Six Wars at a Time: The Life and Times of Gutzon Borglum, Sculptor of Mount Rushmore*. Sioux Falls SD: Center for Western Studies, Augustana College, 1985.

Shullery, Paul. "Theodore Roosevelt: The Scandal of the Hunter as Nature Lover." In Naylor, Brinkley, and Gable, *Theodore Roosevelt*, 221–30.

Sinkler, George. "Theodore Roosevelt and the Black American." In *The Racial Attitudes of American Presidents: From Abraham Lincoln to Theodore Roosevelt*. New York: Doubleday, 1971.

Smith, Rex Alan. *The Carving of Mount Rushmore*. New York: Abbeville Press, 1985.

Stanton, Lucia. "'Those Who Labor for My Happiness': Thomas Jefferson and His Slaves." In Onuf, *Jeffersonian Legacies*, 147–80.

Steele, Brian. "Jefferson's Legacy: The Nation as Interpretative Community." In Cogliano, *Companion to Thomas Jefferson*, 526–50.

———. *Thomas Jefferson and American Nationhood*. Cambridge, UK: Cambridge University Press, 2012.

Stein, Susan R. *The Worlds of Thomas Jefferson at Monticello*. New York: Harry N. Abrams, 1993.

Steinberg, Arthur K. "Presentism, George Washington and Slavery." In Cope, Pederson, and Williams, *George Washington*.

Stephenson, Charles Todd. "Celebrating American Heroes: The Commemoration of George Washington, Abraham Lincoln, Theodore Roosevelt, and Thomas Jefferson, 1832–1943." PhD diss., Brown University, 1993.

Taliaferro, John. *Great White Fathers: The Story of the Obsessive Quest to Create Mount Rushmore*. New York: Public Affairs, 2002.

Taylor, Alan. *American Colonies: The Settling of North America*. New York: Penguin, 2001.

———. *American Republics: A Continental History of the United States, 1783–1850*. New York: W. W. Norton, 2021.

———. *American Revolutions: A Continental History, 1750–1804*. New York: W. W. Norton, 2017.

———. *Thomas Jefferson's Education*. New York: Norton, 2019.

Thomas, Christopher A. *The Lincoln Memorial and American Life*. Princeton NJ: Princeton University Press, 2002.

Thompson, Mary V. *"The Only Unavoidable Subject of Regret": George Washington, Slavery, and the Enslaved Community at Mount Vernon*. Charlottesville: University of Virginia Press, 2019.

Tichi, Cecelia. *Embodiment of a Nation: Human Form in American Places*. Cambridge MA: Harvard University Press, 2001.

"Treaties and Other International Agreements: The Role of the United States Senate: A Study." Prepared for the Committee on Foreign Relations, United States Senate, S. Print 106–71. Washington DC: U.S. Government Printing Office, 2001.

Treuer, David. *The Heartbeat of Wounded Knee*. New York: Riverhead Books, 2019.

Twohig, Dorothy. "'That Species of Property': Washington's Role in the Controversy over Slavery." In Higginbotham, *George Washington Reconsidered*, 114–38.

Usner, Daniel H., Jr. "Iroquois Livelihood and Jeffersonian Agrarianism." In Hoxie, Hoffman, and Albert, *Native Americans and the Early Republic*, 200–225.

Van Alstyne, Richard W. *The Rising American Empire*. New York: W. W. Norton, 1960.

Vaughn, Karen. "Locke on Property: A Bibliographical Essay." *Literature of Liberty* 3, no. 1 (Spring 1980). Full text available at https://oll.libertyfund.org/page/locke-on -property-a-bibliographical-essay-by-karen-vaughn.

Wallace, Anthony J. C. *Jefferson and the Indians: The Tragic Fate of the First Americans*. Cambridge MA: Harvard University Press, 1999.

Warren, Louis A. *Lincoln Memorial Building: Hodgenville, Kentucky*. Hodgenville KY: Herald News, 1921.

Webster, Sally. *The Nation's First Monument and the Origins of the American Memorial Tradition*. Burlington VT: Ashgate, 2014.

Wiencek, Henry. *An Imperfect God: George Washington, His Slaves, and the Creation of America*. New York: Farrar, Straus and Giroux, 2003.

———. *Master of the Mountain: Thomas Jefferson and His Slaves*. New York: Farrar, Straus and Giroux, 2012.

Wills, Garry. *Cincinnatus: George Washington and the Enlightenment*. Garden City NY: Doubleday, 1984.

———. *Inventing America: Jefferson's Declaration of Independence*. New York: Random House, 1977.

———. *Lincoln at Gettysburg: The Words That Remade America*. New York: Simon and Schuster, 1992.

Wilson, Douglas L. "Jefferson and the Republic of Letters." In Onuf, *Jeffersonian Legacies*, 50–76.

Wood, Gordon S. *Empire of Liberty: A History of the Early Republic, 1789–1815*. New York: Oxford University Press, 2009.

———. "The Trials and Tribulations of Thomas Jefferson." In Onuf, *Jeffersonian Legacies*, 395–417.

Woodard, Colin. *Union: The Struggle to Forge the Story of United States Nationhood*. New York: Penguin, 2021.

Woodley, Jenny. "'Ma Is in the Park': Memory, Identity, and the Bethune Memorial." *Journal of American Studies* 52, no. 2 (May 2018): 474–502.

INDEX

Illustrations found in the gallery following page 98 are indexed by figure number (indicated by *fig.*) in *italics*.

INDEX · 215

World War I, 22, 107, 108, 125
World War II, 16, 64, 66–67, 102, 105, 107, 146n38
Wounded Knee massacre, 15
Wovoka (Paiute spiritual leader), 144n13

Wright, Frank Lloyd, 21
Wright brothers, 21

Ziegler, Mary, 136
Ziolkowski, Korczak, and family, 32